Drupal™ 7 Explained

Drupal™ 7 Explained

Your Step-by-Step Guide

Stephen Burge
with Cindy McCourt

PRENTICE
HALL

Upper Saddle River, NJ • Boston • Indianapolis • San Francisco
New York • Toronto • Montreal • London • Munich • Paris • Madrid
Cape Town • Sydney • Tokyo • Singapore • Mexico City

The publisher offers excellent discounts on this book when ordered in quantity for bulk purchases or special sales, which may include electronic versions and/or custom covers and content particular to your business, training goals, marketing focus, and branding interests. For more information, please contact

U.S. Corporate and Government Sales
(800) 382-3419
corpsales@pearsontechgroup.com

For sales outside the United States, please contact

International Sales
international@pearsoned.com

Visit us on the Web: informit.com/aw

Library of Congress Cataloging-in-Publication Data is on file.

ISBN-13: 9780133124231
ISBN-10: 0133124231

Text printed in the United States on recycled paper at R.R. Donnelley in Crawfordsville, Indiana.

Second Printing: September 2014

Editor-in-Chief
Mark Taub

Acquisitions Editor
Debra Williams Cauley

Development Editor
Songlin Qiu

Managing Editor
Kristy Hart

Project Editor
Elaine Wiley

Copy Editor
Apostrophe Editing Services

Indexer
Erika Millen

Proofreader
Sheri Replin

Editorial Assistant
Kim Boedigheimer

Cover Designer
Alan Clements

Compositor
Nonie Ratcliff

*For Stacey, who immeasurably improved my life
and this book.*

Contents

Preface

This book was written for people like you who want to learn Drupal quickly and easily.

We teach Drupal classes across the United States and talk with people like you who have to try to learn Drupal and other software.

They order books, watch videos, read online documentation, and go to live events. Many are frustrated and say the same thing: "Geeks create this training, and geeks don't speak our language."

So, when we were asked to write this book, we wanted to write it in plain English. We wanted to write a book that normal people could read, understand, and enjoy.

Maybe you went to work one day and your boss said, "Surprise! You're now running our Drupal website."

Maybe your career is in an entirely different industry and you're using Drupal for a hobby or a side-project.

Maybe you're a web professional and want to make a career from building Drupal sites.

It doesn't matter. We all want to spend more time building websites and less time struggling with complicated instructions.

We hope this book enables you to create Drupal websites that make you proud.

Acknowledgments

This book is a team effort, and I'm delighted to be able to thank the following people:

Stacey, Eshun, and Evelyn, who allowed me to work on the book through more weekends than I care to count.

Cindy, who was infinitely helpful and patient while we were writing.

Emma Jane and Amye, who provided immensely helpful feedback.

Debra, Songlin, and Kim, who guided the book through to publication.

About the Authors

Stephen Burge has split his career between teaching and web development. In 2007, he combined the two by starting to teach web development. His company, OSTraining, now teaches Drupal classes around the world and online. Stephen travels widely, helping people learn and thrive with open source software. Stephen is originally from England, and now lives in Atlanta.

Cindy McCourt is an experienced Drupal trainer, who coaches clients side-by-side to build internal Drupal capacity while planning and developing their Drupal solution. She specializes in user experience planning, configuration and code strategizing, site building, and project management. Cindy authored *Getting Started with Drupal 7*, a Refcard provided by dzone.com, and offers Drupal insights via her blogs on idcminnovations.com and ostraining.com.

1

Drupal Explained

You can build great websites with Drupal.

Our names are Steve Burge and Cindy McCourt and we're Drupal trainers. During hundreds of Drupal classes in many cities and countries, we've met lots of different types of Drupal learners:

- **Drupal learners come from many different backgrounds:** They are accountants, florists, photographers, secretaries, factory workers, stay-at-home parents, and people from all walks of life.

- **Drupal learners don't need to know anything about websites:** Some Drupal learners are professional web designers, but many others have never built a site before and don't know any website code or jargon.

- **Drupal learners don't need any experience:** We've trained people who went to work the previous week and found their boss saying, "Surprise! You're running our Drupal site!" They often still wore their look of surprise.

- **Drupal learners are of all ages:** We've taught 15-year old students skipping class all the way up to retirees in their 80s.

If any of those descriptions sound like you, you've picked up the right book. Using plain English and straightforward instructions, this book will help teach you how to build great websites using Drupal.

However, before you start, you probably need to know something about Drupal. This chapter is a brief introduction.

The What, When, Where, Who of Drupal

- **What is Drupal?** It's web-publishing software. It's designed for people to publish content online: news, blogs, photos, products, documents, events, or 1,001 other things. Because it enables you to manage your content, you'll often hear it called a Content Management System or CMS.

- **When did Drupal start?** Drupal has been around since 2000.

- **Who started Drupal?** It was created by Dries Buytaert, who at that time was a student in Belgium. Dries is still the leader of Drupal today.

- **Who runs Drupal?** Drupal is run by volunteers. However, many of the volunteers also work for Drupal businesses. They make money from building Drupal websites and that enables them to volunteer some time to help to keep the Drupal project running.

Why Drupal?

- **Drupal is easier:** I can't promise that your Drupal experience will be 100% frustration-free. There will be some moments when you're stuck and feel baffled. However, Drupal is easier to use than many other options for creating websites.

- **Drupal is quicker:** Drupal provides you with many ready-built features. If you want a new site design or to add a calendar or shopping cart to your site, you can often do it with just a few clicks. It may take a few days or even weeks to build a great Drupal site, but you can develop and launch more quickly than with many alternatives.

- **Drupal is cheaper:** Building a Drupal site is unlikely to be completely cost-free because, at a certain point, you may need to spend some money: You may have purchased this book or other training, and you might hire an expert. A good Drupal site can cost between a few dollars and hundreds of thousands of dollars at the top end. However, it costs you nothing to get into Drupal, whereas commercial alternatives to Drupal often cost hundreds of thousands of dollars before you even start.

- **Drupal has more options:** If you'd like extra features on your Drupal site, http://drupal.org is the place to go. It currently lists more than 20,000 options. You can do many, many things by using Drupal without writing a line of code. However, you may have to hire a developer if you have unusual or specific requirements.

How Much Is Drupal?

Free. Yes, 100% free.

The software is free to use, free to download, free to use on your sites, free to use on your customers' sites.

There are also thousands of free features available. You can find designs that people have created and are giving away. You can also find free shopping carts, calendars, photo galleries, and much more.

However, there are companies that make a living by selling services and products for Drupal. For example, if you need somewhere to host your site or someone to help you build it, you will probably need to pay.

What Does Drupal Mean?

Yes, Drupal is an unusual name. Why was it chosen? Dries chose the name Drupal because the domain name was available. That sounds like a joke, but it's partially true. The name went through three variations:

- First, Dries, originally wanted to call the project "dorp," which is Dutch for village.

- Second, when he went to register the domain name, he typed "drop" by accident and so registered drop.org.

- Finally, Dries released his software as "Drupal," which is a misspelling of the Dutch word "druppel," which means drop.

Drupal is often mispronounced. The correct way to say it is "Droo-puhl."

The "drop" meaning of Drupal influenced the mascot, which is shown in Figure 1.1. The overall mascot looks like a drop. The two eyes in the middle were also originally designed as two drops to look like the infinity symbol. The design looked so much like a face that a nose and mouth were added.

Figure 1.1   The Drupal mascot

How Many Versions of Drupal Are There?

In this book, you use Drupal 7, but you may encounter at least three different versions:

- **Drupal 6** was released September 2005. Millions of websites use it, and it will still be actively supported and updated by the Drupal team until the release of Drupal 8. Despite this, there are no plans for new features for this version.

- **Drupal 7** was released January 2008. The latest and greatest version, it's the version used in this book.

- **Drupal 8** will be released in late 2013 or early 2014.

The code in each new Drupal version is substantially different from the last. After you choose a version, it will probably be the version that your site uses for several years. It is difficult to upgrade from version 6 to 7 or from version 7 to 8.

However, the key concepts of Drupal don't change greatly, and this book focuses on those key concepts. After you finish, you can hopefully pick up a site using Drupal 6 or even Drupal 8 when it arrives and learn it quickly.

Learning Drupal actually is like learning to drive. You learn to drive in one type of car, but after you understand how to do it, you can quickly adapt to driving any other type of car.

Who Uses Drupal?

Governments: Drupal is used by many national government sites. International organizations such as the United Nations and the European Union use Drupal, and so do governments from the United States, the U.K. and Portugal to Indonesia, Sri Lanka, and Mongolia. If there is one thing that the ordinary person in the street knows about Drupal, it is that it runs http://www.whitehouse.gov, the official site of the President of United States, as shown in Figure 1.2.

Drupal also powers the official home of the German government at http://www.deutschland.de (see Figure 1.3).

Media: Drupal powers many TV, entertainment, and news websites and can handle large amounts of traffic. Leading newspapers in many other countries use Drupal. *The Economist* is a historic and widely read British publication. Its website http://www.economist.com is built in Drupal.

Figure 1.2   The Drupal website for the President of the United States

Figure 1.3   The Drupal website for the German government

Education: Drupal is particularly popular in education, with everyone from large universities to small schools using it. One of the most famous is the University of Texas. Its website is http://www.utexas.edu, as shown in Figure 1.4.

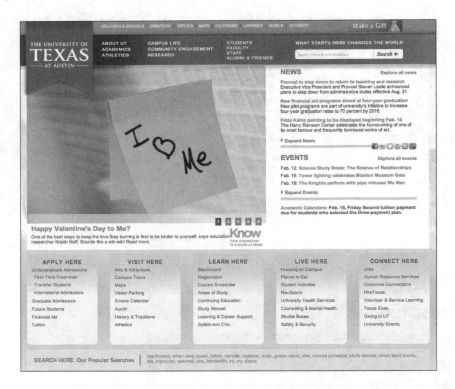

Figure 1.4   The University of Texas website built with Drupal

Sports: Many sports teams and organizations around the world use Drupal. Some of the most famous are the Professional Golfers' Association of America (PGA) and The Bass Anglers Sportsman Society, whose Drupal website at http://www.bassmaster.com is shown in Figure 1.5.

Entertainment: Sony and Warner have both adopted Drupal for many of their artists. If you visit the websites for oldies like Bob Dylan and Eric Clapton or new acts like Beyonce and Kid Rock, you'll find them running on Drupal. You can see a more detailed list of sites built with Drupal at http://www.drupalshowcase.com.

Figure 1.5 The Bassmaster website built with Drupal

This Book Explained

Now that you know a little bit about Drupal, let's talk about this book, *Drupal 7 Explained*.

What You Need

You need only two things to follow along with this book:

- A computer with an Internet connection
- A webhosting account to install Drupal

What This Book Covers

There are 14 chapters in this book:

- Chapter 1, "Drupal Explained," is the first chapter—you've almost finished reading it!

- Chapter 2, "Drupal Planning Explained," explains how to plan your Drupal site before you start building it.

- In Chapter 3, "Drupal Installations Explained," you install Drupal and set it up correctly.

- In Chapter 4, "Drupal Administration Explained," you learn how to navigate around your Drupal site.

- In Chapter 5, "Drupal Content Explained," you practice the three-step workflow that makes creating Drupal site content easy.

- In Chapter 6, "Drupal Fields Explained," you make your content more interesting by adding images and extra information.

- In Chapter 7, "Drupal Modules Explained," you add extra features to your site.

- In Chapter 8, "Drupal Menus Explained," you create the navigation for your site.

- In Chapter 9, "Drupal Themes Explained," you redesign your Drupal site.

- In Chapter 10, "Drupal Blocks Explained," you add extra blocks of information to your site. These allow people to do many different things, including using the search form, seeing your latest articles, or registering on your site.

- In Chapter 11, "Drupal Views Explained," you'll take the information on your site and present it in tables, lists, grids, photo galleries, and more.

- In Chapter 12, "Drupal Layout Modules Explained," you create advanced layouts on your Drupal site, putting content and features in 2- and 3-column designs.

- In Chapter 13, "Drupal Users Explained," you control what users on your site can see and do.

- In Chapter 14, "Drupal Site Management Explained," you set up your site ready for launch and manage your site successfully and safely after it launches.

This Book Is Small

Big books are no fun. They're expensive to buy, heavy to carry, and often written in long, complicated sentences, paragraphs, and chapters that go on and on while the text grows and the words grow longer and more obscure as the author tries to show their verbosity and vocabulary, examining the thesaurus for words that describe, narrate, impress, and fill up space but never quite get to the point so that you end up going back to the beginning of the long confusing text and try to reread, but then you start wondering what's for dinner or what's on TV instead....

This book is small because it leaves things out.

You're going to read that time and time again, but it's worth repeating: This book will leave things out.

You focus on only the most important parts of Drupal so that you can understand them as easily as possible.

This book is not comprehensive. It does not contain everything you could now know about Drupal. It contains only what a Drupal beginner needs to know.

This Book Is Active

You don't learn to ride a bicycle by reading a book: You learn by actually riding. You don't learn to drive a car by reading a book: You learn by actually driving.

A book can help and give some advice, but without actually riding a bike or driving a car, you'll never really learn. The same is true with Drupal. So, throughout every chapter of this book, you're going to be asked to work with Drupal.

This Book Uses Specific Examples

After you master the techniques in this book, you can build your own websites for companies, charities, schools, sports, or whatever else you need.

However, this book uses a specific example site. Asking all the readers of this book to build the same site makes it easy for the author to give you specific instructions, explanations, and screen shots. It's not essential that you follow every step provided, but by following the flow of each chapter you can get a good understanding of all the key Drupal concepts.

The example used is a website. Starting in Chapter 2 and going through to Chapter 14, you create a site with information about Drupal. The project is called Drupalville. That's going to be the project you use to see how to build and run a Drupal site.

You can also find lots of information, including detailed instructions, updates, and corrections for each chapter at http://www.drupal7explained.com.

Things in This Book May Have Changed

The best way to learn Drupal is by building a specific site using detailed instructions and screen shots.

But, there is one downside to this approach that you need to be aware of: Drupal changes but books do not.

Drupal changes and so do the extra features and designs that you add on to it. Everything in this book is correct at the time of writing. But, as the book gets further away from its publication date, it's possible that some of the instructions and screen shots may become out of date.

Be patient with any changes you find. We can help you list changes at http://www.drupal7explained.com, so you can contact us via that site if you find any.

What's Next?

In this chapter, you learned important information about Drupal:

- Drupal is easier, cheaper, and quicker and has more options than many of the alternative ways to build websites.
- Drupal is widely used by businesses, governments, and nonprofit organizations.
- People of all backgrounds, ages, and technology experience have learned Drupal.
- You're going to join them.
- You're going to join them by following clear, step-by-step instructions.
- When you finish this book, you'll have built example websites, but you'll be ready to build your own Drupal sites on many more topics.

The next step is to get you thinking about and planning your Drupal site. Are you ready? If you are, turn the page and let's begin.

2

Drupal Planning Explained

Before you build any website, it's important to plan.

However, it's difficult for you to plan a Drupal site at the moment because you have little or no experience with Drupal.

So, in this chapter we're going to suggest some things you should plan for before you begin building a Drupal site.

We're also going to recommend a workflow that will help you carry out your plan successfully.

At the end of this chapter, you should be able to

- Understand what's involved in a website plan

- Understand what's involved in a project management plan

- Understand what's involved in a development plan

- Understand what's involved in a maintenance plan

- Start to think about the website, project management, development and maintenance plans for the site we'll build in this book

Drupal Site Planning Explained

Planning means different things to different people. Your role in the project, your experience, and your skills all influence your approach to planning:

- If you are a project manager, your thoughts might go directly to scheduling and budgets.

- If you are a designer, your first thoughts might lean more toward how each page of the site will look.

- If you are a content manager, content development workflows might come to mind followed quickly by how the content will be organized on the site.
- If you are a developer, your idea of a plan might be which development methodology you want to use or which strategies are best for implementing the design created by the designer.

There are many things to consider when you plan. For example, if the schedule is tight and the budget is low, the planned design might not be possible. To take another example, if you do not have the appropriate skills on your development team, you might need to change your development strategy to one that meets most of your planned design, leaving the more customized functionality to a time when time, skills, and budget allow.

There are general guidelines, but each plan must be customized to your situation.

To plan a Drupal site, you need four types of plans:

- Website
- Project management
- Development
- Maintenance

Now consider a brief introduction of each type of plan. For a more detailed view into planning Drupal websites, check out Cindy's other book called *Drupal: The Guide to Planning and Building Websites*.

Website Plan

This plan focuses on defining the content and functional requirements, as well as the design (visual, structural, layout, and interaction) aspects of the site. The website plan conveys what you want for your site after it is built. It influences the schedule, required budget, and skills, and provides a way to manage expectations for all involved. The more detailed the plan, the higher probability that you will get the site you want, assuming all things equal.

A website plan commonly includes a requirements document and a design:

- Requirements, which includes but is not limited to the
    - Types of content required
    - Communication strategies the site needs to support
    - Strategies that will support visitors finding the content they need

- Features that add value to users' experiences
- Roles of your users and what they will be allowed to do
- Performance expectations based on projected use
- Security requirements
- Design, which includes but is not limited to the

  - Wireframes for the homepage, the landing pages, and the different types of content
  - Interaction plan describing the behavior of the objects included in the wireframes
  - Style guide to be used when rendering the visual aspects of the site
  - Theme region plan required to support the layout strategies assumed in the wireframes
  - Graphic rendering of the finished pages

Project Management Plan

For this type of plan, you should consider the resources required to meet the website plan and the maintenance plan:

- What skills will you need?
- What order will the website planning and development tasks be accomplished?
- When can the site be launched?
- How much will it cost?
- How will you monitor progress?
- How will you manage expectations if a requirement or design feature cannot be met as originally requested?

These are only some of the questions that fall into the realm of project management. With these questions, you can start a discussion with those involved in the website project, whether you are the client, the developer, or the designer.

The project management plan can include one or more of the following:

- Schedule
- Budget
- Skills
- Expectations

Development Plan

Development plans are a source of much discussion among people who build websites. As you've seen, a simple development plan could be this: Install Drupal. For professionals, entire methodologies have grown up around development plans. Two of the most famous are Agile and Waterfall.

The development plan can document your content strategy. For example, if you add events to your site, you can enter all the event information into one text field or split the information into different fields, such as date, location, and price.

What would influence your decision? For a simple site, it might be sufficient to have all the information in one text field. For a larger, more complex site you may need to filter or sort events by date, location, price, host, and more. To filter and sort in this way, you need to make sure that information is entered into different fields.

Another aspect of a development plan is when each strategy will be implemented. For instance, will each section of the site be implemented one at a time? Or will aspects of each site section be implemented, thus implementing all sections at the same time but in varying degrees of detail?

In the end, the development plan should convey what is needed to implement the requirements and design in the website plan and meet the project management expectations regarding schedule and budget. For example, development plans can include one or more of the following:

- A list of different types of content along with their data fields, features, and user permissions
- A list of features needed on your site together with the modules required to provide those features
- A strategy for the design of your site
- A development methodology
- A test plan that covers each aspect of testing, including integration, regression, security, usability, and accessibility

Maintenance Plan

Maintenance tasks are typically performed after the site is officially launched, but that doesn't mean you start planning your maintenance when the site is about to go live. At least three types of maintenance tasks need to be planned:

- Routine monitoring maintenance
- Planned update maintenance
- Site management

The way you plan to perform each type of maintenance can influence development strategies. For instance, if you plan to maintain the content on your site by allowing particular people to manage specific types of content, the development team needs to be aware of that and provide the necessary functionality.

Our Drupalville Website Plan

As mentioned in the previous chapter, we're going to build a site called Drupalville. By the end of this book, our plan is for the site to look like Figure 2.1.

Figure 2.1   The completed Drupalville site for this book

Content Requirements

The site we're going to build has multiple types of content. Here's a list of the types of content that we'll add to our site:

- News articles
- Static content
- Blog posts
- Documentation
- Information about Drupal companies
- Events
- Discussion forums
- Information about useful Drupal websites
- Information about useful Drupal user groups

Communications Requirements

The site will also have these types of communication:

- The content communicates the message.
- Drupal's default emails communicate account settings actions.
- Comments are allowed for users to respond to the content.
- Social media links provided can help visitors to share pages of the site with others.
- Polls enable users to respond to questions.
- Contact form so that users can reach the administrators on the site.

Navigation Requirements

We're going to provide the following to help visitors navigate the site:

- Menus
- Dynamically generated lists of content that can be filtered
- Breadcrumbs

Feature Requirements

The content, communications, and navigation requirements previously listed hint to many of the features planned for the site. The following list reinforces that which has already been implied and adds additional features. The list could be quite extensive if you include all the default functionality on the site:

- **Weather:** A block that displays the weather
- **Sharing capability:** Functionality that enables users to post to social media sites and email
- **Forum management:** Functionality that organizes forums and their displays
- **Polls:** Functionality that manages the availability and access to the polls
- **Contact Forms:** Enable users to submit an inquiry
- **Search**
- **Site map**

User Requirements

There will be several different groups of users:

- Anonymous visitors who can only look at the site
- Authenticated users who can log in, post comments, and join the discussion forums
- Bloggers who can write blog posts
- Company editors who can manage the Drupal company listings
- Moderators who can manage the comments and discussion forums
- Administrators who have free reign to do anything on the site

Design Requirements

To help you visualize what our Drupalville site can look like at the end of this book, here are screen shots of the landing pages you will be building:

- **News articles:** Displayed in a teaser list layout with comments and social media links. You can see these articles in a slideshow on the author's homepage. There's a preview in Figure 2.2.

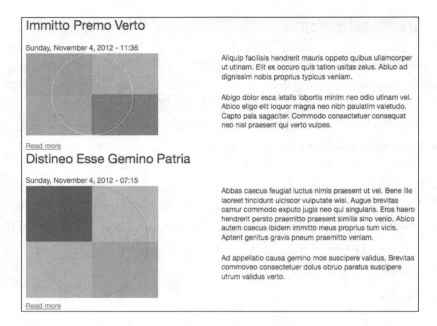

Figure 2.2   A preview of the news layout

- **Blog posts:** Displayed in a blog layout with comments and social media links. There's a preview in Figure 2.3.

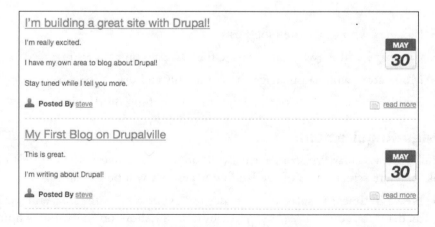

Figure 2.3   A preview of the blog layout

- **Events:** Displayed in a calendar layout, as shown in Figure 2.4.

Figure 2.4   A preview of the calendar layout

- **Discussion forums:** Displayed in a bulletin board layout, as shown in Figure 2.5.

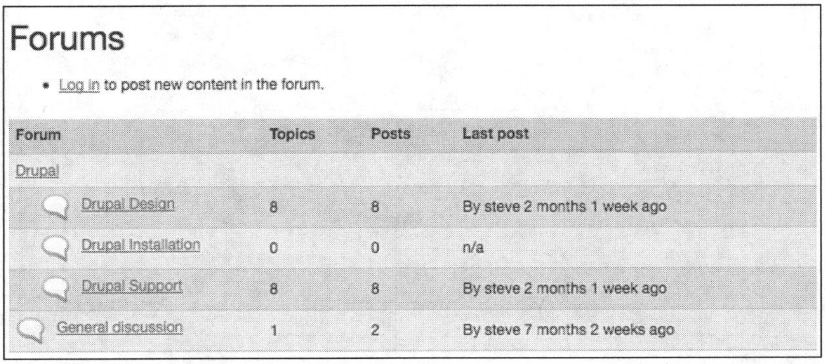

Figure 2.5   A preview of the discussion forum layout

- **Information about Drupal companies:** Displayed with detailed, business directory-style information. There's a preview in Figure 2.6.
- **Information about useful Drupal websites:** Displayed with the name of site and the topic they address, as shown in Figure 2.7.

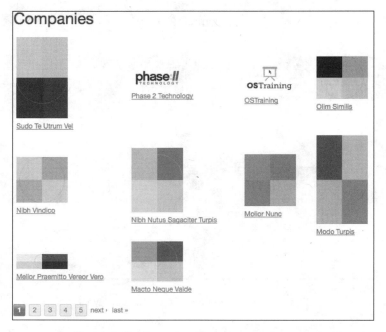

Figure 2.6   A preview of the company's layout

Figure 2.7   A preview of the websites layout

- **Drupal user group listings:** Displayed with location information, as shown in Figure 2.8.

User Groups

User Group Name	User Group Listing Date
Erat Immitto	11/04/2012 - 14:04
Adipiscing At	11/04/2012 - 13:52
Ibidem Populus Velit	11/04/2012 - 13:42
Praesent Volutpat	11/04/2012 - 13:36
Acsi Causa Sed	11/04/2012 - 12:48
Esse Populus	11/04/2012 - 12:40
At Immitto Similis	11/04/2012 - 12:22
Immitto Premo Verto	11/04/2012 - 11:36
Oppeto Proprius Tation Vero	11/04/2012 - 11:17
Mauris Ut	11/04/2012 - 11:14

1 2 3 4 5 6 7 8 9 ... next › last »

Figure 2.8   A preview of the user group layout

Our Drupalville Project Management Plan

Project management plans aren't usually conveyed in four bullet points, but here is a quick summary of what we'll need to complete this book's project successfully:

- **Schedule:** You'll build this site at your own pace. Someone working quickly may finish this book in two days or less. Someone without so much free time can build the site successfully, but more slowly.

- **Budget:** Zero. You won't need to spend any money to build the site for this book.

- **Skills:** Zero. You'll learn everything you need to know to build the site.

- **Expectations:** Your first Drupal site does not come with very complicated expectations. Your Drupalville site won't be the most beautiful Drupal site in the world and it won't make you a million dollars. However, we do expect that it will be a giant step towards helping you learn Drupal.

Our Drupalville Development Plan

In this book, we're going to use a specific development plan. Figure 2.9 shows the plan that we're going to use and refer to throughout the book. Here are the chapters in which each step is detailed. Not every chapter contains a step, but the book does follow the order of the plan:

- Planning (Chapter 2, "Drupal Planning Explained")
- Installation (Chapter 3, "Drupal Installations Explained")
- Content types (Chapter 5, "Drupal Content Explained")
- Fields (Chapter 6, "Drupal Fields Explained")
- Themes (Chapter 9, "Drupal Themes Explained")
- Blocks (Chapter 10, "Drupal Blocks Explained")
- Views (Chapter 11, "Drupal Views Explained")
- Layout modules (Chapter 12, "Drupal Layout Modules Explained")
- Users (Chapter 13, "Drupal Users Explained")

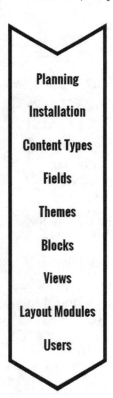

Figure 2.9   Our Development Plan in this book

We recommend that you follow this plan when building your first few Drupal sites.

In a few months' time, when you're more experienced with Drupal, you may find ways to improve this plan, skip some steps, or even rearrange some steps. That's great. However, as a beginner, you should follow these steps closely until you reach that more experienced stage.

Our Drupalville Maintenance Plan

Because the site we're creating is only designed to help you learn, we don't necessarily need an ongoing maintenance plan. At the end of this book, you have two options:

- You can delete the Drupalville site that we've built.
- You can maintain the Drupalville site using the techniques shown in Chapter 14, "Drupal Site Management Explained."

What's Next?

Now that we've discussed planning, you're ready to build your first Drupal site.

Turn the page and let's continue with the next step in our Drupal plan: installation.

3

Drupal Installations Explained

This chapter shows you where and how to install Drupal. When you finish, you should have a Drupal site that you can use through this book. That is where you can practice everything else you do in upcoming chapters.

At the end of this chapter, you should be able to

- Choose the best place to host Drupal.
- Choose the best way to install Drupal.
- Install Drupal automatically.
- Install Drupal manually.
- Get help if you're stuck with installing Drupal.

Hosting Your Drupal Site Explained

Drupal is not like many other software programs. It can't just run on any computer. It requires a server to run successfully. That means you normally have the choice of installing Drupal in one of three places:

- A local server installed on your computer
- A web server that you own or rent
- A web server hosted by Drupal specialists

Choosing the best place to install Drupal is important, so here is an explanation of the difference between the three options.

A Local Server Installed on Your Computer

We do not recommend that beginner Drupal users use a local server.
It can be tempting to choose this route. More advanced users find several useful advantages to working on your computer:

- **Working offline:** You can work without an Internet connection.
- **Privacy:** Your Drupal site will be safe and private, accessible only to people who can access that computer.
- **Free:** There are no fees to pay.

However, there are also several important disadvantages to using a computer:

- **Extra installations needed:** You need to download and configure special software for your computer.
- **Difficult to get help:** You can't easily show it to other people and ask for help.
- **Only one computer:** You can access it only from the computer you used to install it.
- **Need to move to launch:** When you're ready to make your site public, you need to move everything to a web server and adjust for any differences between the two locations.

Because of these disadvantages, installing on your computer can present significant obstacles for a beginner. Do not take this route until you have more experience.

However, if you do feel comfortable overcoming these obstacles, you can find instructions on how to install Drupal on a PC at http://www.drupal7explained.com/pc and on a Mac at http://www.drupal7explained.com/mac.

A Web Server That You Own or Rent

Unlike your computer, a web server is specifically designed for hosting websites so that they are easy to visit for anyone who's online.

If you work for a company, it might provide a server. However, many people need to rent space from a hosting company.

There are two common types of web server: Linux and Microsoft. Both require PHP, because that is the language Drupal is written in, and MySQL, because it is the type of database Drupal normally uses. These are the minimum versions needed:

- **PHP:** 5.3.5 or above
- **MySQL:** 5.0.15 or above

Linux servers also require Apache, a type of web server software. The minimum version for that is 1.3 and above. You can find more details on Drupal's technical requirements at http://drupal.org/requirements.

To run Drupal, Apache has long been the favorite choice. Microsoft is working hard to make Drupal run as smoothly as possible on its servers, but for now, Apache is still recommended.

Most hosting companies now support Drupal, but it's worth choosing carefully. Some hosting companies are much better than others. Here is some advice before picking your host:

- Search http://www.drupal.org/forum for other people's experiences with that host.

- Contact the hosting company's customer support and ask what it knows about Drupal. One of our training students actually called the phone numbers of several hosts and timed their response. After all, in an emergency you don't want to be on hold for an hour or to be talking to someone that knows nothing about Drupal.

For more Drupal hosting advice, visit http://www.drupal7explained.com/hosting.

A Web Server That's Hosted by Drupal Specialists

You just saw that you can install Drupal on almost any server that has PHP and MySQL installed. However, you can also host on servers that are fine-tuned for Drupal.

There are many advantages to choosing Drupal-specific hosting services:

- They are managed by Drupal experts who know exactly what Drupal sites need to run well.

- They can keep your web server up to date, which greatly increases security. Some also keep your Drupal site up to date for you.

- They provide extra features that make it easier to install and manage a Drupal site.

We recommend you consider using a Drupal-specific hosting service. you can find a recommendation at http://drupal7explained.com/hosting. However, we're not going to use one in this book. This is for two main reasons:

- Some of these services add a lot of extra features when they install Drupal. Those features will be confusing as you try to follow along with the book.

- To keep your site safe and secure, these services may restrict access to some of your Drupal site's files, which will cause problems in later chapters of this book.

Installation Recommendations Explained

Although you can install Drupal in other ways, two methods are recommended:

- Install Drupal automatically on a web server.
- Install Drupal manually on a web server.

If you use one of these two methods, it is easier to follow along with this book.

Installing Drupal automatically is a fast and easy method to start with Drupal, but you need to make sure this method is supported by your hosting company.

If you choose to install Drupal manually, you'll be moving Drupal files to the web server. For that, you'll need File Transfer Protocol (FTP) software. One good choice is Filezilla, which is free to download and can work on Windows, Mac, or Linux computers. To download it, go to http://www.filezilla-project. org, and click Download Filezilla Client.

You will see both recommended ways to install Drupal. If you're in a hurry, use the One-Click option explained in the section, "Install Drupal Automatically."

If you'd like to be geeky and take the time to install Drupal yourself, use the steps explained in the section, "Manual Drupal Installations Explained."

Automatic Drupal Installations Explained

Automatic installers are often called One-Click installers. Actually, One Click is a bit of an exaggeration. Installing Drupal this way takes approximately five clicks. There are many different versions of automatic installers. You're going to use perhaps the most popular version, which is called Fantastico. Your hosting company may offer an alternative that looks a little different but works in a similar way.

The following are steps to install Drupal automatically:

1. **Login to your web hosting account:** Each hosting account looks a little different, but there are often similarities. CPanel and Plesk are two popular types of software used for an account. In this example, you use CPanel, as shown in Figure 3.1.

Figure 3.1   CPanel hosting account

2. **Find the Fantastico button and click it:** You can find the button on any of the rows, but you can normally find it by looking for the blue smiley face, as shown in Figure 3.2.

Figure 3.2   Fantastico button

3. **View the Fantastico Control Panel:** After clicking the Fantastico button, the main Fantastico Control Panel displays, as shown in Figure 3.3. Click Drupal on the left.

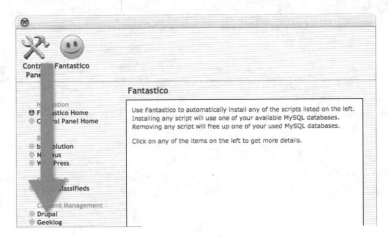

Figure 3.3   Fantastico Control Panel

4. **Choose to install Drupal:** You now see a screen like the one in Figure 3.4 with a brief introduction to Drupal. Click New Installation to proceed.

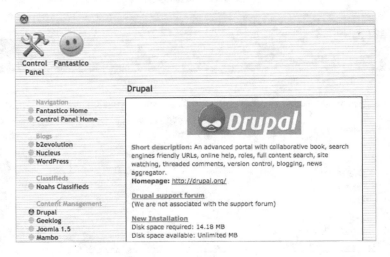

Figure 3.4   Drupal screen in Fantastico

5. **Enter your new site details:** Fantastico now asks for the details of your new site. Here's what you need to know:

   - **Install on domain:** Unless you're an experienced website builder, you can leave this field alone.

   - **Install on directory:** You can leave this blank if you'd like the site to be accessible directly via your domain (for example: http://www.drupal7explained.com). The recommended alternative for learning with this book is to use a subfolder. If you do this, it's not difficult to move your site if you later want to make it accessible directly via your domain. So, go ahead and enter **Drupalville** into this field.

   - **Admin:** This is a username you use on your site. Don't use "admin," because that is too easy for other people to guess.

   - **Password:** This is the password you use to log in. Don't use "admin" here! Don't use "password," "1234," or "iloveyou," either. A good combination of numbers, punctuation, and uppercase and lowercase letters is vital.

   - **Admin email:** Enter your email address here. If you forget your password, this is where it will be sent.

   - **Admin full name:** Enter your name here.

   - **Site name:** Enter **Drupalville** here. This is what people see when they get emails from your site. For example, the email will say: Thank You for Registering at Drupalville.

   - **Install sample data:** Make sure that this box is unchecked. You are not going to use any sample data for your Drupal sites in this book.

   Enter those details in the screen, as shown in Figure 3.5.

6. **Confirm your installation details:** After you enter all your information and click Install, a confirmation screen displays, as shown in Figure 3.6. Click Finish Installation to complete the install.

Figure 3.5   Drupal installation screen in Fantastico

Figure 3.6   Drupal confirmation screen in Fantastico

7. **Bookmark your new site addresses:** The final Drupal screen in
Fantastico displays. Your installation has completed. There will be two links,
as shown in Figure 3.7:

   - The full URL to the admin area (bookmark this!)
   - The full URL to this installation of Drupal

Take its advice, and click both links; then bookmark them in your browser.
You'll use both of those links often!

8. **Visit your new site:** Click the links, as shown in Figure 3.7. In the example you previously saw, the links can take you to http://www. drupal7explained.com/drupalville. You now see a new website, as shown in Figure 3.8.

Install Drupal (3/3)

/home/drupal7e/public_html/drupalville/sites/default
/settings.php configured
/home/drupal7e/public_html/drupalville/data.sql configured

Please notice:

We only offer auto-installation and auto-configuration of Drupal but do not offer any kind of support.

You need a username and a password to enter the admin area. Your username is   . Your password is   The full URL to the admin area (**Bookmark this!**): http://drupal7explained.com /drupalville/

[Back to Drupal overview]

Email the details of this installation to:

[   ]

[Send E-mail]

Figure 3.7   Final Drupal screen in Fantastico

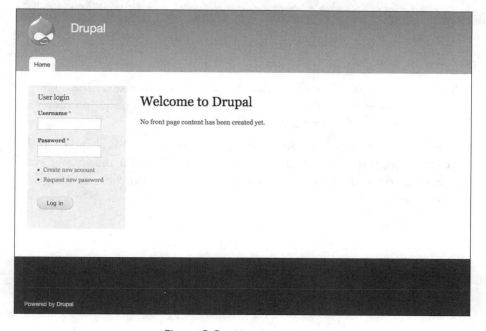

Figure 3.8   Your New Drupal site

9. **Try logging in to your new site:** You can log in to your site by using the login area shown in Figure 3.9. Log in using the username and password you created earlier.

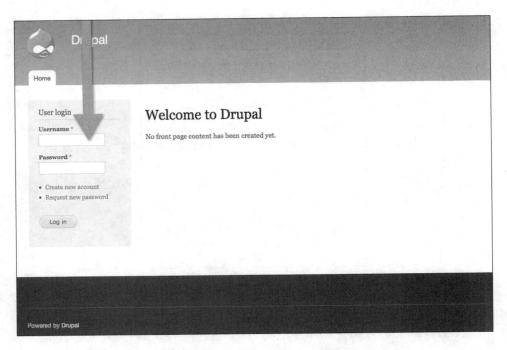

Figure 3.9   Drupal Administrator Login screen

10. **View the Drupal Control Panel:** If you entered your username and password correctly, you'll now see a black and gray administration menu across as the top of your site, as shown in Figure 3.10.

11. Congratulations! You can now go straight to the end of this chapter. Most of the rest of this chapter will be spent installing Drupal manually, but even many experienced Drupal users prefer to do things automatically using an automatic installer.

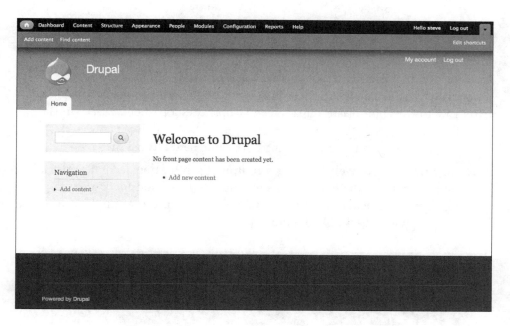

Figure 3.10   Drupal Administrator Control Panel

Manual Drupal Installations Explained

An old-fashioned HTML website consists only of one part: files. It doesn't need anything else to run.

However, a Drupal website is different because it consists not only of files but also includes a database to store all the site's information. You must set up both the files and the database and then connect them together. So, the process of installing Drupal manually is like this:

Step 1: Create a database.

Step 2: Download the Drupal files, and upload them to your web server.

Step 3: Complete the Drupal installation by connecting the database and files together.

Step 1: Create a Database

The first step is to create a database to store all the unique information about your site.

A database is basically a group of tables with letters and numbers stored in its rows and columns. Think of it as several spreadsheets. There's a spreadsheet with all the articles you write. There's another for all of the users who register on your site. The database makes it easy for Drupal to easily handle large amounts of data. If a new article or user is added, Drupal just needs to add an extra row to the appropriate spreadsheet. Drupal uses a particular type of database known as MySQL.

Now go ahead and set up a database for your new Drupal site:

1. **Log in to your web hosting account:** Each hosting account looks a little different, but there are often similarities. CPanel and Plesk are two popular types of software used for hosting accounts. In this example, you use CPanel, which looks like Figure 3.11.

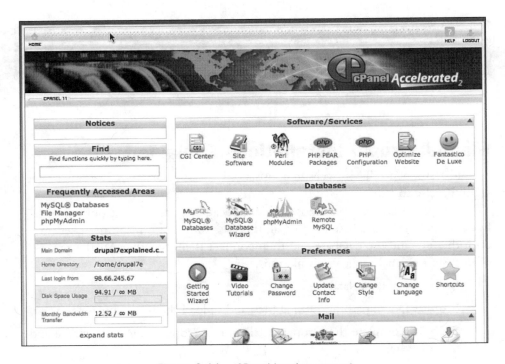

Figure 3.11   CPanel hosting account

2. **Find the button that says MySQL Databases and click it:** The button has the MySQL name and the blue dolphin logo, as shown in Figure 3.12.

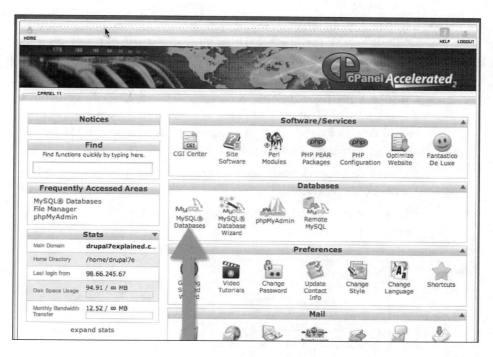

Figure 3.12   MySQL Databases button

3. **Create a new database:** Choose a name that is relatively easy to remember, and click Create Database. Be sure to write this name down and note that it's likely to have your hosting account name before it. In Figure 3.13, your new database is called drupal7e_drupalville.

Figure 3.13   Create a new database

4. **Create a database user:** The next step is to create a user account so that you can access the database. Without password protection, anyone might log in and see your site's important information. Here's what you need to do:

- **Choose a username:** Enter a short username here, different from anything you've used before. This example uses **dbuser**. The username is a little confusing because your hosting account name is added also, so in Figure 3.14, your full username will be drupal7e_dbuser.

- **Choose a password:** Some versions of CPanel can help you choose a password that is difficult to guess. If you set your own choice, use a combination of numbers, punctuation, and uppercase and lowercase letters so that the password is hard to guess.

- **Be sure to record both your username and password safely:** You need them again soon.

- **Click Create User:** You should see a message saying the user has been created successfully.

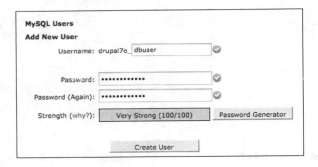

Figure 3.14   Creating a new database user

5. **Allow the new user access to the database:** Now you need to allow your new user to log in to the database. There should be an area called Add User to Database. Choose your database name and then your username before clicking Add, as in Figure 3.15.

Figure 3.15   Adding user to the database

6. **Give your user permission to modify the database:** The final step in this process is to decide what your new user can and cannot do with the database. Give them All permissions so that your Drupal site can make whatever changes it needs to the database. Click Make Changes to finish the process, as shown in Figure 3.16.

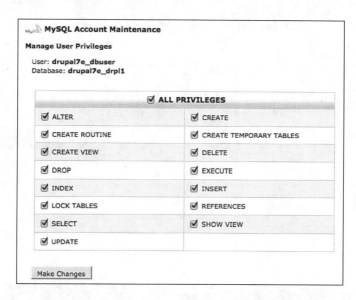

Figure 3.16   Giving user permissions to modify the database

Step 2: Download the Drupal Files and Upload Them to Your Web Server

Now that you have the database ready, you can upload the Drupal files. These contain all the code and images that Drupal needs to run:

1. **Find the Drupal download area:** Go to http://www.drupal.org and click the Get Started with Drupal button, as shown in Figure 3.17.

2. **Find the Drupal download page:** You now see a page with information on getting started with Drupal. Click the Download Drupal 7.14 button, as shown in Figure 3.18. The number 7.14 may have increased by the time you read this, but don't fear: Click this button, and you can always download the latest and recommended version of Drupal.

Figure 3.17   Download Drupal button

Figure 3.18   Finding the Drupal download page on Drupal.org

3. **Download Drupal:** Drupal download pages have green, yellow, and red areas. It works like a traffic light. The green areas have safe downloads; the yellow areas have downloads you should be cautious about; and the red areas have experimental downloads that shouldn't be used on a live site. Remember also that you're using Drupal 7. So, you want the download for Drupal 7 from the green area, as shown in Figure 3.19. Click the zip link, and a download starts. You receive a .zip file with a name like this: drupal–7.14.zip. It contains all the files you need to install Drupal, so look after it! Save it to your desktop, your downloads folder, or somewhere you can find it easily.

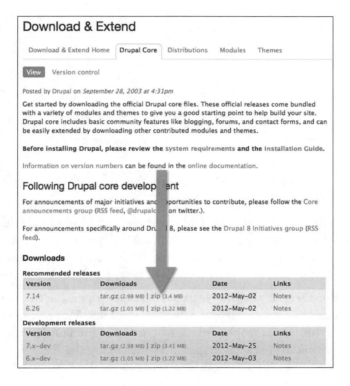

Figure 3.19   Download Drupal link

4. **Uncompress the .zip file:** On a Windows computer you can right-click the file and choose Extract Here. On a Mac you can click File, Open With, and choose Archive Utility. When that's complete, you should have a folder on your desktop that looks like Figure 3.20. The folder should have a name similar to drupal-7.14.

Figure 3.20   Drupal files on your computer

5. **Access your web server:** You're now going to start the process of moving your files on to your web server.

   The first step is to open your FTP software such as Filezilla. Then log in to your FTP account, and browse to the folder where you want to install Drupal. Often, this is the root directory, which often has a name such as /public_html/, /www/, or /htdocs/.

6. **Move the Drupal files to your webserver:** Open the folder that just downloaded and extracted and Select All the Files. Move all the files, via your FTP software, into the folder where you're installing Drupal. With Filezilla, this is as simple as dragging and dropping the files. Uploading might take from 5 to 30 minutes or more depending on your Internet connection.

7. **Double-check your database information:** Before you go any further, stop to make sure you have all the information. Here's what you need:

   - **Hostname:** This is often localhost, but some hosting companies such as GoDaddy have a different hostname. You can find it in your hosting account or by contacting customer support.

- **Username:** The username for your database. In this example, it was Drupalex_dbuser.

- **Password:** The password for your database.

- **Database name:** The name of your database. In this example, it was Drupalex_dbuser.

Got all that? Then move to Step 3 and wrap up your Drupal installation.

Step 3: Complete the Drupal Installation by Connecting the Database and Files Together

You've now successfully set up the two halves of your Drupal site: the database (Step 1) and the files (Step 2). The final step is to connect those two halves together. You do that now:

1. **Drupal Web Installer Step 1: Select an installation profile.** Start your browser and visit the URL where you uploaded the files. In the example used, that was http://www.drupal7explained.com/drupalville/.

   You should see an installation screen like Figure 3.21. This is the first step in Drupal's easy-to-use installation manager. There are several steps to go through. The first one is simple: You just need to choose the Standard installation option and then click Save and Continue.

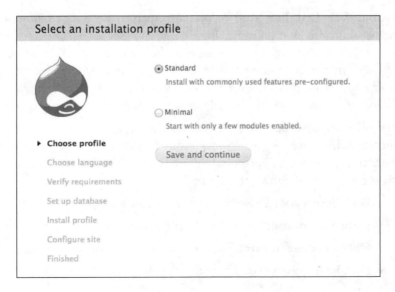

Figure 3.21   Drupal Web Installer Step 1

2. **Drupal Web Installer Step 2: Choose language.** If you have been following along, you have the option to install only English. Click Save and Continue, as shown in Figure 3.22.

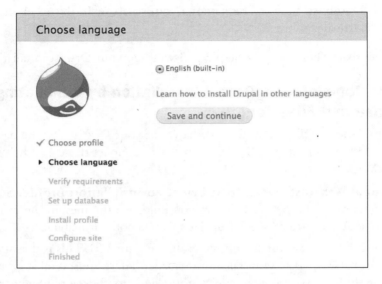

Figure 3.22   Drupal Web Installer Step 2

3. **Drupal Web Installer Step 3: Verify requirements.** For many of you, Drupal skips this step entirely. However, if your server isn't correctly set up for Drupal, you see an error message, as shown in Figure 3.23. Drupal explains what needs to be fixed before you can proceed. If the instructions don't make sense to you, your best options are to talk to the people running your server or to ask for help at http://www.drupal.org/forum/1.

4. **Drupal Web Installer Step 4: Set up database.** This is the most important step. This is where you connect your files and database together. You need the details you collected when you created the database earlier. You can see a screen, as shown in Figure 3.24:

   - **Database type:** Leave this as the default setting.
   - **Database name:** Enter the details you collected earlier.
   - **Database username:** Enter the details you collected earlier.
   - **Database password:** Enter the details you collected earlier.

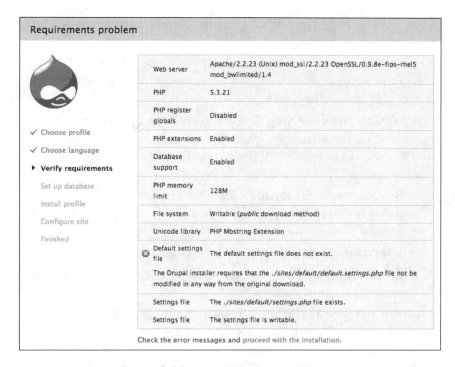

Figure 3.23   Drupal Web Installer Step 3

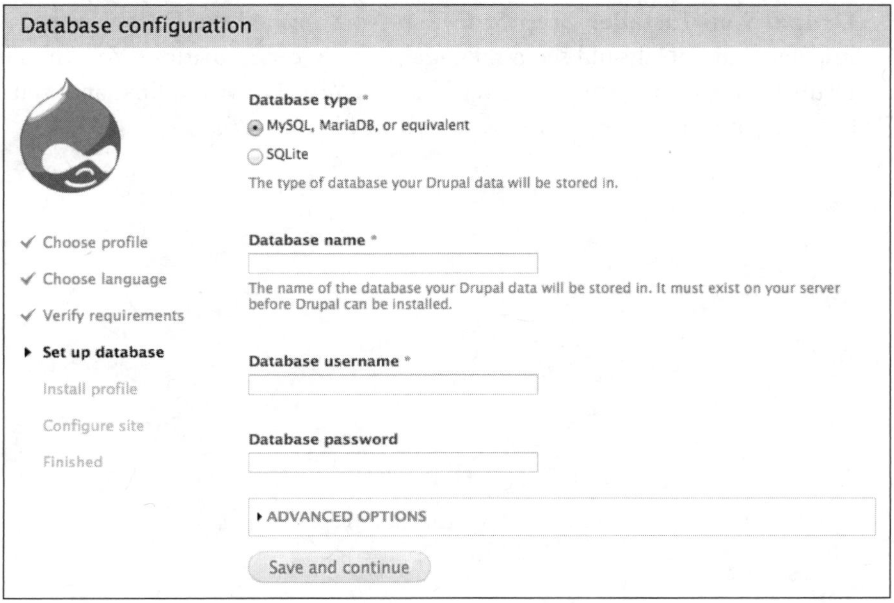

Figure 3.24   Drupal Web Installer Step 4

Click Save and Continue when you finish. If you made a mistake, Drupal sends you back to try again.

There are also some advanced options. If you have serious problems getting passed this step, talk with your hosting company and ask them for help filling in the Database host and Database port fields.

5. **Drupal Web Installer Step 5: Configuration.** The screen shown in Figure 3.25 is the final place where you need to enter any information. Be sure to make a careful note of the email, username, and password that you enter:

   - **Site name:** Enter **Drupalville** here. This is what people see when they get emails from your site. For example, the email will say, Thank you for Registering at Drupalville.

   - **Username:** This is the username you use on your site.

   - **Email address:** Enter an email address that you want to use for your personal account on the site.

   - **Admin password:** This is the password you use to log in. Please don't use "admin" here! Don't use "password," "1234," or "iloveyou" either. There are plenty of good free password generators available if you do a quick look on your favorite search engine.

   Click Save and continue.

6. **Drupal Web Installer Step 5: Finish.** You finished the Drupal web installer, and you should see a message saying Congratulations, You Installed Drupal! Visit Your New Site. Click the Visit Your New Site link, and you can see your new Drupal site, as shown in Figure 3.26.

Figure 3.25   Drupal Web Installer Step 5

Figure 3.26   Drupal Web Installer Step 6

If you're in the right place, you'll see a login screen, as shown in Figure 3.27. Log in using the username and password you created earlier.

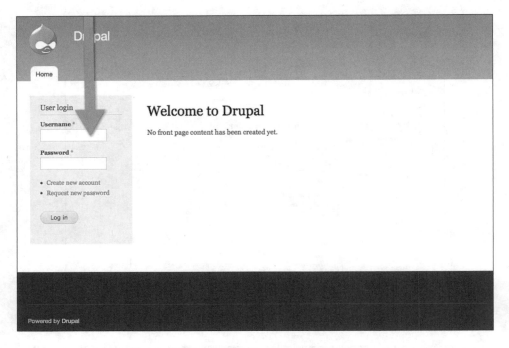

Figure 3.27   Drupal Administrator Login Screen

7. **View the Drupal Control Panel**. If you entered your username and password correctly, you'll now see a black and gray administration menu across as the top of your site, as shown in Figure 3.28.

8. Congratulations! You've installed Drupal, and you're ready for the rest of this book.

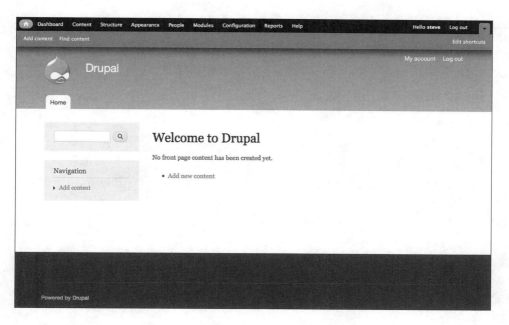

Figure 3.28   Drupal Administrator Control Panel

Getting Help with Installations

There are three places you should go if you need help at any point during this chapter:

- **The Drupal Forum:** It's almost guaranteed that someone has experienced the same Drupal installation problem as you and has asked about it on http://www.drupal.org/forum/1/. It's a great place to search for solutions and ask for help.

- **The Drupal help site:** There's an installation manual available for Drupal 7 at http://www.drupal.org/documentation/install.

- **Drupal 7 Explained:** http://www.drupal7explained.com has video tutorials and more to help with your installation.

What's Next?

You now have a Drupal site ready to use. In the next chapter, you tour your new site and are introduced to the most important things you need to know. Are you ready? Turn the page to continue.

4

Drupal Administration Explained

This chapter explains the basic concepts of your Drupal site. When you finish, you'll understand how to navigate around your site and how administrators manage your site.

At the end of this chapter, you should be able to

- Understand the difference between the administrator and visitor areas of your Drupal site.
- Understand the visitor area of your Drupal site.
- Understand the administrator area of your Drupal site.
- Make your first Drupal site changes.

The Administration Menu Explained

At the end of Chapter 3, "Drupal Installations Explained," you installed your new Drupal site and logged in. Congratulations! You're now ready to explore your Drupal site.

Across the top of the site, you now see a horizontal, black administration menu, as shown in Figure 4.1. This menu is the most important part of your site. Almost everything you want to change and modify on your site can be accessed from here.

The links in this menu are organized according to how often they're used.

On the left side of your menu, you can see a Home icon, plus a Dashboard and Content link. These are three of the links you click most often.

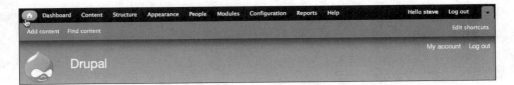

Figure 4.1   The administration menu in your Drupal site

On the right side of your menu, you can see Configuration, Reports, and Help links. Configuration and Reports are links that are used less frequently. These contain settings and maintenance functions. The Help link contains documentation.

Now take a look at each link in turn.

Home Icon

Click the Home icon, as shown in Figure 4.2.

Figure 4.2   The Home icon on the administration menu

Whenever you click this Home icon, you'll always be taken back to your site's front page, as shown in Figure 4.3.

Dashboard

Click the Dashboard link, as shown in Figure 4.4.

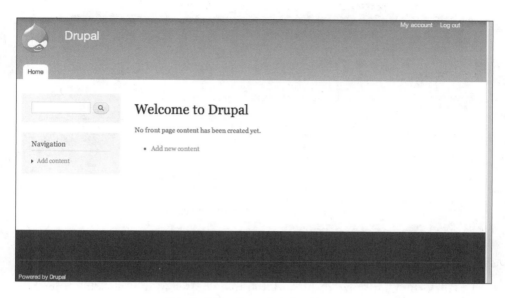

Figure 4.3   Your site's front page

Figure 4.4   The Dashboard link on the administration menu

You can now see three boxes on the screen, as shown in Figure 4.5. This screen gives you helpful information about what's going on with your site:

- The Recent Content box shows what's new.
- The Search Form box enables you to search for any content on the site.
- The Who's New box shows you new site members.

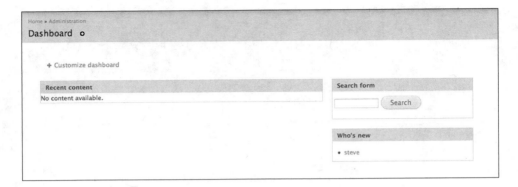

Figure 4.5   The Dashboard screen

You can also customize this screen to show the information that you want. To do so, follow these steps:

1. Click the Customize dashboard link that you see in the top-left corner of Figure 4.5. You now see a screen, as shown in Figure 4.6. There are two more boxes available: Recent Comments and Who's Online.

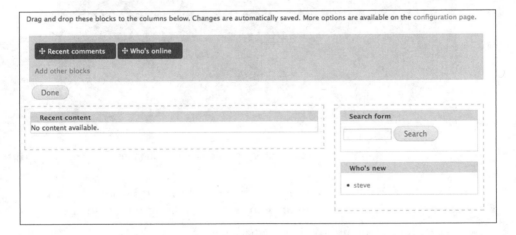

Figure 4.6   Customizing the Dashboard screen

2. Drag and drop the Recent Comments and Who's Online boxes into the main area so it now looks like Figure 4.7.

3. Click the Done button to finish customizing the dashboard.

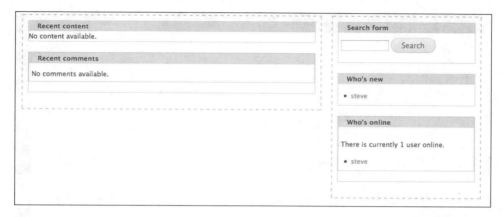

Figure 4.7   New areas on your Dashboard screen

It is also possible to add more boxes to this screen. We'll show you how to create those boxes, called "blocks," in Chapter 10, "Drupal Blocks Explained."

Content

Click the Content link, as shown in Figure 4.8.

Figure 4.8   The Content link in the administration menu

You can now see the screen shown in Figure 4.9.

This screen gives you a list of all the content that has been added to your site. At the moment, that's a grand total of zero content items. However, if you have a lot of content, you can use the filters at the top of the page to find content easily. Figure 4.10 shows how you can search by the status of the content.

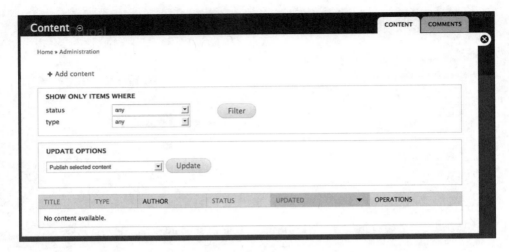

Figure 4.9   The Content screen

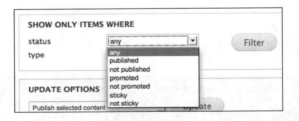

Figure 4.10   Searching for content of a particular status

You can also search for content of a particular type, as shown in Figure 4.11. Chapter 5, "Drupal Content Explained," explains the difference between an Article and a Basic page. In Chapter 5 you also see how to create more types of content.

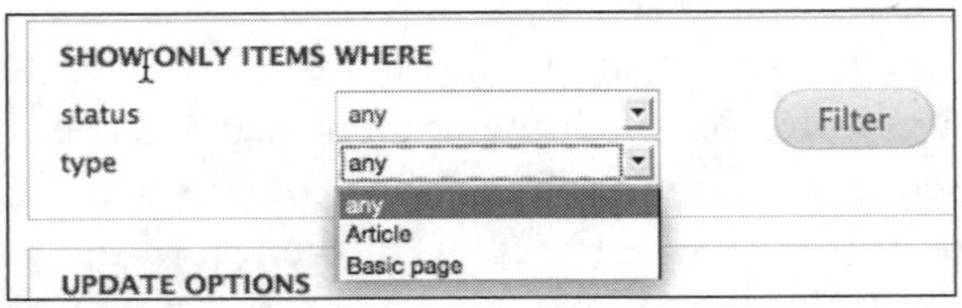

Figure 4.11   Searching for content of a particular type

On this screen, you can find and manage your content. The Update Options drop-down, as shown in Figure 4.12, enables you to manage your content in bulk.

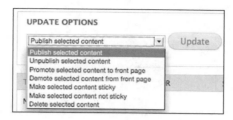

Figure 4.12   Options for managing your content

Finally, on this screen, you can manage comments on your site. You can access the comments area via the tab in the top-right corner, as shown in Figure 4.13.

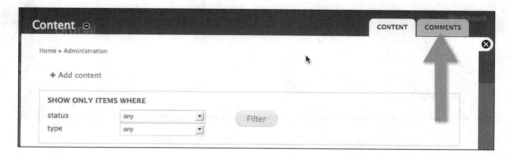

Figure 4.13   The Comments tab

You can see tabs like this often during this book. It's a common method of navigation in Drupal 7.

Click the Comments tab. You'll now see the screen, as shown in Figure 4.14.

In the top-right corner, there are also some smaller links, as shown in Figure 4.15. These enable you to access either Published Comments or Unapproved Comments.

You can also see smaller links like this throughout this book. Be careful and look out for these because they're often easy to miss.

Figure 4.14   The Comments screen

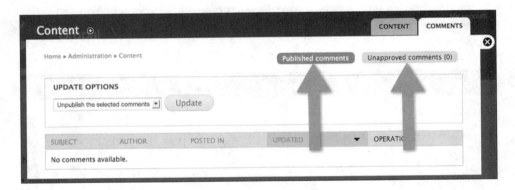

Figure 4.15   Links on the Comments screen

There are also two other Content links in the administration menu: Add Content and Find Content. These are marked in Figure 4.16.

Figure 4.16   Add Content and Find Content links in the administration menu

The Find content link takes you back to the Content screen you have been looking at already.

The Add Content link is the most important link in the entire site. After all, you are using a Content Management System (CMS). Everything you do with Drupal in this book is designed to help you add content to your website.

Click Add Content, and you see a screen like Figure 4.17. As mentioned earlier, Drupal provides two types of content: Article and Basic page.

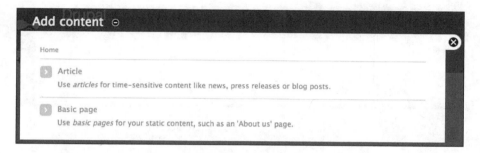

Figure 4.17   Add Content and Find Content links in the administration menu

Underneath the two content types, you see a brief explanation of what their purposes are. The Article is described as being for time-sensitive content such as news, press releases, or blog posts. The Basic page is described as being for your static content, such as an About Us page.

The next chapter creates several examples so that you can understand the difference between these two.

Structure

Click the Structure link, as shown in Figure 4.18.

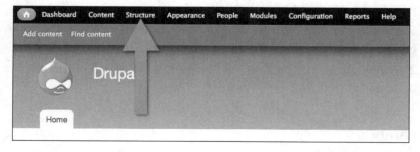

Figure 4.18   The Structure link in the administration menu

You can now see the screen shown in Figure 4.19. By default, the Structure screen has four links: Blocks, Content types, Menus, and Taxonomy.

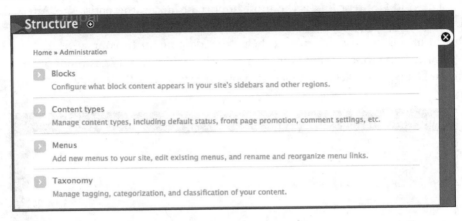

Figure 4.19   The Structure screen

The short explanation of this Structure screen is that it contains the main fundamental building blocks of your site.

The long explanation of this Structure screen will take several chapters. You explore blocks in Chapter 10, "Drupal Blocks Explained," Content types in Chapter 5, "Drupal Content Explained", menus in Chapter 8, "Drupal Menus Explained," and taxonomy in Chapter 6, "Drupal Fields Explained." In this book, you also add several links to this page.

For now, notice that, as with the Add content screen, there are short explanations under each link:

- **Blocks:** Configure what content appears in your site's sidebars and other regions.

- **Content types:** Manage content types, including default status, front page promotion, comment settings, and so on.

- **Menus:** Add new menus to your site, edit existing menus, and rename and reorganize menu links.

- **Taxonomy:** Manage tagging, categorization, and classification of your content.

Appearance

Click the Appearance link in the administration menu. You can now see the screen shown in Figure 4.20.

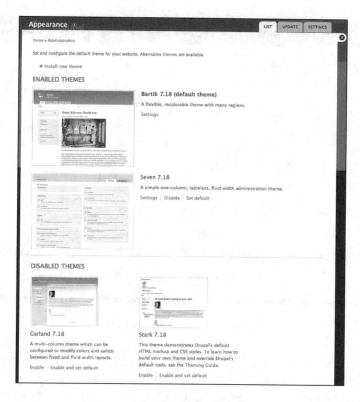

Figure 4.20   The Appearance screen

This screen contains the design for your site. Designs are provided by themes.

Bartik is the theme used by your site at the moment. Bartik is responsible for the blue-and-white color scheme, plus your site's layout.

Seven is the theme used for your administration area. Seven is responsible for the white background and gray tabs in the top-right corner.

Drupal provides you with two more options for your colors and layout: Garland and Stark. Both are currently in the Disabled Themes area.

Chapter 9, "Drupal Themes Explained," shows you how to modify and replace your theme.

People

Click the People link in the administration menu. You now see the screen shown in Figure 4.21.

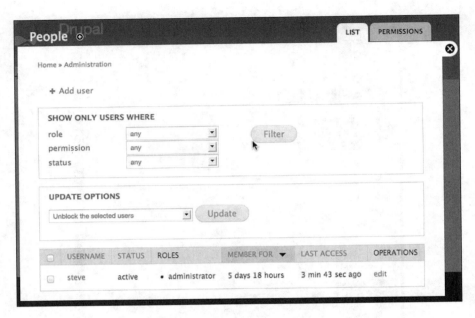

Figure 4.21   The People screen

This People screen has a list of all the users who are registered on your site. You can create new user accounts via the Add User link.

As with the Content screen, there are filters at the top to help you search for users, and there also Update Options to help you manage users. These are shown in Figure 4.22.

Figure 4.22   Filters and options on the People screen

Finally, there is a top-right tab called Permissions. Chapter 13, "Drupal Users Explained," goes into that area and shows you how to control user permissions on your site.

Modules

Click the Modules link in the administration menu. You can now see the screen shown in Figure 4.23. This area contains all the features on your Drupal site. Each module has a description beside it showing what it does.

This list is sorted alphabetically at the moment, so it starts with Aggregator and ends with User. Your version of Drupal might have more modules than this lower down the page; however, the modules between Aggregator and User are the default modules shared by all Drupal sites.

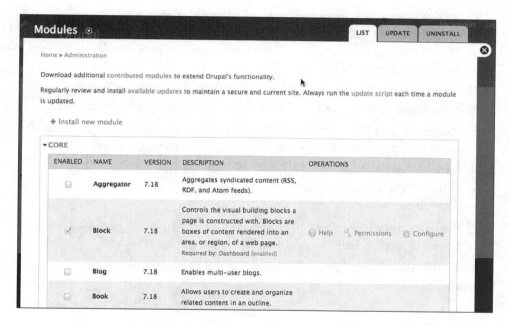

Figure 4.23   The Modules screen

You can add more modules via the Install New Module link in the top-left corner. You see how to do that in Chapter 6, "Drupal Fields Explained," and then Chapter 7, "Drupal Modules Explained," gives you even more details.

For now, take a look at one module in detail. The Comment module is shown in Figure 4.24. There are eight pieces of information or useful links:

1. **Check box:** Is this module enabled? If you don't want anyone commenting on your site, you can uncheck this box and click Save Configuration at the bottom of the screen. Comments will be instantly turned off for your whole site.

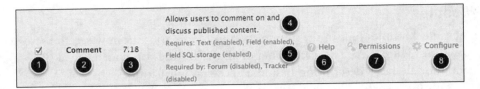

Figure 4.24   The Comment area in the Modules screen

2. **Comment:** The module's name!

3. **7.18:** The module's version number. This will increase while you use Drupal because new versions will be released with improvements and bug fixes. You see how to update to those new versions in Chapter 14, "Drupal Site Management Explained."

4. **Description:** This explains what the module does. This explanation is fairly clear; although, not all descriptions will be so easy to understand.

5. **Requires and Required By:** This area tells you if the Comment module needs other modules to operate. This area also tells you if the Comment module is needed by other modules to function.

6. **Help:** If you are unsure how to use a module, click this link for a more detailed explanation.

7. **Permissions:** This takes you to the Permissions area you just saw on the People screen. It enables you to decide who uses this module.

8. **Configure:** If there are any settings for this module, you can find them by clicking this link.

Configuration

Click the Configuration link on the administration menu. You can now see the screen shown in Figure 4.25.

This area has the settings for the main features in your site. As you add more features to your site (and remember, you do that by adding modules), this area becomes larger.

Often, these settings are the same that you can get to from the Configure link (refer to Figure 4.24).

This book doesn't have a whole chapter dedicated to this Configuration area, but you visit it throughout this book, often when you set up new features.

Now take a look at just one of these configuration options. Click the Shortcuts link, as shown in Figure 4.26.

Figure 4.25   The Configuration screen

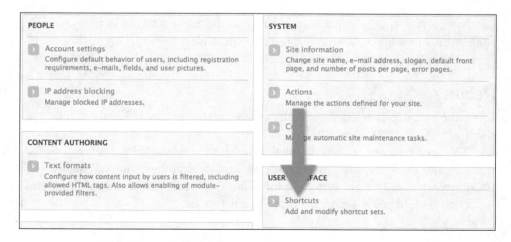

Figure 4.26   The Shortcuts link on Configuration screen

Click List Links in the center of the next screen. You now see a screen, as shown in Figure 4.27. Notice that there are two links: Add Content and Find Content. These are the same two links that you can see in the gray area of your administration menu.

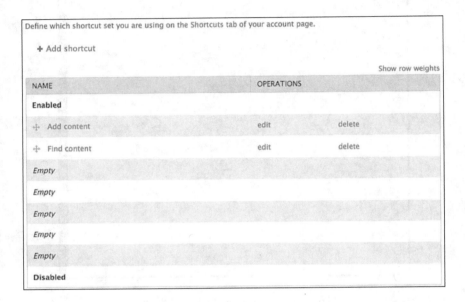

Figure 4.27   The Shortcuts screen

As you've seen, it can sometimes take two, three, or four clicks to reach some areas of your site. If you link to those areas from these Shortcuts, you can access those areas more easily and quickly.

Reports

Click the Reports link on the Administration menu. You now see the screen shown in Figure 4.28.

This area contains reports about the health of your site. Here, you can find out whether there are any problems with your site, whether your site needs updating, what people are searching for using your search box, and similar useful information. Chapter 14 explains more about this area.

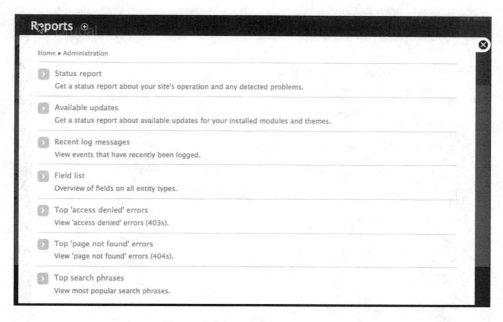

Figure 4.28   The Reports screen

Help

Click the Help link on the Administration menu. You can now see the screen shown in Figure 4.29.

Now look at one example. Click the Dashboard link under Help topics, as shown in Figure 4.30.

You now see the screen shown in Figure 4.31 with an explanation of the Dashboard that you saw earlier in this chapter.

This Help area is something that can become more useful as you become more experienced. When you first use Drupal, some of the terminology here may be confusing. However, by the end of this book, you will hopefully understand the large majority of these terms.

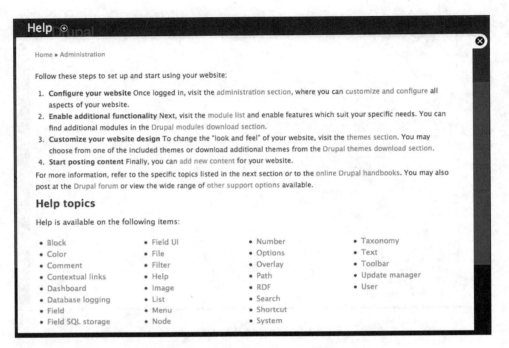

Figure 4.29   The Help screen

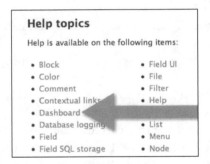

Figure 4.30   The Dashboard link on the Help screen

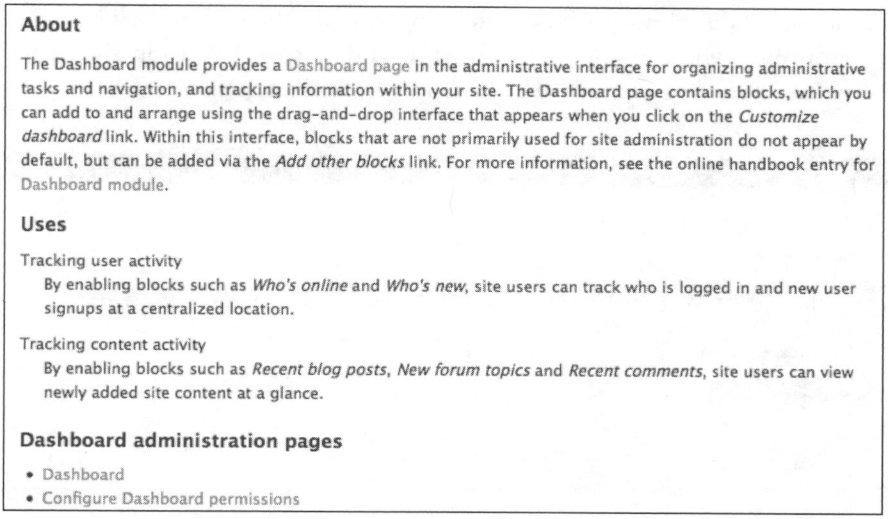

About

The Dashboard module provides a Dashboard page in the administrative interface for organizing administrative tasks and navigation, and tracking information within your site. The Dashboard page contains blocks, which you can add to and arrange using the drag-and-drop interface that appears when you click on the *Customize dashboard* link. Within this interface, blocks that are not primarily used for site administration do not appear by default, but can be added via the *Add other blocks* link. For more information, see the online handbook entry for Dashboard module.

Uses

Tracking user activity

By enabling blocks such as *Who's online* and *Who's new*, site users can track who is logged in and new user signups at a centralized location.

Tracking content activity

By enabling blocks such as *Recent blog posts*, *New forum topics* and *Recent comments*, site users can view newly added site content at a glance.

Dashboard administration pages

- Dashboard
- Configure Dashboard permissions

Figure 4.31   About the Dashboard

Hello

Click the Hello link on the Administration menu, as shown in Figure 4.32.

Figure 4.32   The Hello link

You now see the screen shown in Figure 4.33. This is your own user profile.

Figure 4.33   Your own user profile

Click the Edit tab under your name, and you see the screen shown in Figure 4.34. From here you can edit your username and password. You can also change the email address that your site uses to send you notifications.

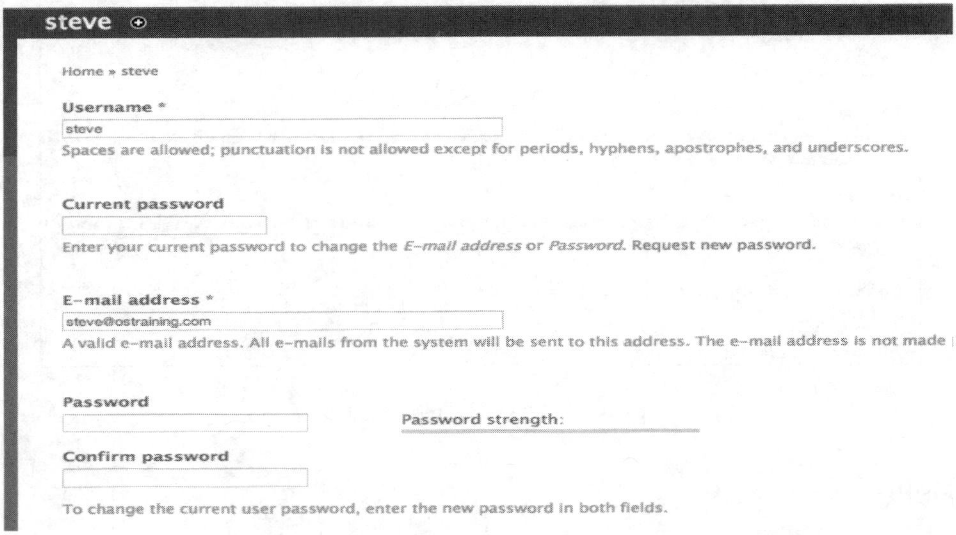

steve ⊕

Home » steve

Username *

steve

Spaces are allowed; punctuation is not allowed except for periods, hyphens, apostrophes, and underscores.

Current password

Enter your current password to change the *E-mail address* or *Password*. Request new password.

E-mail address *

steve@ostraining.com

A valid e-mail address. All e-mails from the system will be sent to this address. The e-mail address is not made

Password   Password strength:

Confirm password

To change the current user password, enter the new password in both fields.

Figure 4.34   Editing your own user profile

There are only two other settings that you should change for now, both of which are lower down on the screen. Those are both shown in Figure 4.35:

- **Upload picture:** You can click Browse and add an image to your profile.
- **Locale settings:** You can choose your time zone.

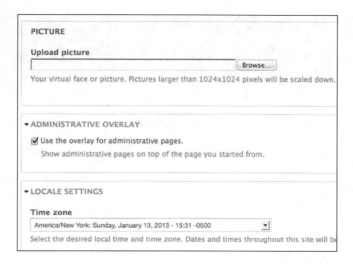

Figure 4.35   More editing of your user profile

The Administration and Visitor Areas Explained

This chapter ends by showing you the difference between Drupal's administration and visitor areas.

Log Out

This is the final link on the right side of the Administration menu. Go ahead and click that link. Your site now appears as shown in Figure 4.36; although, with some Drupal installations, there may be different text on this homepage. Regardless, this is what people see if they visit your site without an administrator username and password.

Now log in again. Use the User Login box on the left side, and enter the username and password that you created when installing the site. Your screen should now look like Figure 4.37.

Notice how similar the images are in Figures 4.36 and 4.37. This similarity is an important point because it can be confusing to beginners. It is also different from many other types of website software.

When using other software, the visitor area and the administrator area of your site are completely different. Other software often provides a Control Panel that has a distinctive look and feel. This is not true in Drupal.

Figure 4.36   The Visitor Area of Your Site

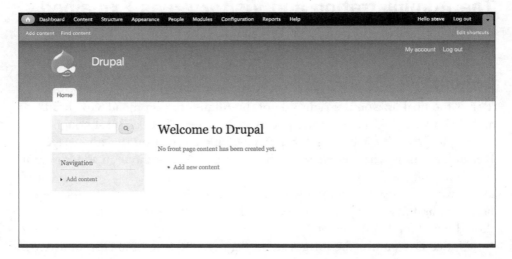

Figure 4.37   The Administration area of your site

In Drupal, the visitor area and the administration area are closely linked. Often, an ordinary user of your site will use the same login box as the administrator of your site. There are two infallible ways to tell that you are using the site as an administrator, not a visitor:

- You can see the black administration menu.

- The main part of your screen appears in the pop-up/overlay that you've used several times already. You can see the overlay in Figure 4.38. The black X mark enables you to close this overlay. Also, you can still faintly see the site behind the overlay.

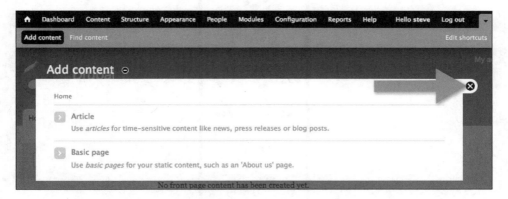

Figure 4.38   The overlay in administration area of your site

When you start with Drupal, it's sometimes confusing to understand what is visible to visitors and what is visible only to administrators. There are some ways around this.

The simplest solution is to have two browsers open. In one browser, you can log in as the administrator of your site. In the other browser, don't log in and you can see your site as a visitor would.

Chapter 13 recommends a more advanced feature called Masquerade, which enables you to see your site through the eyes of any visitor.

What's Next?

You've now had a tour of Drupal's administration area. You've had a brief look inside all the important screens in your site. Now it's time to start using Drupal.

As mentioned in Chapter 2, "Drupal Planning Explained," we recommend that you use the workflow in Figure 4.39 to build your first Drupal sites. This workflow helps overcome much of the confusion that beginners face when building their first Drupal sites.

In Chapter 2 and Chapter 3, you covered the first steps in the Drupal work-flow: planning and installation. In Chapter 5, you take the next step: content types.

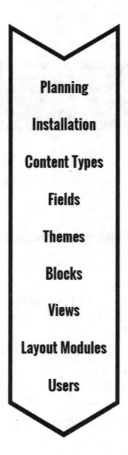

Figure 4.39   The Drupal workflow we use in this book

Drupal Content Explained

The most important thing on your website is the content.

Drupal itself is called a Content Management System, and the most important way that Drupal helps you manage content is with content types.

In this chapter, we explore the content types available on a new Drupal site.

We're also going to show you how to create and edit your own content types.

At the end of this chapter, you should be able to

- Add content.
- Find content.
- Create an Article.
- Create a Basic page.
- Enable more content types.
- Create more content types.
- Edit content types.
- Describe the purpose of a content type.

Content Types

There is one important thing to think about before using Drupal content: Different types of content have different features.

Your site might contain many different content types, from news, blogs, and events to opinion polls, e-commerce products, staff member profiles, and more. Each of those is a different content type and will likely need different features.

When you first install Drupal, it gives you an Article and a Basic page content type.

Drupal also provides four other content types ready for you to enable and use: Blog, Book, Forum, and Poll. Each content type has unique features and serves a unique purpose on the site.

In addition to the content types that Drupal provides, you can also create your own. For instance, imagine you want to sell products on your site. You can create a Product content type. This unique content type can feature photos of the product, its price, and shipping information. You probably don't want to add a price and shipping information to staff member profiles, so you can create a separate Staff Members content type for them! Perhaps your site is going to help your team run events. You can create an Events content type and include a date and a location. The possibilities are endless.

Default Content Types Explained

The best way to learn about content types is to start using them. Let's start with the two default content types: Article and Basic page.

Creating an Article

Articles are where you can put all your news and topical information. In our Drupalville site, we will use articles to publish news and information about Drupal.

We're going to start simply and walk through the process of creating an Article. After you are familiar with the style of the content form, you can speed up the process and explore more options:

1. Log into your site and see the black menu bar across the top.

2. Under that menu is a gray menu bar, which contains just two links: Add Content and Find Content.

3. Click Add Content, which you can see highlighted in Figure 5.1.

4. You'll see a screen like Figure 5.2.

   You'll see two options: Article and Basic Page. You can see that Drupal explains an Article in this way: "Use *articles* for time-sensitive content like news, press releases or blog posts."

Figure 5.1   The Add content link

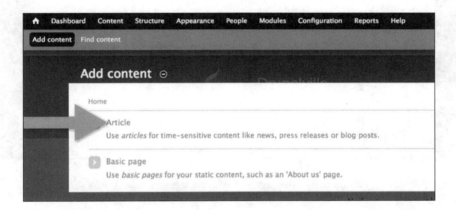

Figure 5.2   Choosing which content type to create

5. Click Article, and you see a screen like Figure 5.3. This is the main screen for creating content in Drupal. You'll be coming back here time and time again throughout the book.

6. There are only two fields that are essential to enter: Title and Body. You can also enter Tags, which are keywords you can use to categorize the content. You can enter as many as you want. Simply add a comma and a space after each one. Here are the details of what to enter. You can see the results in Figure 5.4:

   - **Title:** Welcome to Drupalville
   - **Tags:** Drupalville, Introduction
   - **Body:** Welcome to Drupalville. This is a great place to spend time!

Figure 5.3   The content creation screen for an Article

Figure 5.4   Creating your Welcome to Drupalville content

7. Scroll to the bottom of the page, and click Save, as shown in Figure 5.5.

You can now see your first Drupal article live on your site, as shown in Figure 5.6.

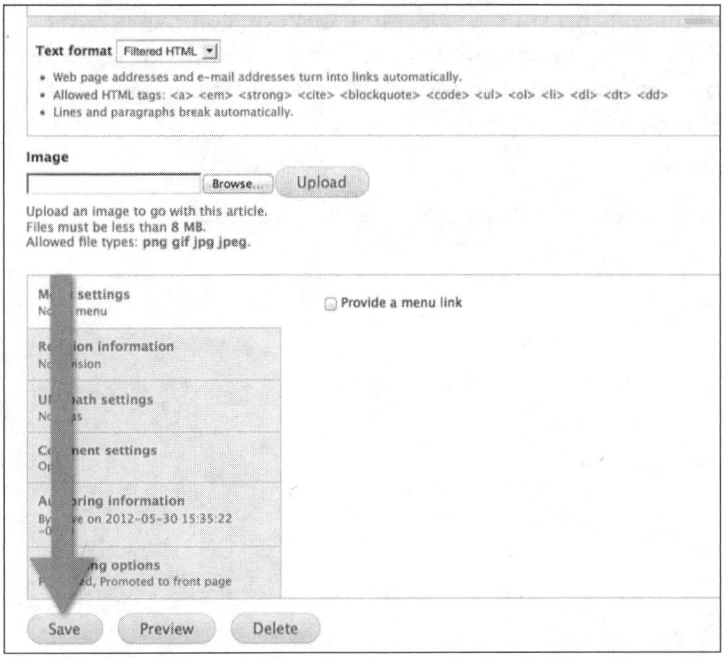

Figure 5.5
The Save button
for Drupal content

Figure 5.6
The Welcome to
Drupalville content
after saving

8. You can leave comments on your article. Now give the comments a test.
   You must enter a comment but don't have to enter a title. If you leave the
   title blank, then Drupal will fill it in for you. As you enter the comment,
   your screen will look like Figure 5.7:

   - **Subject:** I agree
   - **Comment:** I'm excited to see how this site turns out.

Figure 5.7   Adding a new comment

9. Click Save under the comment, as shown in Figure 5.8.

   Your Welcome to Drupalville article should now look like Figure 5.9.

   That was easy, right? You've just published your first Drupal article. Now do
it again. Now you create an article about the Drupal mascot:

1. Go to http://drupal.org/node/9068 and download the Drupal mascot
   from the top of the page. Save the mascot onto your computer desktop.

2. In your Drupal site, click Add content.

3. Click Article.

Add new comment

Your name   steve

Subject   [I agree]

Comment *

[I'm excited to see how this site turns out]

Text format   [Filtered HTML ▾]   More information about text formats ⓘ

- Web page addresses and e-mail addresses turn into links automatically.
- Allowed HTML tags: <a> <em> <strong> <cite> <blockquote> <code> <ul> <ol> <li> <dl> <dt> <dd>
- Lines and paragraphs break automatically.

[Save]   [Preview]

Figure 5.8   Saving a comment

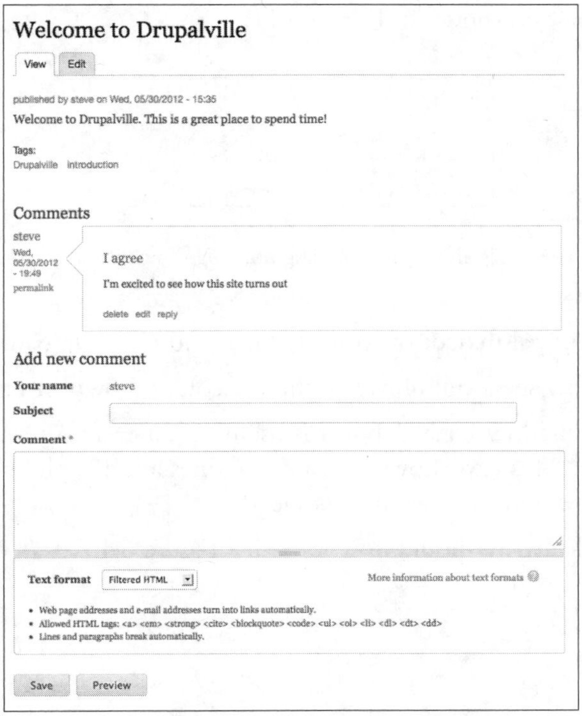

Welcome to Drupalville

[View] [Edit]

published by steve on Wed, 05/30/2012 - 15:35

Welcome to Drupalville. This is a great place to spend time!

Tags:
Drupalville   Introduction

Comments

steve
Wed,
05/30/2012
- 19:49   I agree
permalink
                I'm excited to see how this site turns out

                delete edit reply

Add new comment

Your name   steve

Subject   [   ]

Comment *

[   ]

Text format   [Filtered HTML ▾]   More information about text formats ⓘ

- Web page addresses and e-mail addresses turn into links automatically.
- Allowed HTML tags: <a> <em> <strong> <cite> <blockquote> <code> <ul> <ol> <li> <dl> <dt> <dd>
- Lines and paragraphs break automatically.

[Save]   [Preview]

Figure 5.9   Your first comment

4. Enter the following information:

- **Title:** Have You Seen The Drupal Mascot?
- **Tags:** Drupal, mascot, introduction
- **Body:** The Drupal mascot is designed to look like a drop of water.

You might notice that the Tags box will make suggestions for you as you type. Enter the letters "in" and Drupal will suggest "introduction," as shown in Figure 5.10.

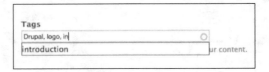

Figure 5.10   Adding tags to content

Now upload your mascot to the article:

1. Find the image field.

2. Click Browse, as shown in Figure 5.11.

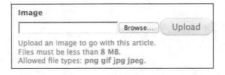

Figure 5.11   Adding an image to content

3. Find the Drupal mascot on your desktop, and click Upload.

4. You can now see a thumbnail of the mascot, as shown in Figure 5.12.

   It isn't required by Drupal, but it is useful to enter an Alternate Text description. This text shows to search engines and people who may be partially sighted and can't see images clearly.

   Your whole article should now look like Figure 5.13.

Figure 5.12   An image successfully uploaded to content

Figure 5.13   A content item with an image and tags added, before saving

5. Click Save at the bottom of the page.

Your article should now look like Figure 5.14.

Figure 5.14   A content item with an image and tags added, after saving

Creating a Basic Page

Now that you've created two Articles, you can see what the other default content type looks like.

You can create an About Us page on your Drupalville site, as shown in Figure 5.15. When people are discussing websites, pages like this are often called static pages. Static refers to content that seldom or never changes. In Drupal, static pages are called Basic pages.

About Us is a great example. You might write your About Us page once and then not update it for months or years.

You can walk slowly through the process of creating a Basic page. We will explore the screen in front of you and introduce you to the options you see. After you are familiar with the style of the content form, you can speed up the process, slowing only when something new comes along:

1. Notice the black menu bar across the top of your site. Under that menu is the gray menu bar with two links: Add Content and Find Content. Click Add Content.

2. You now see your two content types: Basic Page and Article. Click Basic Page, as marked in Figure 5.15.

   You now have a screen that looks like Figure 5.16.

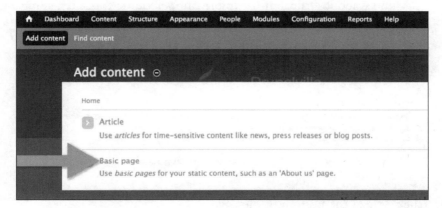

Figure 5.15   Creating a Basic page

Figure 5.16   The content creation screen for a Basic page

3. Here are the details of what to enter. You can see the results in Figure 5.17:

   - **Title:** About Us

   - **Body:** Drupalville is a great resource for everything you want to know about Drupal. It has information about events, sites, companies, and more.

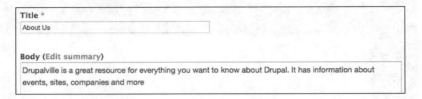

Figure 5.17   Text entered for the Basic page

4. Click Save at the bottom of the page.

   Now that you've finished your first Basic page, your screen will look like Figure 5.18.

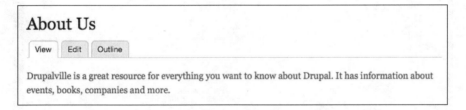

Figure 5.18   A Basic page after saving

Notice anything missing? What did you have on Articles that you don't have on your Basic page? Let's see an Article and Basic page side-by-side, as shown in Figure 5.19.

The Article has the title, author name, the publishing date, an image, body, tags, and comments. The Basic page has only the title and body.

1. Click the Home link on the Main menu, as highlighted in Figure 5.20.

Figure 5.19   Comparing an Article and a Basic page

Figure 5.20   The Home link

Your site's homepage should look like Figure 5.21. What's missing? Your Basic Page again. The Articles are there, but the Basic Page is missing.

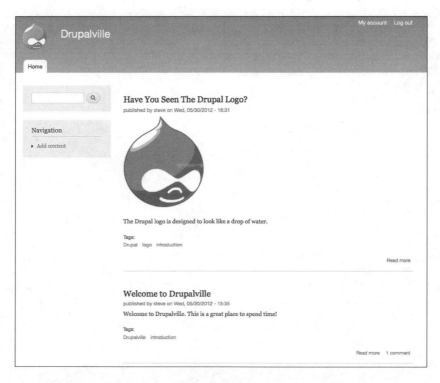

Figure 5.21   The homepage of your Drupal site

Fortunately, there is one place where you can find all the content on your Drupal site.

2. Click Find Content, as highlighted in Figure 5.22.

Figure 5.22   The Find content link

You'll now see a list of all the content on your site, as shown in Figure 5.23. If you ever get stuck looking for content on your site, this is the place to come.

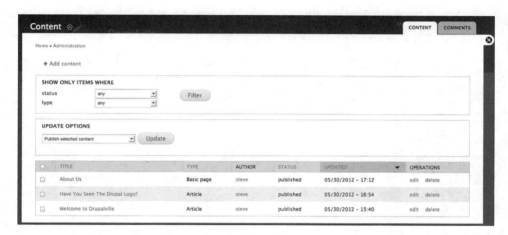

Figure 5.23   The Find Content screen

3. Edit your About Us page so that it's easier to find. Click the Edit link in the About Us row, as shown in Figure 5.24.

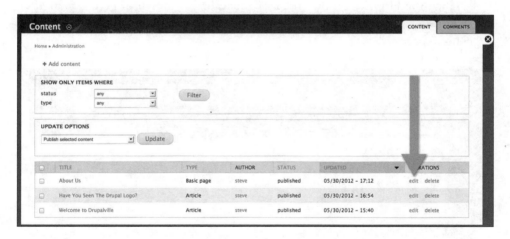

Figure 5.24   Editing content via the Find Content screen

Add a menu link so that this Basic page is easy to find:

1. Scroll down to the bottom of the page and click the Provide a Menu Link box.

2. You'll see some more options appear. You won't need to change these options. Simply confirm that they look like Figure 5.25.

Figure 5.25   Provide a Menu Link option

3. Click Save.

4. Click the Home icon on the black menu bar, as shown in Figure 5.26. If you ever get lost in Drupal's admin area, click this icon to go back to the homepage.

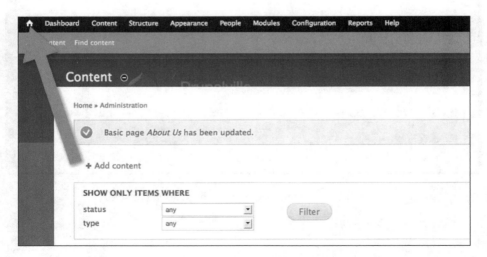

Figure 5.26   The home icon on Drupal's admin menu bar

There will now be a Main Menu link to your About Us page, as shown in Figure 5.27. By default, menus are ordered alphabetically. You learn how to change the order of menu links in Chapter 8, "Drupal Menus Explained."

Figure 5.27   About Us menu link

What Have We Learned?

Let's recap. Drupal comes with two content types: Articles and Basic pages.

Why does Drupal come with two content types? Because different types of content require different features.

What are the different features on these content types? Look at Table 5.1.

Table 5.1   **The Features of the Basic Page and Article Content Types**

Features	Basic Page	Article
Title	Yes	Yes
Author Name	No	Yes
Publishing Date	No	Yes
Image	No	Yes
Body	Yes	Yes
Tags	No	Yes
Comments	No	Yes
Published to front page?	No	Yes

Why do you think that the Basic page has all these features removed? It is because static, unchanging content probably doesn't need those features.

We recently spoke with a student who admitted not updating his About Us page since 2000. It certainly would be embarrassing if visitors saw that as the publishing date for that page.

On the other hand, if you have topical news and use an Article, you probably need the publishing date. It's important to know if the information in the Article is fresh or out of date.

Repeat after us, "Different types of content have different features."

The wonderful thing about Drupal content is that it's possible to expand the previous chart in both directions. You can add more content types and features.

In the next section, you see how to add more content types and more features.

Extra Content Types Explained

You've seen that Drupal provides two default content types: Article and Basic page. There are also more content types available but not yet enabled. Now see how to enable those extra content types.

Creating a Blog Entry

A blog entry is similar to an article, but is likely to contain more of the author's own personal opinion. Because of this, blog posts are often organized by author rather than topic.

Drupal provides a blog content type, but it is disabled by default. Let's see how to enable the Blog content type for our site:

1. On the black menu bar located at the top of your screen, click Modules. Your screen should look like Figure 5.28.

   A lot of information is conveyed on this Module page, which Chapter 4, "Drupal Administration Explained," briefly covers and Chapter 7, "Drupal Modules Explained," further explores. For now, we're simply going to enable the Blog module.

2. Check the box next to Blog, as highlighted in Figure 5.29.

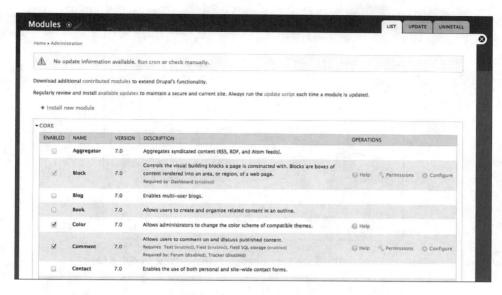

Figure 5.28   The Modules screen

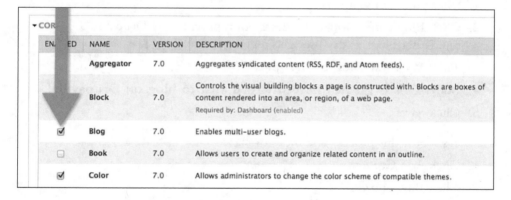

Figure 5.29   Checking the box next to the Blog module

3. Scroll to the bottom of the page, and click Save Configuration, as high-lighted in Figure 5.30.

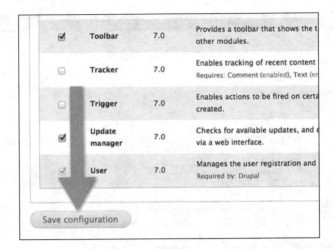

Figure 5.30   The Save Configuration button on the Modules page

Now use exactly the same processes you used when creating an Article and a Basic page:

1. Click Add Content.

2. Click Blog entry. Notice the description provided by Drupal is "Use for multi-user blogs. Every user gets a personal blog."

3. Title: **My First Blog on Drupalville**

4. Body: **This is great. I have my own area to blog on Drupaville!**

5. Click Save.

Let's repeat this process one more time:

1. Click Add Content.

2. Click Blog entry.

3. Title: **I'm building a great site with Drupal!**

4. Body: **We're underway. I'm excited to get this site built.**

5. Click Save.

6. Look for the new addition on the blog entries, which is highlighted in Figure 5.31.

7. The new feature provided by the Blog module is a simple link. Click the link highlighted in Figure 5.31, and you see a list of all the blog posts provided by the author, as shown in Figure 5.32.

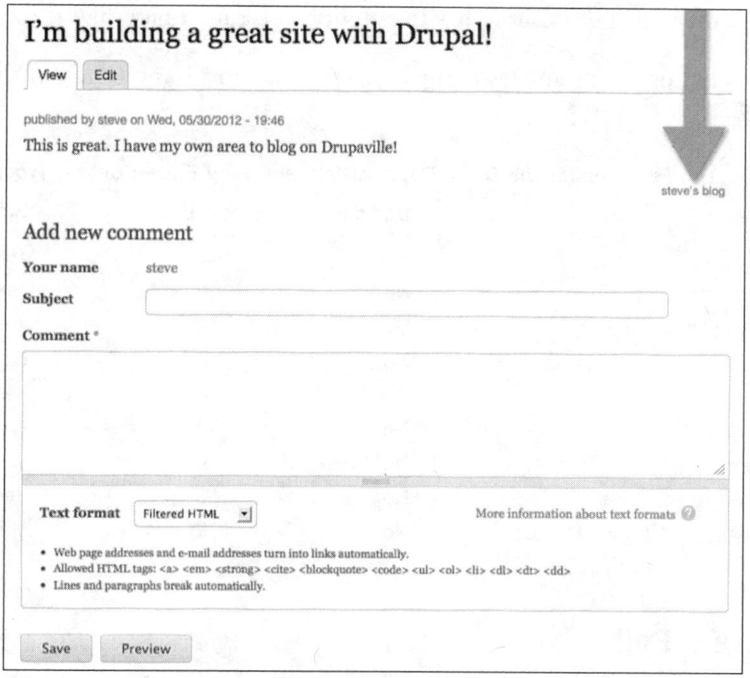

I'm building a great site with Drupal!

View Edit

published by steve on Wed, 05/30/2012 - 19:46

This is great. I have my own area to blog on Drupaville!

steve's blog

Add new comment

Your name   steve

Subject

Comment *

Text format   Filtered HTML ▾   More information about text formats ⓘ

- Web page addresses and e-mail addresses turn into links automatically.
- Allowed HTML tags: <a> <em> <strong> <cite> <blockquote> <code> <ul> <ol> <li> <dl> <dt> <dd>
- Lines and paragraphs break automatically.

Save   Preview

Figure 5.31   A Blog entry

steve's blog

✦ Post new blog entry.

I'm building a great site with Drupal!

published by steve on Wed, 05/30/2012 - 19:46

This is great. I have my own area to blog on Drupaville!

Read more

My First Blog on Drupalville

published by steve on Wed, 05/30/2012 - 19:38

This is great. I have my own area to blog on Drupaville!

Read more

Figure 5.32   All blog entries for one user

Each user on the site now has the ability to create a blog like this.

Now see how Blog entries compare to Articles and Basic pages, as shown in Table 5-2.

Table 5-2   **The Features for the Basic Page, Article and Blog Entry Content Types**

Features	Basic Page	Article	Blog Entry
Title	Yes	Yes	Yes
Author Name	No	Yes	Yes
Publishing Date	No	Yes	Yes
Image	No	Yes	No
Body	Yes	Yes	Yes
Tags	No	Yes	No
Comments	No	Yes	Yes
Published to Front Page?	No	Yes	Yes
Link to All the Author's Entries	No	No	Yes

Creating a Poll

Do you want to find what your site visitors are thinking on a certain topic? Would it help you to ask them questions?

You can do that with Drupal's Poll module. Poll enables you to ask simple questions with multiple choice answers.

It might seem strange to include Poll in a chapter on content types, but it is relevant. You see, Polls are content in the same way as Articles, Blogs, and Basic Pages.

Here's how to enable the Poll module and add a Poll:

1. Click Modules on the black menu bar.

2. Check the box next to Poll in the module list.

3. Click Save Configuration.

4. Click Add Content.

5. Click Poll. You'll now see a screen shown in Figure 5.33.

6. Here are the details to fill in when creating a poll:

   - Question: How long have you been using Drupal?

   - Choice: One day

   - Choice: One week

   - Click More Choices

- Choice: One month
- Click More Choices
- Choice: One year

When you finish, your screen should look like Figure 5.34

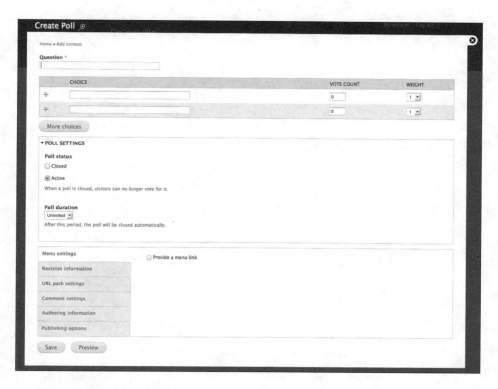

Figure 5.33   Creating a Poll

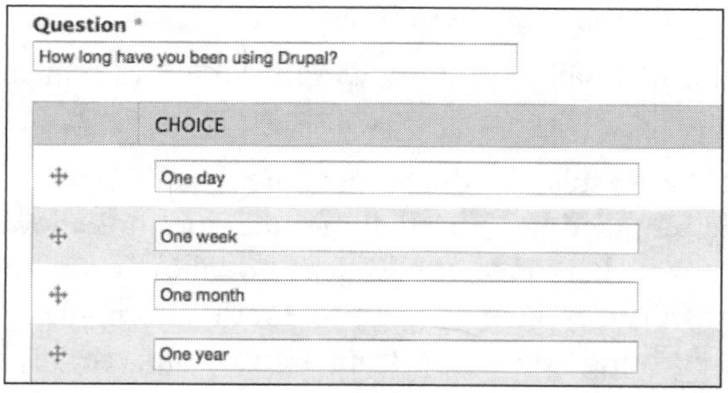

Figure 5.34   Creating Poll choices

7. Click Save.

Your Poll will appear, as shown in Figure 5.35.

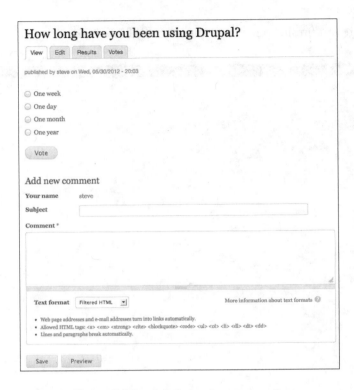

Figure 5.35   A Poll showing on your site

8. Notice the two new tabs: Results and Votes. Click Results and you can see all the totals for each answer. Click Votes and you see each individual vote.

9. Click View and choose one response.

10. Click Vote. Drupal will now show you the results of your poll, as in Figure 5.36.

Notice that the Results tab disappears. The default view of the poll for you becomes the results. Why? The Poll module does not allow users on the site to vote more than once. It also does not allow anonymous visitors to vote more than once unless they go to another computer. Okay, so it isn't perfect at preventing vote scams from anonymous visitors, but it does quite well.

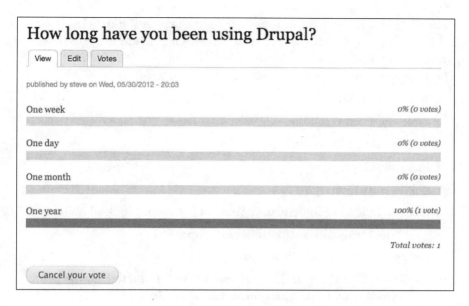

Figure 5.36   Poll results

Table 5-3 shows how Polls compare to Articles, Basic pages, and Blog entries.

Table 5-3   **The Features for the Basic Page, Article, Blog Entry, and Poll Content Types**

Features	Basic Page	Article	Blog Entry	Poll
Title	Yes	Yes	Yes	Yes
Author Name	No	Yes	Yes	Yes
Publishing Date	No	Yes	Yes	Yes
Image	No	Yes	No	No
Body	Yes	Yes	Yes	Yes
Tags	No	Yes	No	No
Comments	No	Yes	Yes	Yes
Published to Front Page?	No	Yes	Yes	Yes
Link to All the Author's Entries	No	No	Yes	No
Opinion Questions	No	No	No	Yes

Creating a Forum

On your site, you want to encourage visitors to post questions and respond to other visitor questions, so your plan includes a discussion forum. You can find a great example of a discussion forum using Drupal at http://drupal.org/forum.

Forum topics are content in exactly the same way as the Articles, Basic pages, Blog entries, and Polls you've seen before. The Forum module simply organizes the content into a discussion forum layout.

Now, create some discussion posts. Here are the steps:

1. Go to the Modules page.

2. Enable the Forum module.

3. Click Save Configuration.

4. Click Add Content.

5. Click Forum Topic.

6. Enter the following information. Your screen should look like Figure 5.37.

   - Title: **How did you discover Drupal?**

   - Forums: **General discussion**.

   - Body: **What's your Drupal story? Me: I started using it at school and have been addicted ever since.**

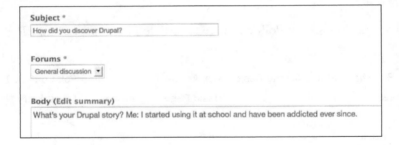

Figure 5.37   Creating a Forum topic

7. Click Save. Your forum topic should look like Figure 5.38.

8. Post a reply in the comments for this forum post.

9. When you save your forum topic, it should look like Figure 5.39.

Figure 5.38
Forum topic content
after saving

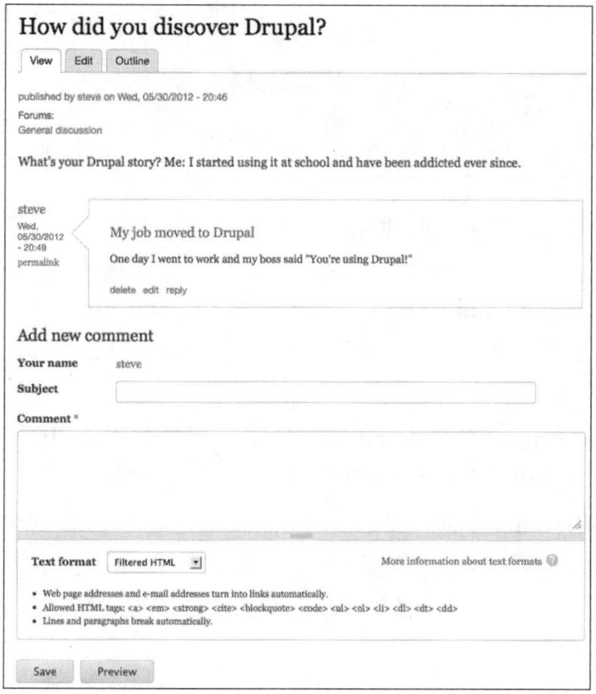

Figure 5.39   A Forum topic
with a reply

10. To be honest, this looks identical to the Article with a comment you cre-
    ated at the beginning of this chapter. Where is the discussion forum? You
    can see it by clicking the General discussion link, which is highlighted in
    Figure 5.40.

Figure 5.40   Link from a Forum topic to the main forum area

You now see your forum topic organized into a discussion forum layout, as
shown in Figure 5.41.

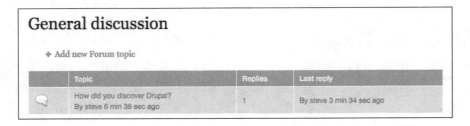

Figure 5.41   The main forum area

Click Add new Forum topic and add some new posts. No matter how
many you add, the topics stack up on the main General Discussion page, as
shown in Figure 5.41.

By default, all Drupal forum topics are entered into General Discussion. If
you want a more elaborate organization for your topics, follow these steps:

1. Click Structure on the black top menu.

2. Click Forums. You now see a screen that looks like Figure 5.42.

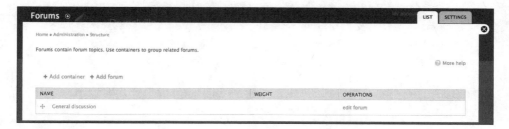

Figure 5.42   Move Drupal forums

There are two things to know here:

- **Container:** This includes the top level categories such as Drupal or Sports.
- **Forum:** This includes the subcategories such as Drupal Installation, Drupal Design and Drupal Support or Tennis, Golf, and Football.

Now see how that works in practice:

1. Click Add container.

2. Container name: **Drupal**.

3. Click Save.

4. Click Add Forum.

5. Forum name: **Drupal Installation**.

6. Parent: **Drupal**.

7. Click Save.

8. Click Add Forum.

9. Forum name: **Drupal Design**.

10. Parent: **Drupal**.

11. Click Save.

12. Click Add Forum.

13. Forum name: **Drupal Support**.

14. Parent: **Drupal**.

15. Click Save.

    Your forum organization should now look like Figure 5.43.

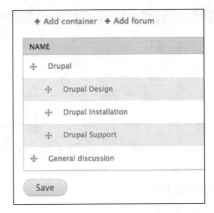

Figure 5.43   Forum categories organized on your site

Now that you've seen how your fifth content type works, let's recap. How do Forum topics compare to Articles, Basic pages, Blog entries, and Polls? See Table 5-4.

Table 5-4   **The Features for Our Five Content Types**

Features	Basic Page	Article	Blog Entry	Poll	Forum Topics
Title	Yes	Yes	Yes	Yes	Yes
Author Name	No	Yes	Yes	Yes	Yes
Publishing Date	No	Yes	Yes	Yes	Yes
Image	No	Yes	No	No	No
Body	Yes	Yes	Yes	Yes	Yes
Tags	No	Yes	No	No	No
Comments	No	Yes	Yes	Yes	Yes
Published to Front Page?	No	Yes	Yes	Yes	No
Link to All the Author's Entries	No	No	Yes	No	No
Opinion Questions	No	No	No	Yes	No
Discussion Forum Format	No	No	No	No	Yes

Creating a Book

Now let's turn our attention to the last of the six content types available with Drupal by default.

We're going to create a Drupal User Manual as a section for your site. As the name suggests, a user manual is an organized set of pages. For an example of an online book created using Drupal's Book module, visit http://drupal.org/documentation/. Click through the pages using the navigation links at the bottom of the page content. You can see that content is organized using links like those shown in Figure 5.44.

- The five links organized vertically are to pages in a lower level in the documentation.

- The Up link takes you to a higher level in the documentation.

- The Administration Guide and Working with the toolbar links enable you to browse through pages in the same level of the documentation.

Figure 5.44   Part of the documentation area on Drupal.org

To add a manual like this to your site, you need to enable the Book module; then you can create some pages for your book. Follow these steps:

1. Click Modules on the black menu bar at the top of your screen.

2. Check the box next to Book in the module list.

3. Click Save Configuration.

4. Click Add Content.

5. Click Book Page.

6. Enter the following information:

   - Title: **Drupal User Manual**.

   - Body: **Welcome to the Drupal manual provided by Drupalville**.

   - Menu settings: Check the Provide a Menu link box.

   - Book outline: Create a new book. Your screen should look like Figure 5.45. This is where you tell Drupal that the page you are creating is the page that defines the book.

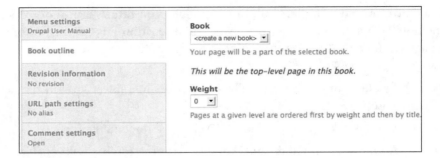

Figure 5.45   Creating a new book for documentation purposes

7. Click Save. Your book page should look like the image in Figure 5.46.

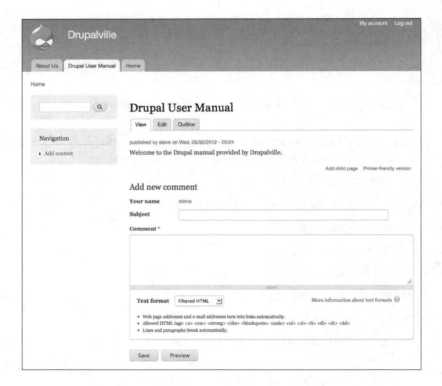

Figure 5.46   Creating Book page content

The Book module is called Book for a reason. Book is designed to link content together like the table of contents in a book. The process ends with a series of pages with parent and child relationships. For example, book pages are parents to chapter pages. In turn, chapter pages are parents to topic pages. In this next activity, you create child pages to the book you just defined. Now create the first chapter:

1. Click Add Child Page, as highlighted in Figure 5.47.

Figure 5.47   Adding a child page to a Drupal book

2. Enter the following information:
   - Title: **Chapter 1: How to Install Drupal**.
   - Body: **This part of the Drupal User Manual will show you how to install Drupal**.
   - Book Outline > Book: **Drupal User Manual**.
   - Book Outline > Parent Item: **Drupal User Manual**.
3. Click Save.
4. Click Add Child Page.
5. Enter the following information to create a child page for your documentation:
   - Title: **How to Install Drupal Automatically**
   - Book Outline > Book: **Drupal User Manual**
   - Parent Item > Book: **Chapter 1: How to Install Drupal**
6. Click Save.

7. Click Up. This link is highlighted in Figure 5.48.

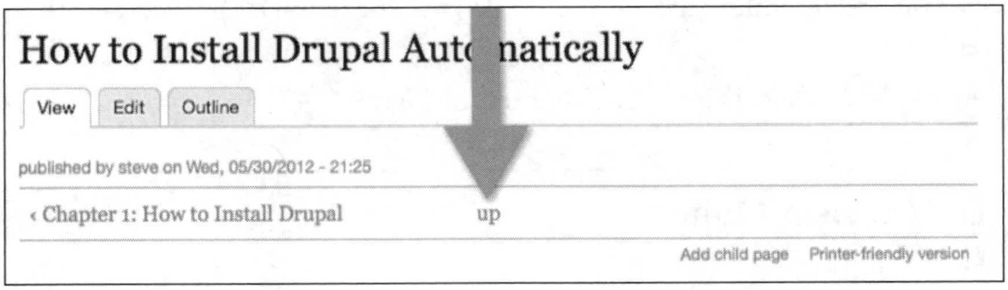

Figure 5.48   Navigating through Book content

8. Enter the following information to create another child page:
    - Click Add Child Page.
    - Title: **How to Install Drupal Manually**.
    - Book Outline > Book: **Drupal User Manual**.
    - Parent Item > Book: **Chapter 1: How to Install Drupal**.

9. Click Save.

10. Click Up.

11. Enter the following information to create another child page:
    - Click Add Child Page.
    - Title: **How to Install Drupal on a Mac**.
    - Book Outline > Book: **Drupal User Manual**.
    - Parent Item > Book: **Chapter 1: How to Install Drupal**.

12. Click Save.

13. Click Up.

14. Enter the following information next:
    - Click Add Child Page.
    - Title: **How to Install Drupal on a PC**.
    - Book Outline > Book: **Drupal User Manual**.
    - Parent Item > Book: **Chapter 1: How to Install Drupal**.

15. Click Save.

16. Click Up.

You can now see that your User Manual is starting to take shape, as shown in Figure 5.49.

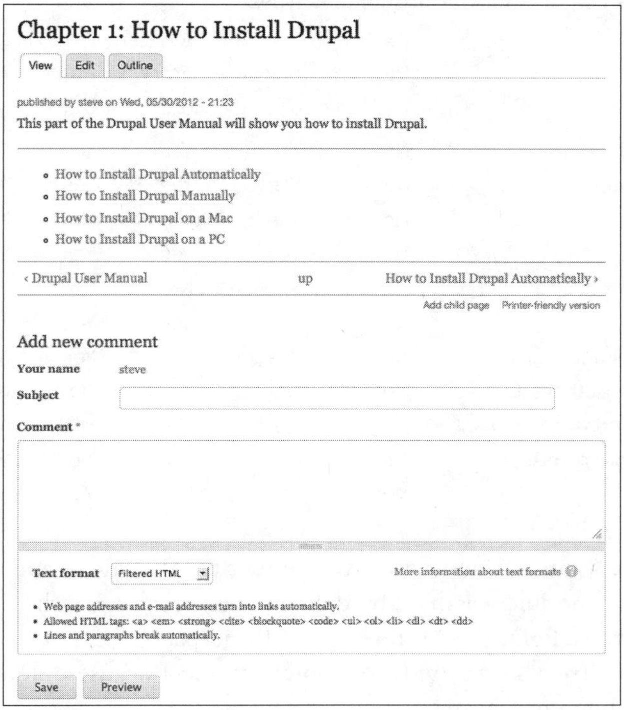

Figure 5.49   The organization of content provided by the Book module

If your pages don't end up where you want them, you can move them around easily, as follows:

1. Click the Outline tab on one of your book pages.

2. Click Reorder an Entire Book in the top-right corner.

3. Click Edit Order and Titles.

4. Find the + symbol next to each page. If you click, hold and drag the + symbol, you can rearrange the pages up, down, in, and out.

5. Click Save Book Pages.

Now we've seen how your sixth content type works. How do Book pages compare to Articles, Basic pages, Blog entries, Polls, and Forum topics?

Table 5.5 shows the extra features provided by the Book module are automatically available to all your content types.

Table 5.5   **The Features for Our Six Content Types**

Features	Basic Page	Article	Blog Entry	Poll	Forum Topics	Book Pages
Title	Yes	Yes	Yes	Yes	Yes	Yes
Author Name	No	Yes	Yes	Yes	Yes	Yes
Publishing Date	No	Yes	Yes	Yes	Yes	Yes
Image	No	Yes	No	No	No	No
Body	Yes	Yes	Yes	Yes	Yes	Yes
Tags	No	Yes	No	No	No	No
Comments	No	Yes	Yes	Yes	Yes	Yes
Published to Front Page?	No	Yes	Yes	Yes	No	No
Link to All the Author's Entries	No	No	Yes	No	No	No
Opinion Questions	No	No	No	Yes	No	No
Discussion Forum Format	No	No	No	No	Yes	No
Book outline	Yes	Yes	Yes	Yes	Yes	Yes

Let's recap. Drupal comes with two content types: Articles and Basic pages. If you enable four modules disabled by default, you can also use these content types: Blog entries, Polls, Forum topics, and Book pages.

Why does Drupal come with six content types? Because different types of content need different features.

In the final section, we see how to add new content types and customize the ones you already have.

Custom Content Types Explained

Now that you are familiar with several types of content, you can create custom content types.

In your Drupalville site, you're going to create content types called Events, Sites, User Groups, and Companies. Before diving in and creating them, let's talk briefly about each content type:

- **Events:** This content type can be used to post Drupal-related events, such as the annual DrupalCons and regional Drupal Camps.

- **Sites:** This content type can be used to post sites that provide information, tutorials, modules, or themes for Drupal.

- **User Groups:** This content type can be used to post sites for local groups that meet to talk and learn about Drupal.

- **Companies:** This content type can be used to post businesses that provide Drupal-related services.

Creating the Events Content Type

Create your first custom content type: Events.

1. Click Structure on the black menu bar.

2. Click Content Types. You see that all the content types used so far are now available here, as shown in Figure 5.50.

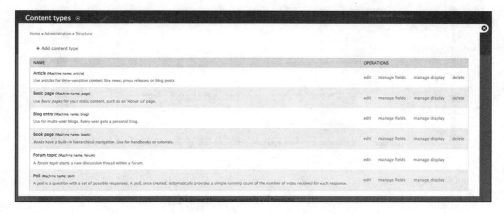

Figure 5.50   A list of all current content types

3. Click Add Content Type in the top-left of the screen. Take a moment and compare the Add Content Type link on the screen and the Add Content on the menu bar at the top of the page. These links are often confused. Pay close attention going forward because you create a content type and then add content using that content type. Add Content Type always comes before Add Content.

   You now see a screen like the one in Figure 5.51.

4. Enter the following information. The title will be shown to your visitors but your screen will look like Figure 5.52:

- Name: **Events**.

- Description: **This is where we enter information about Drupal events around the world**.

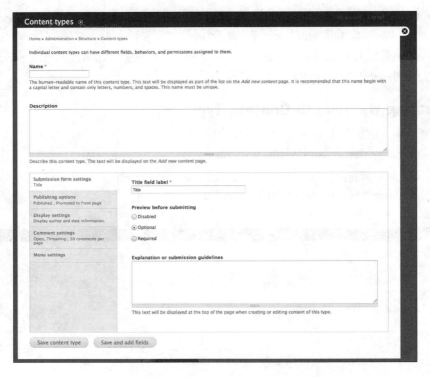

Figure 5.51   The new Content Types screen

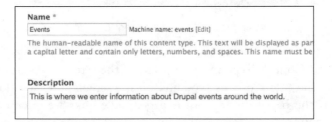

Figure 5.52   Adding a name and description to a new content type

Although the description is private and won't be made public, try to use it. The name of the content type might seem obvious when you create it and remain so for the life of the project. But, I've been on several projects where the name was not so obvious 6 months later. Thus, try to clearly explain the purpose of the content type.

Further down the screen, there are five areas with options to configure your content type. Now look at them one-by-one.

Submission Form Settings

This area controls the form that users see when they add Events content.

Enter the following information. Note that the Title field label is an important setting. It often shows on the screen. The Explanation won't be made public. Your screen should look like Figure 5.53:

- **Title:** Name of Event.

- **Explanation:** Make sure that you fill in all the fields. Make sure to include as much information as possible about why someone should attend this event.

Figure 5.53   Submission form settings for a content type

Publishing Options

This area controls the default publishing options for Events content. Consider each option:

- **Published:** Will Events content be published automatically? This is one way to moderate the content submitted to your site. Each time a page is created with a content type that has this option unchecked, the page will be saved but the page will not be available. The administrators can use the Find Content administrative page to locate unpublished pages and manually edit and publish them.

- **Promoted to Front Page:** Will Events content be published to the front page automatically?

- **Sticky at Top of List:** This is most useful for keeping forum guidelines at the top of the list of new forum posts. You probably won't use this setting for other content types.

- **Create New Revision:** Now this is an important feature. If you check this box, Drupal saves a copy of your article every time you make a change. If the new version has a problem, you can easily roll back to the previous version.

So, here are the boxes we recommend checking, as shown in Figure 5.54:

- **Published:** Yes

- **Promoted to Front Page:** Yes

- **Sticky at Top of Lists:** No

- **Create New Revision:** Yes

Submission form settings	Default options
Name of Event	☑ Published
Publishing options	☑ Promoted to front page
Published , Promoted to front page , Create new revision	☐ Sticky at top of lists
Display settings	☑ Create new revision
Display author and date information.	Users with the *Administer content* permission will be able to override these options.
Comment settings	
Open, Threading , 50 comments per page	
Menu settings	

Figure 5.54   Publishing options for a content type

Display Settings

This option simply asks whether you want the author name and published date shown on the article. Unfortunately, you can't easily split these up. You have to choose both or none.

Uncheck the following box (as shown in Figure 5.55):

- Display Author and Date Information: No

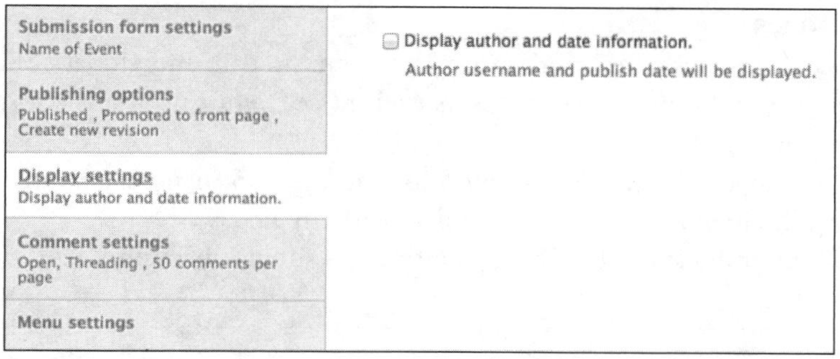

Figure 5.55   Display settings for a content type

Comment Settings

This option asks if you want people to comment on your content. Think carefully before turning this on. Comments will probably be appropriate for some content, such as Articles, Blogs, and Events. You probably don't want comments for your About Us page or if you add pages for your staff members.

The most confusing setting is first. Here's the meaning of the three options:

- **Open:** People can post new comments.
- **Closed:** People can see previously posted comments but can't post new ones.
- **Hidden:** Neither comments nor the comment form show on the site.

I recommend leaving the default settings, as shown in Figure 5.56.

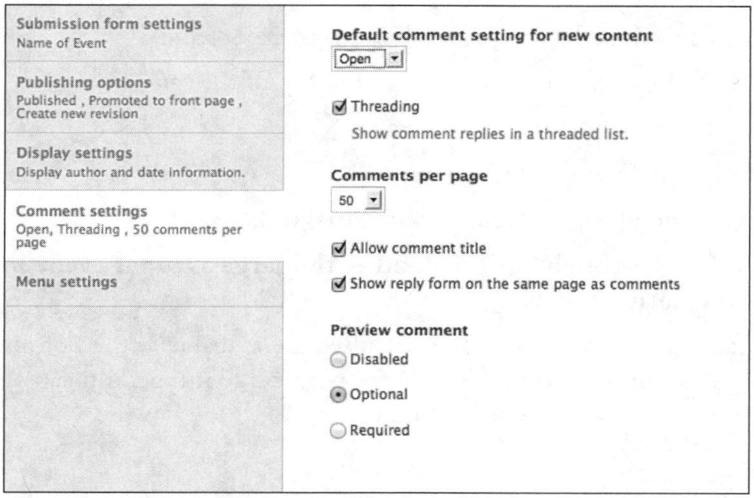

Figure 5.56   Comment settings for a content type

Menu Settings

This area controls whether users can make menu links to individual content items. The key question to ask is this: Is each new Event important enough to make into a menu link?

In this case, the answer is possibly No. There are so many events that it would be difficult to provide menu links for them all.

I recommend leaving the default settings, as shown in Figure 5.57.

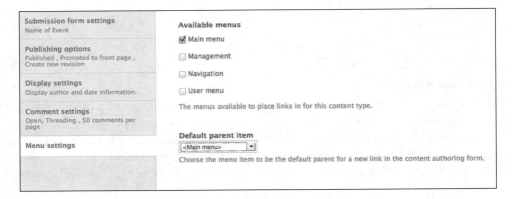

Figure 5.57   Menu settings for a content type

Creating an Events Content Item

Now that you have set up your Events content type, you can use it to create a content item:

1. Click Save Content Type at the bottom of the screen.

2. Click Add Content on the menu at the top of the screen.

3. Click Events.

4. Enter the following information:

   - Name of Event: **DrupalCon Portland**.

   - Body: **DrupalCon Portland is the large Drupal event in North America for 2013**.

Notice that all the options just discussed are available at the bottom of this page. You can set options globally for your content type. You can also set options for each individual content item.

In addition to the options just discussed, there are additional options, including Book outline and URL path settings. Those options are controlled in other parts of the site, often under the Configuration link in the top menu.

5. Click Save.

Now test Revisions, which is a new feature you have turned on for Events:

1. Click the Edit tab under the DrupalCon Portland title.

2. Make a small change to the content. For example, change the word large to **huge**.

3. Click Save.

4. Click the new Revisions tab under the DrupalCon Portland title.

5. You can now see a screen like the one in Figure 5.58. You can click the date of the revision to see the previous content. You can click the revert link to restore that previous version of the content.

   There are some extra features available for Drupal that enable you to take even greater control over this Revision feature. Visit http://www. Drupal7Explained.com/chapter5 for more details.

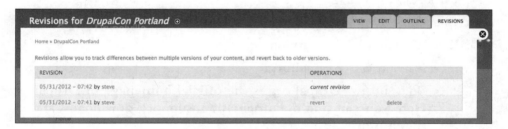

Figure 5.58   Revisions to a Drupal content item

Creating the Sites Content Type

Now create your second custom content type: Sites. This gives your visitors information about useful Drupal sites:

1. Click Structure on the black menu bar.

2. Click Content Types.

3. Click Add Content Type.

4. Enter the following information.

   - Title: **Sites**

   - Description: This is where you enter information about useful Drupal websites and resources.

5. Find the Submission form settings area and enter this information:

   - Title: **Site Name**

6. Find the Publishing options area and enter this information:

   - Published: Yes

   - Promoted to front page: Yes

   - Sticky at top of list: No.

   - Create new revision: Yes.

7. Find the Display settings area and enter this information:

   - Display author and date information: Yes

8. Comments settings: Leave as default.

9. Menu settings: uncheck Main menu.

10. Click Save.

11. Click Add Content.

12. Click Sites.

13. Enter the following information:

    - Name of Site: **Drupal.org**.

    - Body: **http://Drupal.org is the official homepage of Drupal. Here you can find documentation, support, downloads, and much more**.

14. Click Save.

15. The first Site you add will look like Figure 5.59.

Notice that Drupal has automatically converted http://Drupal.org into a link. At the moment, Drupal allows only a small amount of HTML code. Chapter 7 shows you how to allow more code in the body. You also see how to add a text editor.

Figure 5.59   A new content item created with the Sites content type

Creating User Groups

Now create another content type: User Groups. This content type can help your visitors to find a Drupal User Group near them:

1. Click Structure on the black menu bar.

2. Click Content Types.

3. Click Add Content Type.

4. Enter the following information:

   - Title: **User Groups**

   - This is where you enter information about Drupal User Groups around the world.

5. Find the Submission Form Settings area and enter this information:

   - Title: **User Group Name**

6. Find the Publishing options area and enter this information:

   - Published: Yes

   - Promoted to Front Page: Yes

   - Sticky at Top of List: No

   - Create New Revision: Yes

7. Find the Display settings area and enter this information:

   - Display Author and Date Information: Yes

8. Comments settings: Leave as default.

9. Menu settings: Uncheck Main menu.

10. Click Save.

11. Click Add Content.

12. Click User Groups.

13. Enter the following information:

    - User Group name: **Drupal Atlanta**.

    - Body: **This group meets at least once a month and attracts people from all over the Atlanta area**.

14. The first User Group you have added should look like Figure 5.60.

Congratulations. You now have multiple content types on your site!

Creating Companies

Now create your final custom content type: Companies.

1. Click Structure on the black menu bar.

2. Click Content Types.

3. Click Add Content Type.

4. Enter the following information:

   - Title: **Companies**

   - Description: This is where you enter information about Drupal companies.

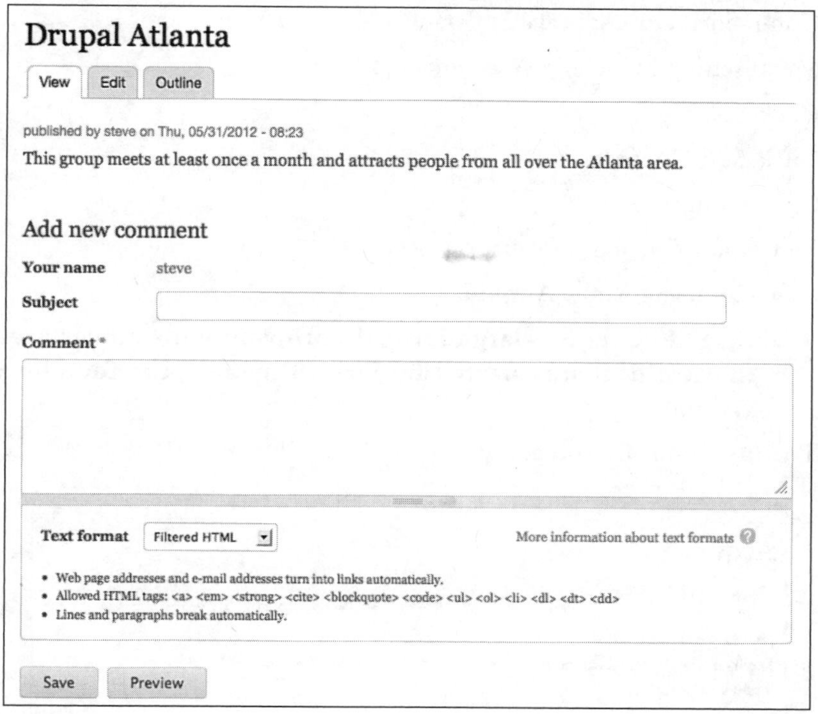

Figure 5.60   A new content item created with the User Group content type

5. Submission form settings:

   - Title: **Company name**

6. Publishing options:

   - Published: Yes

   - Promoted to Front Page: Yes

   - Sticky at Top of List: No.

   - Create New Revision: Yes.

7. Display settings:

   - Display author and date information: Yes

8. Comments settings: Leave as default.

9. Menu settings: Uncheck Main menu.

10. Click Save.

11. Click Add Content.

12. Click Companies.

13. Enter the following information:

    - Company name: **Acquia**.

    - Body: **Acquia is a large Drupal company with offices around the world. It was started by Dries Buytaert, the founder of Drupal**.

14. The first company you add should look like Figure 5.61.

Figure 5.61   A new content item created with the Companies content type

Editing Content Types

If you want to change any of the settings for any of your 10 content types, here is what you do:

1. Click Structure.

2. Click Content Types.

3. Click Edit next to the content type you want to change.

One thing to note: If you do change any content types settings, the changes will apply only for new content items in that content type. For example, if you make a change to the Events content type, it can impact future Events content that you add, but it does not change your DrupalCon Portland content. You must open and change that manually.

What Have You Learned?

Now recap what you've learned during this chapter:

- Content types are crucial for setting up content on your Drupal site. Why? Because different types of content need different features.

- Drupal comes with two content types enabled by default: Basic Page and Article.

- Drupal comes with four modules that add four more content types: Blog entry, Book page, Forum topic, and Poll.

- You can create your own custom content types.

- You can edit existing content types.

You now have 10 different content types on your site. Each of those 10 has a customized set of features. You started with two default content types, enabled four more content types, and now added four custom content types.

Click Add Content on the black menu bar, and you can now see all 10 content types with a description of what they do, as shown in Figure 5.62.

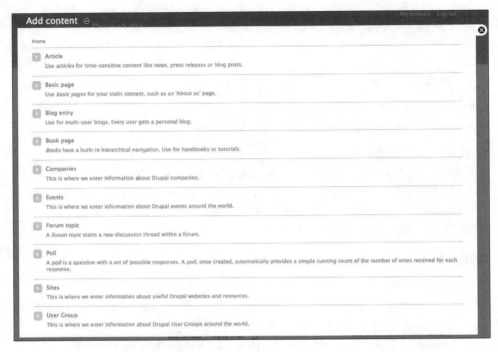

Figure 5.62   A list of all your current content types

Table 5.6 shows a detailed list of all the features for those 10 content types. The wonderful thing about Drupal content is that you can expand the Table 5.6 in both directions by adding more content types and more features.

Table 5.6 The Features of All Your Current Content Types

Features	Basic Page	Article	Blog Entry	Poll	Forum Topics	Book Pages	Events	Sites	User Groups	Companies
Title	Yes	Yes	Yes	Yes	Yes	Yes	Yes	Yes	Yes	Yes
Author Name	No	Yes	Yes	Yes	Yes	Yes	Yes	Yes	Yes	Yes
Publishing Date	No	Yes	Yes	Yes	Yes	Yes	Yes	Yes	Yes	Yes
Image	No	Yes	No	No	No	No	No	No	No	No
Body	Yes	Yes	Yes	Yes	Yes	Yes	Yes	Yes	Yes	Yes
Tags	No	Yes	No	No	No	No	No	No	No	No
Comments	No	Yes	Yes	Yes	Yes	Yes	Yes	Yes	Yes	Yes
Published to Front Page?	No	Yes	Yes	Yes	No	No	Yes	Yes	Yes	Yes
Link to All the Author's Entries	No	No	Yes	No	No	No	No	No	No	Yes
Opinion Questions	No	No	No	Yes	No	No	No	No	No	No
Discussion Forum Format	No	No	No	No	Yes	No	No	No	No	No
Book Outline	Yes	Yes	Yes	Yes	Yes	Yes	Yes	Yes	Yes	Yes
Revisions	No	No	No	No	No	No	Yes	Yes	Yes	Yes

What's Next?

See what our Drupalville site looks like at the end of this chapter. It should look similar to Figure 5.63.

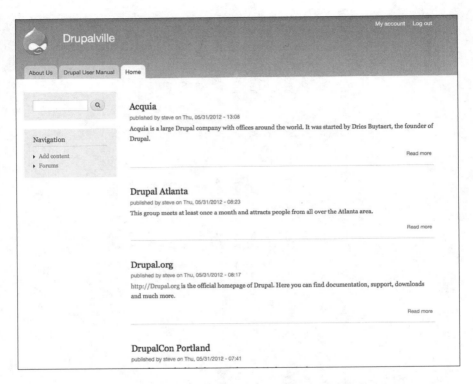

Figure 5.63   Your Drupalville site at the end of this chapter

Don't worry if your site doesn't match this exactly. If you understand the concepts that we covered in this chapter, you can move on to Chapter 6, "Drupal Fields Explained."

At the moment, our new content types still look almost identical. There's little to distinguish between our Events, Sites, User Groups, and Companies.

What do we need to do to make our content types more interesting and useful?

- We need to add specific information to each content type.
- We need to add dates and locations to our events.
- We need to add screenshots and site information to our sites.

- We need to add meeting locations and organizer details to our User Groups.

- We need to add company logos and addresses to our Companies.

That's what you do in Chapter 6. You make your content types more interesting by using Fields. Fields are the next step in the Drupal workflow, which you can see in Figure 5.64.

Figure 5.64   Your Drupal site workflow

6

Drupal Fields Explained

In Chapter 5, "Drupal Content Explained," we explored content types, and you created Articles, Basic Pages, Events, Sites, User Groups, Companies, and more.

The limitation we found at the end of Chapter 5 is that there were few or no differences between those content types.

This chapter shows you how to make your content types unique, interesting, and useful by adding fields.

In this chapter, you'll use many different types of fields. To use all those different types of fields, you also expand your skills by downloading modules from Drupal.org.

At the end of this chapter, you should be able to

- Add different types of fields to a content type.

- Share a field across multiple content types.

- Manage the display of fields in the full content view and teaser.

- Understand Taxonomy and how Drupal categorizes content.

- Download and install modules from Drupal.org.

Planning Your Fields

Fields provide almost unlimited possibilities for adding information to your content. Here are just a few of the many possibilities:

- Text
- Whole numbers
- Decimal numbers
- Images

- Files such as PDFs and Microsoft Word documents
- A pre-defined list of options
- Addresses
- Phone numbers
- Dates and times

However, not all of these field types are available with a new Drupal site.

In Chapter 5, we saw that there are six default content types in Drupal. In this chapter, we will see that there are 13 default field types. All other field types must be added to your site by installing new modules.

We currently have four content types from Chapter 5 that need to be made more interesting. Those content types are Drupal Sites, Events, Companies, and User Groups. To be more useful, they need more information. They need fields.

Table 6.1 describes the fields we'll use for each content type. Sometimes, we'll use one of the existing field types. Other times we'll set up new field types.

Table 6.1:   **Our Plan for Adding Fields to Content Types**

Fields	Sites	Companies	Events	User Groups
Title (Default Field) Name	Site Name	Name	Event Name	User Group
Body (Default Field)	Description	Description	Description	Description
Image	Screenshot	Logo	Event Logo	
Term Reference	Tags	Tags Language Spoken	Tags What topics will be covered?	Tags
List (Text)	Topics	Services		
Boolean	Official Site			
Decimal			Event Price	
URL Link		Link	Link	User Group Website
Location				User Group Location
Date			Event Date	
Entity Reference			Sponsors	Organizers

Sites Fields Explained

The Site content type has five fields planned. Four will be created using fields that come with default Drupal. The Link field needs to be added to the site, requiring you to add a module from Drupal.org.

Here's what you're going to do:

- Edit field labels for title and body.
- Add four fields that come with Drupal.

First, you need to set up the two fields that come with every content type: Title and Body.

Editing a Field: Title

When you created the Sites content type in Chapter 5, we suggested that you change the Title field to Site Name. Now make sure that was done:

1. Click Structure on the black menu bar.
2. Click Content Types.
3. Click Edit for the Sites content type, as shown in Figure 6.1.

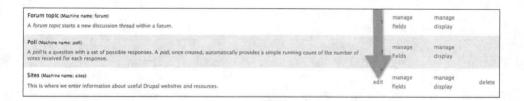

Figure 6.1   Edit link for the Sites content type

4. Scroll down to the Submission form Settings tab.
5. Make sure that the Title field label now reads Site Name, as shown in Figure 6.2.
6. Click Save Content Type.

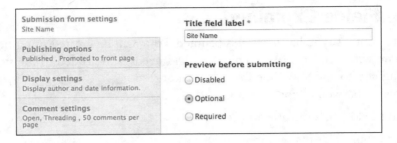

Figure 6.2   The Title field label for your Sites content type

Editing a Field: Body

When you created the Sites content type, you weren't given an opportunity to choose the label of the Body field, so do that now:

1. Click Manage Fields for the Sites content type, as shown in Figure 6.3.

Figure 6.3 Manage Fields link for the Sites content type

2. Click Edit for the Body field, as shown in Figure 6.4.

Figure 6.4 Edit the link for Body field in the Sites content type

3. Change the label from Body to Description, as shown in Figure 6.5.

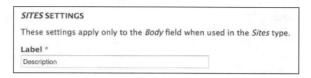

Figure 6.5 The Label for the Body field

4. Click Save Settings at the bottom of the page.

5. Check that both your Title and Body fields have now been updated to Site Name and Description, as shown in Figure 6.6.

LABEL	MACHINE NAME	FIELD	WIDGET
✛ Site Name	title	Node module element	
✛ Description	body	Long text and summary	Text area with a summary

Figure 6.6 Your Sites content type with updated labels

Reusing a Field: Image

You saw in Chapter 5 that the Article content type has an image field. You used it to upload the Drupal mascot. That image field is available for you to reuse on other content types if you choose. Or you can create another image field. How do you decide? Let's see.

Figure 6.7 shows the Image field configuration page from the Article content type. Notice the page is divided into two sections: Article Settings and Image Field Settings.

If you decide to reuse the image field, you cannot change the Image Field Settings without making those changes for all the content types that use this field. That isn't a major hurdle because there are only three things you change in Image Field Settings:

- How many images can be uploaded

- Where the images will be stored

- What the default image will be if none is chosen

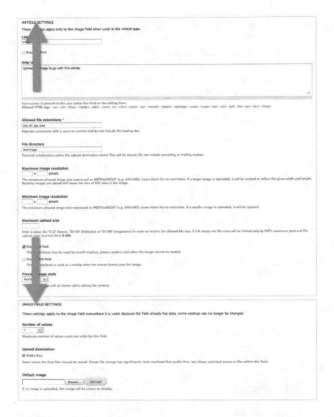

Figure 6.7 The Article Settings and Image Field Settings

Because you don't need to customize any of those three settings, you can reuse the existing Image field. Here's how to do it:

1. Click Structure on the black menu bar, and then click Content Types.

2. Click Manage Fields for the Sites content type.

3. Look for the Add Existing Field area, as shown in Figure 6.8.

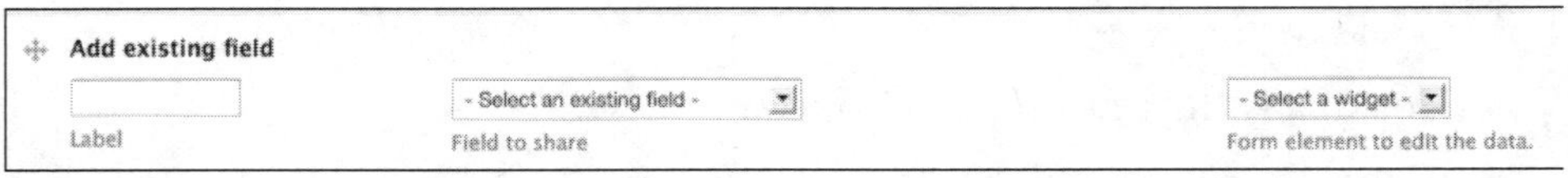

Figure 6.8 The Add Existing Field area

4. Enter **Screenshot** for the Label.

5. Choose Image: field_image (image) from the Field to share option.

   Image will automatically be filled in for the Form element to edit the data option because it is the only choice.

6. Check that your settings look like Figure 6.9.

Figure 6.9 The initial settings for the Screenshot field

7. Click Save and you see a screen similar to Figure 6.10.

Figure 6.10 The full settings for the Screenshot field

8. Enter **Upload a screenshot of the home page for this site** in the Help text field. This help message will appear under the Image field when people upload screenshots.

9. Review the Setting options on the page for future reference.

10. Click Save Settings.

Reusing a Field: Term Reference

When you created a page using the Article content type, you enter relevant words into a field called Tags. This allowed you to group your Articles according to these keywords.

Rather than re-create this field, you can reuse it. If you reuse this field, there are only two options that, if changed, will change for all content types using this field:

- How many tags can be used.

- Which group of tags can be used. Later, in the "Taxonomy Explained" section, we explain how you can manage these groups.

Now repeat the process you used to reuse the Image field, but reuse the Tags field for the Sites content type:

1. Click Structure on the black menu bar, and then click Content Types.

2. Click Manage Fields for the Sites content type.

3. Enter Tags for the Label.

4. Choose Term Reference: field_tags (Tags) from the Field to share option.

5. Choose Autocomplete Term Widget (Tagging) for the Form element to edit the data option.

6. Check that your settings look like Figure 6.11.

Figure 6.11 Reusing a Term Reference field

7. Click Save.

8. Keep the default settings and click Save Settings.

Observe that the Tags field is now added to the list of other fields on the Sites content type, as shown in Figure 6.12.

LABEL	MACHINE NAME	FIELD	WIDGET	OPERATIONS	
✛ Site Name	title	Node module element			
✛ Description	body	Long text and summary	Text area with a summary	edit	delete
✛ Screenshot	field_image	Image	Image	edit	delete
✛ Tags	field_tags	Term reference	Autocomplete term widget (tagging)	edit	delete

Figure 6.12 The Tags field has been added to your Sites content type

Adding a Field: Boolean

In addition to reusing fields, you can create new ones.

Your plan has a field that enables the content author to show whether the site is an official Drupal site. The Boolean field option would be perfect for this because it provides an either/or choice. A Boolean field is perfect for choices such as Yes/No and True/False.

For the Official site field, the site will be listed as either an official site (true) or not an official site (false). Now add this field:

1. Make sure you are on the Manage Fields page for Sites content type. As a reminder, you can get there by clicking Structure, Content Types, and then Manage Fields for Sites.

2. Look for the Add New Field, as shown in Figure 6.13.

Figure 6.13 The Add New Field area

3. Enter **Official Site** as the field label.

4. Enter **sites_officialsite** for the field name.

5. Select Boolean as the type of data to store.

6. Select Check Boxes/Radio Buttons as the form element to edit the data.

7. Make sure that your settings match Figure 6.14.

Figure 6.14 Adding a new Boolean field

8. Click Save.

9. On the next screen, enter **Yes** for On value and **No** for Off value, as shown in Figure 6.15.

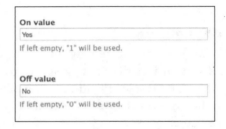

Figure 6.15 The Boolean field settings

10. Click Save Field Settings.

11. Scroll down the next screen and click Save Settings again.

12. Notice the new field is now added to the list, as shown in Figure 6.16.

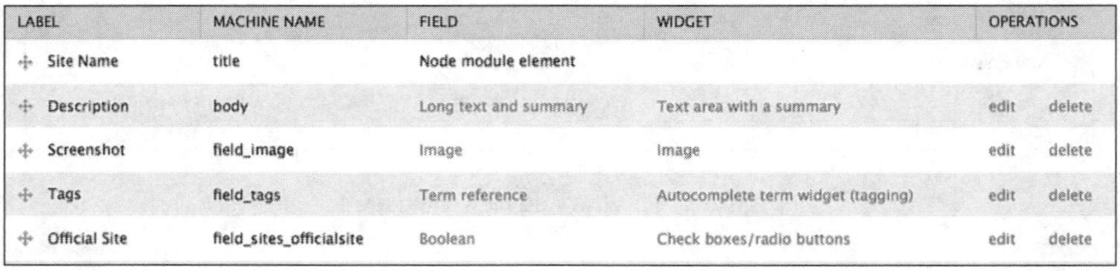

LABEL	MACHINE NAME	FIELD	WIDGET	OPERATIONS	
⊹ Site Name	title	Node module element			
⊹ Description	body	Long text and summary	Text area with a summary	edit	delete
⊹ Screenshot	field_image	Image	Image	edit	delete
⊹ Tags	field_tags	Term reference	Autocomplete term widget (tagging)	edit	delete
⊹ Official Site	field_sites_officialsite	Boolean	Check boxes/radio buttons	edit	delete

Figure 6.16 The Official Site field has been added to your Sites content type

One question you might have is about the Machine Name, which in this example was sites_officialsite. The naming convention is up to you but here is a tip. If you are creating a field that is unique to a specific content type, inserting the content type name in the field name is a good idea. For example, field_sites_image will be used only for Sites, but field_image will be reused by multiple content types. This can help you distinguish between fields that are unique and fields that are reused.

Adding a List (Text) Field

Now you can create a Topics field. This allows people to choose what topics you'll find on each site. There are a variety of ways to do this, but here's one of the simplest options: List (Text):

1. Make sure you are on the Manage Fields page for Sites content type. (As a reminder, you can get there by clicking Structure, Content types, and then Manage Fields for Sites.)

2. Look for the Add New Field area.

3. Enter **Topics** as the field label.

4. Enter **sites_topics** for the field name.

5. Select List (text) as the type of data to store.

6. Select Check Boxes/Radio Buttons as the form element to edit the data.

7. Make sure that your settings match Figure 6.17.

Figure 6.17 Adding a new List (Text) field

8. Click Save.

9. On the next screen, enter the various topics that a Drupal site can address. In Figure 6.18, we entered News, Tutorials, Groups, Events, Modules, and Themes. Each topic is on a new line.

10. Click Save Field settings.

11. Scroll down the next screen and click Save Settings again.

12. Notice the new field is now added to the list, as shown in Figure 6.19.

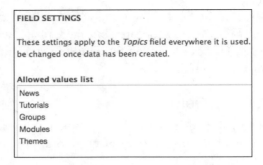

FIELD SETTINGS

These settings apply to the *Topics* field everywhere it is used.
be changed once data has been created.

Allowed values list

News
Tutorials
Groups
Modules
Themes

Figure 6.18 The settings for a List (Text) field

LABEL	MACHINE NAME	FIELD	WIDGET	OPERATIONS	
✛ Site Name	title	Node module element			
✛ Description	body	Long text and summary	Text area with a summary	edit	delete
✛ Screenshot	field_image	Image	Image	edit	delete
✛ Tags	field_tags	Term reference	Autocomplete term widget (tagging)	edit	delete
✛ Official Site	field_sites_officialsite	Boolean	Check boxes/radio buttons	edit	delete
✛ Topics	field_sites_topics	List (text)	Check boxes/radio buttons	edit	delete

Figure 6.19 The Topics field has been added to your Sites content type

Creating New Sites Content

In Chapter 5, when you created the Sites content type, you added Drupal.org as an example. Now add a new Site using all your new fields:

1. Click Add Content.

2. Click Sites.

   Your content creation page should look like Figure 6.20.

3. Complete the content type form with the following:

   - Site Name: **Groups.Drupal.org**.

   - Body: http://groups.drupal.org is the official Drupal community site.

- Thumbnail: If you are comfortable creating your own screenshots, you can visit http://groups.drupal.org and capture a screenshot. Otherwise, you can download a screenshot at http://www.drupal7explained.com/chapter6.

- Tags: Drupal, Groups, Community.

- Official site: Yes.

- Topics: Groups.

Figure 6.20 The content creation screen for your Sites content type

Figure 6.21 shows what your new fields should look like.

4. Click Save. Your new content should look like Figure 6.22.

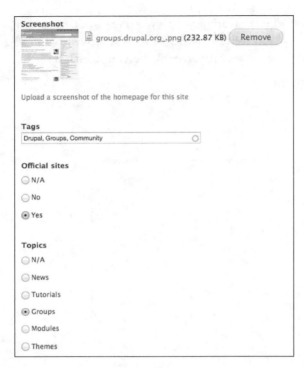

Figure 6.21 Using the new fields for your Sites content type

Figure 6.22 A content item published using your Sites content type

Repeat this process for http://DrupalModules.com. This site offers ratings and reviews on Drupal modules, but it is not an official site. There is a screenshot at http://www.drupal7explained.com/chapter6 if you need it. Figure 6.23 shows how your content should look when it has been created.

Figure 6.23 Another content item published using your Sites content type

Companies Fields Explained

The Companies content type reuses several fields created on other content types and adds one more type of field. Using the same processes you used so far, you can edit and/or add the following fields:

- **Title:** Company Name
- **Body:** Description
- **Image:** Logo
- **Term reference:** Tags

- **List (Text):** Services
- **Link:** Link

Now set up those fields.

Editing a Field: Title

1. Click Structure on the black menu bar and then Content types.
2. Click Edit for the Companies content type.
3. Scroll down to the Submission Form Settings tab.
4. Make sure that the Title field label now reads Company Name.
5. Click Save Content Type.

Editing a Field: Body

1. Go to the Manage Fields page for the Companies content type.
2. Click Edit for the Body field.
3. Change the label from Body to Description.
4. Click Save Settings at the bottom of the page.
5. Check that both your Title and Body fields have now been updated to Company Name and Description, as shown in Figure 6.24.

LABEL	MACHINE NAME	FIELD	WIDGET
⊹ Company name	title	Node module element	
⊹ Description	body	Long text and summary	Text area with a summary

Figure 6.24 The edited fields for your Companies content type

Reusing a Field: Image

1. Make sure you are on the manage fields page for the Companies content type.
2. Look for the Add Existing Field area.
3. Enter **Logo** for the Label.
4. **Choose Image:** field_image (screenshot) from the Field to Share option.

Image will automatically be filled in for the Form Element to Edit the Data option because it is the only choice.

5. Click Save.

6. **Default image:** You can download this from http://www.drupal7explained.com/chapter6. This image shows if someone adds a Company but does not add a logo. Notice that there are two Default images settings. You want the one that is at the top of the screen. If you use the setting at the bottom of the screen, that change will apply to all other content types using this field.

7. Click Save Settings.

8. Check that your Image field has been successfully reused, as shown in Figure 6.25.

LABEL	MACHINE NAME	FIELD	WIDGET
⊹ Company name	title	Node module element	
⊹ Description	body	Long text and summary	Text area with a summary
⊹ Logo	field_image	Image	Image

Figure 6.25 The Logo field added to your Companies content type

Reusing a Field: Term Reference

1. Make sure you are on the manage fields page for the Companies content type.

2. Look for the Add Existing Field area.

3. Enter **Tags** for the Label.

4. Choose Term reference: field_tags (Tags) from the Field to share option.

5. Choose Autocomplete Term Widget (Tagging) for the Form element to edit the data option.

6. Click Save.

7. Keep the default settings and click Save Settings.

8. Check that your Tags field has been successfully reused, as shown in Figure 6.26.

LABEL	NAME	FIELD	WIDGET
⊹ Company name	title	Node module element	
⊹ Description	body	Long text and summary	Text area with a summary
⊹ Logo	field_image	Image	Image
⊹ Tags	field_tags	Term reference	Autocomplete term widget (tagging)

Figure 6.26 The Tags field added to your Companies content type

Adding a List (Text) Field

1. Make sure you are on the Manage Fields page for the Companies content type.

2. Look for the Add New Field area.

3. Enter **Services** as the field label.

4. Enter **companies_services** for the field name.

5. Select List (Text) as the type of data to store.

6. Select Check Boxes/Radio Buttons as the form element to edit the data.

7. Click Save.

8. On the next screen, enter the various services that a Drupal company can provide: Coding, Themes, Hosting, Training, and Support. Make sure that each service is listed on a new line.

9. Click Save Field Settings.

10. Scroll down the next screen and click Save Settings again.

11. Notice the new field is now added to the list, as shown in Figure 6.27.

LABEL	NAME	FIELD	WIDGET
⊹ Company name	title	Node module element	
⊹ Description	body	Long text and summary	Text area with a summary
⊹ Logo	field_image	Image	Image
⊹ Tags	field_tags	Term reference	Autocomplete term widget (tagging)
⊹ Services	field_companies_services	List (text)	Check boxes/radio buttons

Figure 6.27 The Services field added to your Companies content type

Adding a Link Field

Now try something different. Break out of the field options that you have seen so far and add a new field option.

You can add a new type of field by going to Drupal.org and downloading a module. The module that is going to enable you to add links as fields is called (simply) Link.

Here's the workflow you can use. We call it the FITS workflow because using it means that your new feature FITS nicely inside your site:

1. Find the module.

2. Install the module.

3. Turn on the module.

4. Set up the module.

Step 1: Find the Module

1. Open another tab in your browser.

2. Go to http://drupal.org/project/link, as shown in Figure 6.28.

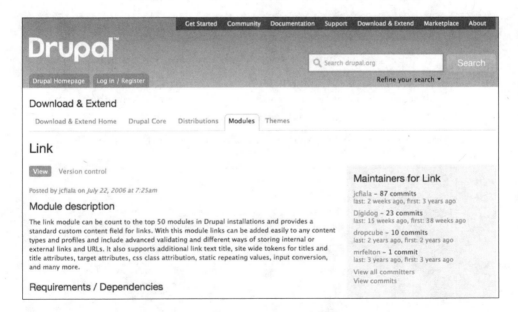

Figure 6.28 The Drupal.org page for the Link module

3. Scroll down to the bottom of the screen and find the Downloads area, as shown in Figure 6.29.

Downloads

Recommended releases

Version	Downloads	Date	Links
7.x–1.0	tar.gz (30.7 KB) | zip (37.47 KB)	2011–Oct–23	Notes
6.x–2.9	tar.gz (39.65 KB) | zip (56.22 KB)	2010–Jun–14	Notes

Development releases

Version	Downloads	Date	Links
8.x–1.x–dev	tar.gz (30.71 KB) | zip (37.48 KB)	2011–Oct–24	Notes
7.x–1.x–dev	tar.gz (31.89 KB) | zip (39.23 KB)	2012–Jun–02	Notes
6.x–2.x–dev	tar.gz (29.26 KB) | zip (37.01 KB)	2012–Feb–28	Notes

Figure 6.29 The Drupal.org download area for the Link module

Here's what to look for when finding the right file:

- You need to look at the files that are in the green area. If files are in the green area, that means they are the recommended version.

- You need to look for the files labeled 7, rather than 5, 6, or 8. If files are labeled with 7, that means they work with Drupal 7.

- It doesn't often matter if you choose the tar.gz or zip files.

- Don't worry if the version numbers have changed since the screenshots in this book were created. You will be fine if you choose the latest release in green, which is marked for Drupal 7.

Figure 6.30 shows the marked recommended version for Drupal 7.

Downloads

Recommended releases

Version	Downloads	Date	Links
7.x–1.0	tar.gz (30.7 KB) | zip (37.47 KB)	2011–Oct–23	Notes
6.x–2.9	tar. (9.65 KB) | zip (56.22 KB)	2010–Jun–14	Notes

Development releases

Version	Downloads	Date	Links
8.x–1.x–dev	tar.g 0.71 KB) | zip (37.48 KB)	2011–Oct–24	Notes
7.x–1.x–dev	tar.g 1.89 KB) | zip (39.23 KB)	2012–Jun–02	Notes
6.x–2.x–dev	tar. 9.26 KB) | zip (37.01 KB)	2012–Feb–28	Notes

Figure 6.30 The correct Drupal 7 download link for the Link module

4. Right-click the tar.gz link as marked in Figure 6.30, and copy the link or copy the shortcut. The exact command depends on the browser you use. The URL that you copy should look like this: http://ftp.drupal.org/files/projects/link-7.x-1.0.tar.gz. If you have any problems doing this and want help or another way to install your files, visit http://www.drupal7 explained.com/chapter6.

5. Return to the browser tab that has your site.

Step 2: Install the Link Module

1. Click the Modules link on the black menu bar.

2. Click Install New Module, as shown in Figure 6.31.

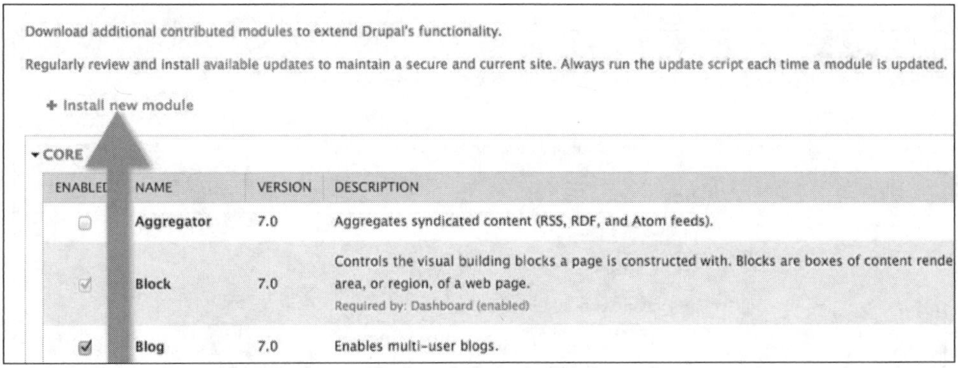

Figure 6.31 The Install New Module link

3. Click in the Install from a URL area, and paste the URL you captured when you copied the link, as shown in Figure 6.32.

4. Click Install. You'll see a screen such as the one in Figure 6.33, which says Installation Was Completed Successfully.

5. Click Enable Newly Added Modules. Clicking this link doesn't actually enable any modules, but it takes you back to the Module page where you can turn on the module.

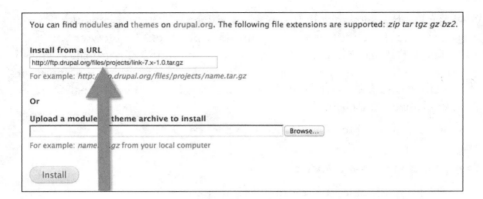

Figure 6.32 Entering the Link module's URL into the Install from a URL area

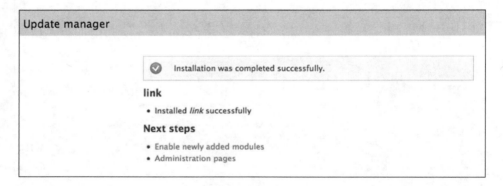

Figure 6.33 The success screen after installing a module

Step 3: Turn on the Module

1. Scroll down the page and check the box next to the Link module, as shown in Figure 6.34.

2. Click Save Configuration.

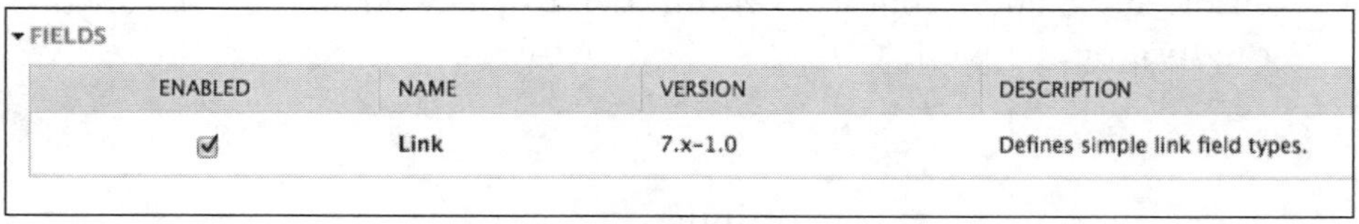

	ENABLED	NAME	VERSION	DESCRIPTION
▾ FIELDS				
	☑	Link	7.x-1.0	Defines simple link field types.

Figure 6.34 Edit link for the Sites content type

Step 4: Set Up the Module

1. Click Structure on the black menu bar.

2. Click Content Types.

3. Click Manage Fields for the Companies content type.

4. Add the Link field:

   - **Label:** Site; Figure 6.35 then shows label as "Link"

   - **Field name:** link (Each content type will have a link field so plan on reusing this field.)

   - **Type of data to store:** Link

   - **Form element to edit data:** Link

5. Click Save.

6. Scroll down and click Save Settings.

7. Check that Link has been successfully added to your Companies content type, as shown in Figure 6.35.

LABEL	MACHINE NAME	FIELD	WIDGET	OPERATIONS	
Company name	title	Node module element			
Description	body	Long text and summary	Text area with a summary	edit	delete
Logo	field_image	Image	Image	edit	delete
Tags	field_tags	Term reference	Autocomplete term widget (tagging)	edit	delete
Services	field_companies_services	List (text)	Check boxes/radio buttons	edit	delete
Link	field_link	Link	Link	edit	delete

Figure 6.35　The Link field added to your Companies content type

Creating New Companies Content

In Chapter 5, when you created the Companies content type, you added Acquia as an example. Now add a new Company, using all your new fields:

1. Click Add Companies.

2. Click Companies.

   Your Content Creation page should look like Figure 6.36.

3. Complete the content type form with the following:

   - Company Name: **OSTraining**

   - Body: http://ostraining.com is the company run by Steve, who co-authored this book. Yes, he is sneaking in a mention of his company.

- Logo: You can download this from http://www.drupal7explained.com/chapter6.
- Tags: Atlanta, Training
- Services: Training
- Link Title: **OSTraining**
- URL: http://OSTraining.com

Figure 6.36 The content creation screen for your Companies content type

4. Click Save. Your new content should look like Figure 6.37.

5. Repeat this process for Phase 2 Technology. Here are the details:

- **Title:** Phase 2 Technology
- **Body:** Phase 2 Technology is based in Washington DC and has been involved with many of the largest Drupal projects. It has also written a lot of code for Drupal.

- **Logo:** You can download this from http://www.drupal7explained.com/chapter6.

- **Tags:** Washington DC, Large Projects

- **Services:** Coding

- **Link Title:** Phase 2 Technology

- **URL:** http://phase2technology.com

Figure 6.37 The OSTraining content item live on your site

Figure 6.38 shows how your content should look when it has been created.

Editing Fields

After using your Companies content type twice, you might feel that some of the fields could be improved. For example, there are at least two possible improvements to the Services field:

- Currently N/A is an option. You might want to force companies to tell you what services they provide.

- Many companies might provide more than one service.

Figure 6.38 Edit link for the Sites content type

It is possible to go back and edit fields and fix these problems; however, you can't change the type of field. For example, you can't change an Image field to a Text field. But you can edit the settings of each field. A word of warning before you start: You can safely change these settings before you enter all of your site's content, but be careful about making changes after your content has been added:

1. Go to Structure, Content Types, and click on Manage Fields for the Companies content type.

2. Click Edit next to Services. You now see the options that you can change.

3. To remove N/A as an option, check the box that says Required field, as shown in Figure 6.39.

   To allow companies to provide more than one service, change the Number of Values list further down the page, as shown in Figure 6.40.

   Click Save.

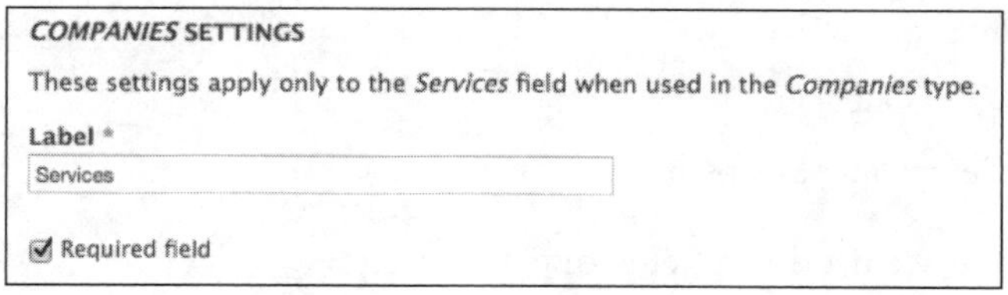

COMPANIES SETTINGS

These settings apply only to the *Services* field when used in the *Companies* type.

Label *

Services

☑ Required field

Figure 6.39 Making the Services field into a Required field

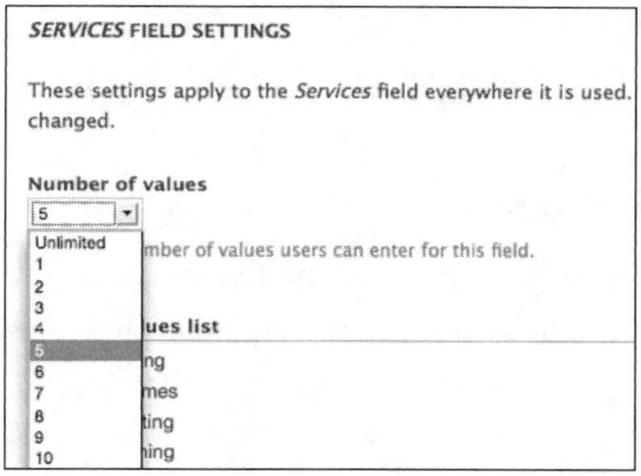

SERVICES FIELD SETTINGS

These settings apply to the *Services* field everywhere it is used. changed.

Number of values

5

Unlimited   mber of values users can enter for this field.
1
2
3
4   ues list
5
6   ng
7   mes
8   ting
9
10   hing

Figure 6.40 Changing the number of values allowed for the Services field

Events Fields Explained

Now that you have created two new content types, you can be a little more adventurous. The Events content type will have more fields and you can modify them.

Here are the fields for your Events content type:

- Title: Event Name
- Body: Description
- Image: Event Logo
- Term Reference: Tags
- Link: Registration

- Decimal: Event Price
- Date: Event Date
- Entity Reference: Sponsors

Let's go and set up those fields one-by-one:

Editing a Field: Title

1. Go to Structure, Content types, and then click Edit for the Events content type.
2. Make sure that the Title field label now reads Event Name.

Editing a Field: Body

1. Go to the Manage Fields page for the Events content type.
2. Click Edit for the Body field, and change the label from Body to Description.

Reusing a Field: Image

1. Make sure you are on the Manage Fields page for the Events content type.
2. Look for the Add Existing field area.
3. Enter Event Logo for the Label.
4. Choose Image: field_image (image) from the Field to share option.
5. Click Save and then Save Settings.

Reusing a Field: Term Reference

1. Look for the Add Existing Field area.
2. Enter Tags for the Label.
3. Choose Term reference: field_tags (Tags) from the Field to share option.
4. Choose Autocomplete term widget (tagging) for the Form element to edit the data option.
5. Click Save and then Save Settings.

Reusing a Field: Link

1. Look for the Add Existing Field area.

2. Enter **Link** for the Label.

3. Choose Link: field_link (Link) from the Field to share option.

4. Choose Link for the Form element to edit the Data option.

5. Click Save and then Save Settings.

Adding a Field: Decimal

There are three types of number fields provided by default: Integer, Float, and Decimal. You need a field for the price of your event.

An Integer field enables only whole numbers, so if you use that you cannot enter 9.95 for your price. You would have to enter 9 or 10.

The Float field and Decimal give you the option to have a decimal. The difference is that a Float field is generally used for numbers where exact precision is not so important. However, you know the exact price of your events, so add a Decimal field for your event price.

1. Make sure you are on the Manage Fields page for the Events content.

2. Locate the Add New Field. Here are the choices to make when adding this next field:

   - **Label:** Event Price.
   - **Field name:** events_price.
   - **Type of data to store:** Decimal.
   - **Form element to edit the data:** Text field.

3. Click Save.

4. On the next screen, keep the default settings.

5. Click Save Field Settings.

6. Prefix: $. This dollar sign appears in front of the field.

7. Click Save Settings again.

You've now modified, reused, or added six new fields. Check that your fields match those shown in Figure 6.41.

LABEL	MACHINE NAME	FIELD	WIDGET	OPERATIONS	
✛ Event Name	title	Node module element			
✛ Description	body	Long text and summary	Text area with a summary	edit	delete
✛ Event Logo	field_image	Image	Image	edit	delete
✛ Tags	field_tags	Term reference	Autocomplete term widget (tagging)	edit	delete
✛ Link	field_link	Link	Link	edit	delete
✛ Event Price	field_events_price	Decimal	Text field	edit	delete

Figure 6.41 The fields for your Events content type

Adding a Field: Date

When you added fields to your Companies content type, you installed a module called Link to allow you to add Link fields.

For your Events content type, use exactly the same process: FITS. This process enables you to install the Date module and make sure it FITS into your site.

Use the Date module to add Date fields. As a reminder, here is how the FITS process works:

1. Find the module.

2. Install the module.

3. Turn on the module.

4. Set up the module.

Step 1: Find the Date Module

1. Open another tab in your browser.

2. Go to http://drupal.org/project/date. The screen should look like Figure 6.42.

3. Scroll to Downloads area and the Locate the tar.gz link associated with Drupal 7. The correct link is highlighted in Figure 6.43.

4. Right-click the tar.gz link, and copy the link or copy the shortcut. The exact command depends on the browser you use. The link should look like this: http://ftp.drupal.org/files/projects/date-7.x-2.5.tar.gz.

5. Return to the browser tab that has your site.

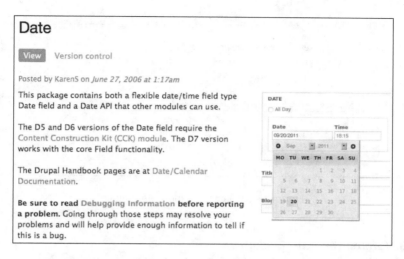

Figure 6.42 The Drupal.org page for the Date module

Downloads

Recommended releases

Version	Downloads	Date	Links
7.x–2.6	tar.gz (208.3 KB) | zip (247.62 KB)	2012–Aug–13	Notes
6.x–2.9	tar.gz (7.13 KB) | zip (300.09 KB)	2012–Apr–27	Notes

Development releases

Version	Downloads	Date	Links
8.x–1.x–dev	tar.gz (1.04 KB) | zip (227.35 KB)	2012–Oct–28	Notes
7.x–2.x–dev	tar.gz (8.38 KB) | zip (247.68 KB)	2012–Sep–30	Notes
6.x–2.x–dev	tar.gz (7.34 KB) | zip (300.31 KB)	2012–May–12	Notes

Figure 6.43 The Drupal 7 download link for the Date module

Step 2: Install the Date Module

1. Click Modules on the black menu bar.
2. Click Install New Module.
3. Click in the Install from URL field, and paste the URL you captured when you copied the link. Your screen should look like Figure 6.44.
4. Click Install.
5. Click Enable Newly Added Modules.

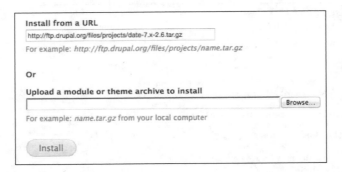

Figure 6.44 Installing the Date module

Step 3: Turn on the Date Module

When enabling modules earlier in this book, you had to check only one box.
The Date module is different. Look at the screen in Figure 6.45 to see the Date
module provides many boxes to check. However, you don't need to check all
those boxes. To set up a date field for your Events, you need to check only three
boxes.

1. Check the box next to the Date, Date API, and Date Popup modules.

2. Click Save Configuration.

Step 4: Set Up the Date Module

1. Click Structure and then Content Types. Then click Manage Fields for the
   Events content type.

2. Add new field label: Event date

   - **Field name:** events_date.

   - **Type of data to store:** Date

   - **Form element to edit the data:** Popup calendar

3. Click Save.

4. Check Collect an End Date, as shown in Figure 6.46.

5. Click Save Field Settings; then click Save Settings.

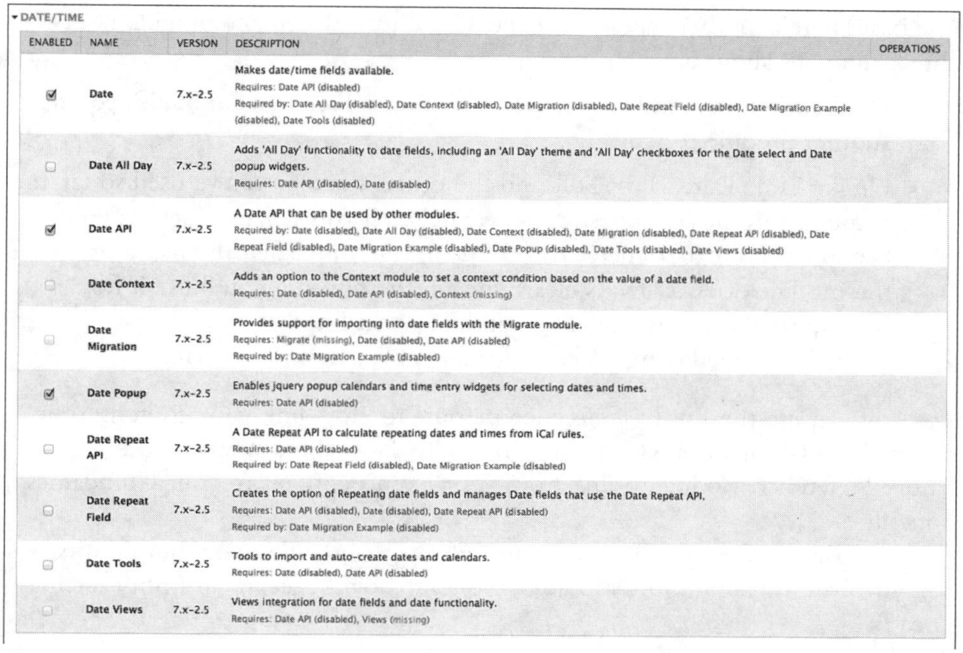

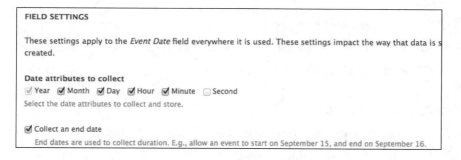

Figure 6.45 The options for the Date module

FIELD SETTINGS

These settings apply to the *Event Date* field everywhere it is used. These settings impact the way that data is s
created.

Date attributes to collect

☑ Year ☑ Month ☑ Day ☑ Hour ☑ Minute ☐ Second
Select the date attributes to collect and store.

☑ Collect an end date
End dates are used to collect duration. E.g., allow an event to start on September 15, and end on September 16.

Figure 6.46 The Field Settings for the Date field

Adding a Field: Entity Reference

When you installed the Date module, you saw that it was different from the
other modules you had used before. The Date module was different because it
came with a variety of features and you didn't need to turn them all on.

Now, here's another type of module. The Entity Reference module has two things different about it:

- Unlike the Link and Date module, the Entity Reference module requires another module to work.

- Unlike Link, Date, Blog, Poll, and the other modules you've used so far, the name of this module doesn't immediately tell you what it does. As you become more experienced with Drupal, you'll find that the name of the module doesn't always clearly match the purpose you'll use it for. Regarding the Entity Reference module, visit http://www. drupal7explained.com/chapter6 for an explanation of the name.

You can use the Entity Reference module to cross-link your content. Your Events have Companies who sponsor them. To show these sponsors, use the Entity Reference module to link from your Events content to your Companies content.

You still use the FITS workflow to make your module work, but the first part involves installing more modules. Now see how to set up an Entity reference field.

Step 1: Find the Modules

Go to Drupal.org and find the Drupal 7 download URLs for these three modules:

1. **Entity reference:** http://drupal.org/project/entityreference.

2. **Entity API:** http://drupal.org/project/entity

3. **CTools:** http://drupal.org/project/ctools

Step 2: Install the Modules

1. Click Module on the black menu bar.

2. Click Install new module.

3. Click in the Install from URL area and paste in the download URL for the Entity reference module that you captured in Step 1.

4. Click Install.

5. Repeat this process. Click Enable newly added modules.

6. Repeat this process for the Entity API and CTools modules.

Step 3: Turn on the Modules

1. Check the Chaos Tools box.

2. Check the Entity Reference box.

3. Check the Entity API box.

4. Click Save configuration.

Step 4: Set Up the Modules

1. Click Structure, Content types, and then manage fields for the Events content type and locate the Add New Field option.

2. Add new field label: Sponsors:

   - Field name: **events_sponsors**.
   - Type of data to store: Entity reference.
   - Form element to edit data: Select list.

3. Click Save.

4. Target Bundles: Choose Companies, as shown in Figure 6.47.

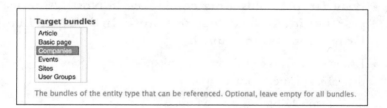

Figure 6.47   Linking your Events content to your Companies content

5. Click Save Field Settings.

6. Number of values: Unlimited.

7. Click Save Settings.

Check that your Events content type looks like Figure 6.48.

LABEL	MACHINE NAME	FIELD	WIDGET	OPERATIONS	
⊹ Event Name	title	Node module element			
⊹ Description	body	Long text and summary	Text area with a summary	edit	delete
⊹ Event Logo	field_image	Image	Image	edit	delete
⊹ Tags	field_tags	Term reference	Autocomplete term widget (tagging)	edit	delete
⊹ Link	field_link	Link	Link	edit	delete
⊹ Event Price	field_events_price	Decimal	Text field	edit	delete
⊹ Event Date	field_events_date	Date	Pop-up calendar	edit	delete
⊹ Sponsors	field_events_sponsors	Entity Reference	Select list	edit	delete

Figure 6.48 The Sponsors field added to your Events content type

Creating Content: Events

In Chapter 5, when you created the Events content type, you created a content item for DrupalCon Portland. Now that you've added all your extra fields, go back and add another event:

1. Click Add content and then click Events.

2. Complete the content type form with the following:

   - Title: **DrupalCon Munich**.

   - Body: **Drupal holds a big conference in North America every year, but it also holds one in Europe. In 2012, the European DrupalCon was in Munich**.

   - Event Logo: You can download this from http://www. drupal7explained.com/chapter6.

   - Tags: DrupalCon, Europe, Munich

   - Registration Title: DrupalCon Munich

   - URL: http://munich2012.drupal.org

   - Event Price: **$450.00**

   - Event Date: **August 20, 2012 at 09:00 to August 24, 2012 at 16:00**

   - Sponsors: **Acquia, Phase 2 Technology**

3. Before you click Save, make sure that your content looks like Figure 6.49.

Figure 6.49 Adding content to your Events content type

4. After you click Save, your content should look like Figure 6.50.

Editing the Default Field Display

When you were creating Companies, you saw that you could go back and edit the settings of fields. It is also possible to alter the display of fields. For example, your fields take up two lines at the moment, with the label on one line and the field content on the next line. You may want to place all the details for a field onto just one line. Also, your Sponsor names don't link back to the relevant Companies content.

Figure 6.50 Edit link for the Sites content type

Here's how you can make your fields look better:

1. Go to Structure, Content types, and click Manage Display for the Events content type.

   You'll see a screen like the one shown in Figure 6.51.

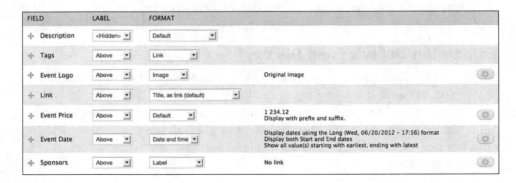

Figure 6.51 The Manage Display screen for the Events content type

2. Using the Label column, you can control the display of your labels. Choosing Inline puts the label and field content on one line. Choosing Hidden removes the label entirely. Figure 6.52 shows some recommended settings.

Figure 6.52 The Label settings for the Events content type

3. Using the Format column, you can change some options about how each field displays. For example, the Link field offers a variety of ways that you can mix-and-match the Label and URL parts of the field, as shown in Figure 6.53.

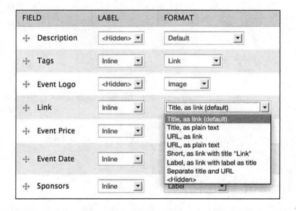

Figure 6.53 The Format settings for the Events content type

Also, some fields have gear icons on the right side of the screen, as marked in Figure 6.54. These gear icons provide extra display setting for your fields.

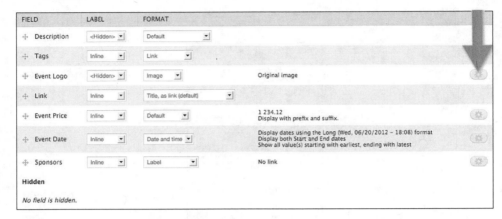

Figure 6.54 The gear icon to change display settings

4. Now, automatically link your Sponsor information to their profiles. To do that, click the gear icon in the Sponsor's row and check the box that says Link Label to the Referenced Entity. This is shown in Figure 6.55. Click Update to complete the change.

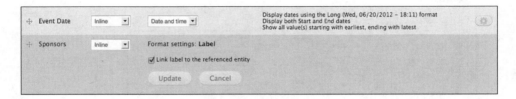

Figure 6.55 Edit link for the Sites content type

5. Click Save to make sure that your changes aren't lost.

Editing the Teaser Display

In the previous section, you controlled how your Events appear when someone sees all the content. Sometimes, however, they see only part of the content. A great example is the homepage. Figure 6.56 shows how your DrupalCon Munich content appears on the homepage.

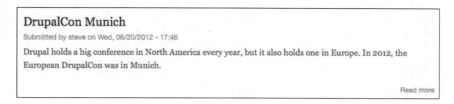

Figure 6.56 The Teaser for the Events content type

The limited homepage display is done for a good reason. If you put all the fields from all of your content on the homepage, it would make one long page. So, Drupal uses Teasers, which contain only part of the content. Here's how you can control what's in the Teaser:

1. Go to Structure, Content types, and then the Manage Display screen for Events.

2. Click the Teaser button in the top-right corner, as shown in Figure 6.57. Drupal uses these top-right buttons often, and they can be easy to miss.

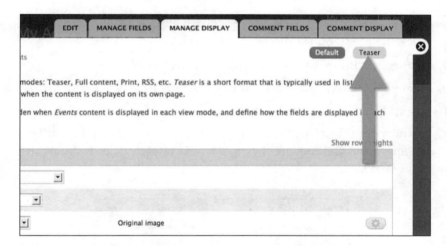

Figure 6.57 The Teaser link on the Manage Display page

3. Notice that almost all the fields are placed in the Hidden area, as shown in Figure 6.58. This means that they will not currently show in the Teaser area.

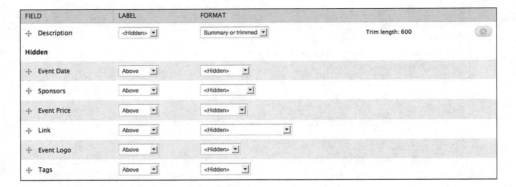

Figure 6.58 The Manage Display page for the Events content type

4. Change the Label for the Event Date field to Inline.

5. Change the Format for the Event Date field to Date and Time. The Date now jumps to the top area of the screen.

6. Change the Label for the Event Logo field to Hidden.

7. Change the Format for the Event Logo field from Hidden to Image.

8. Click the gear icon for the Event Logo.

9. Change the Image style from original to thumbnail.

10. Change the Link Image to Field to Content.

11. Click Update.

   If you want to rearrange the order of these fields, you can do that by holding down and moving the crosses next to each field, as shown in Figure 6.59.

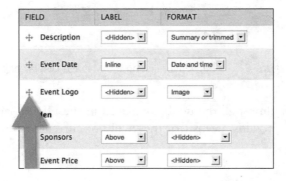

Figure 6.59 The arrow used to rearrange fields

12. Click Save.

13. Return to the homepage and observe your DrupalCon Munich teaser, as shown in Figure 6.60.

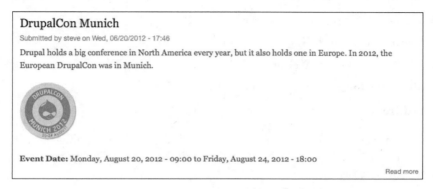

Figure 6.60 The teaser for your Events content type

14. Click the title of the content or click the Read more link and you can see the full content together with your display changes. It should look like Figure 6.61.

Figure 6.61 The default display for your Events content type

User Groups Fields Explained

Here are the fields for your User Groups content type:

- **Title:** User Group Name
- **Body:** Description
- **Term Reference:** Tags
- **Link:** User Group Website
- **Entity reference:** Organizers
- **Address:** User Group Location

Now set up those fields one by one. This time, you can simplify the instructions. If you get stuck, look back to earlier sections in this chapter, and you'll see how to do these tasks.

Editing a Field: Title

Edit the Title field label so that it reads Event Name.

Editing a Field: Body

Edit for the Body field and change the label from Body to Description.

Reusing a Field: Term Reference

Reuse the Tags field and give it the label **Tags**.

Reusing a Field: Link

Reuse the Link field and give it the label **User Group Website**.

Adding a Field: Entity Reference

When you created your Events field, you used Entity Reference to link between your content. Now with your User Groups, you can use Entity Reference to link to users. The goal is that when people register on your site, you can link to them as group organizers:

1. Add new field label: **Organizers**
   - **Field name:** user_groups_organizers
   - **Type of Data to Store:** Entity reference
   - **Form Element to Edit Data:** Autocomplete

2. Click Save.

    ▪ **Target Type:** User

3. Click Save Field settings.

    ▪ **Number of Values:** Unlimited

4. Click Save Settings.

Adding a Field: Address

To add addresses to content, install the Address Field module. Address Field does rely on the Chaos Tools (CTools) module but you already have that installed.

    Use the FITS workflow to make sure it FITS nicely inside your site.

Step 1: Find the Module

1. Open another tab in your browser.
2. Go to http://drupal.org/project/addressfield.
3. Locate the tar.gz file associated with Drupal 7.
4. Right-click the tar.gz link and copy the link or copy the shortcut. The exact command depends on the browser you use.
5. Return to the browser tab that has your site.

Step 2: Install the Module

1. Click Module and then Install New Module.
2. Click in the Install from URL field and paste the URL you captured when you copied the link.
3. Click Install.
4. Click Enable Newly Added Modules.

Step 3: Turn on the Module

1. Check the box next to Address field.
2. Save configuration.

Step 4: Set Up the Module

1. Click Structure, Content types, and then manage fields for the User Groups content type:

   - **Label:** User Group location
   - **Field name:** Address (you can easily reuse this field on other content types.)
   - **Type of Data to Store:** Postal address
   - **Form Element to Edit Data:** Dynamic address form

2. Click Save.

3. Click Save Field Settings.

4. Review your options, but stay with default for this activity.

5. Click Save Settings.

   Check your User Group fields. They should now look like Figure 6.62.

LABEL	MACHINE NAME	FIELD	WIDGET
User Group Name	title	Node module element	
Description	body	Long text and summary	Text area with a summary
Organizers	field_user_group_organizers	Entity Reference	Autocomplete
Tags	field_tags	Term reference	Autocomplete term widget (tagging)
User Group Website	field_link	Link	Link
User Group Location	field_address	Postal address	Dynamic address form

Figure 6.62 The fields for your User Groups content type

Creating Content: User Groups

In Chapter 5, when you created the User Groups content type, you created a content item for Drupal Atlanta. Now that you've added all your extra fields, go back and add another user group:

1. Click Add content, and then click User Groups.

2. Complete the content type form with the following:

   - Title: **Washington D.C. Drupal**.
   - Body: **This group is for everyone living in the Washington D.C. metro area who's interested in Drupal**.

- Tags: Washington D.C.
- Link Title: Washington D.C. Drupal.
- Link URL: http://groups.drupal.org/washington-dc-drupalers.
- Organizers: Choose yourself because you are the only current user.
- Address: Stetson's Famous Bar & Grill, 1610 U St, Washington, District of Columbia, 20009.

After you click Save, your content should look like Figure 6.63.

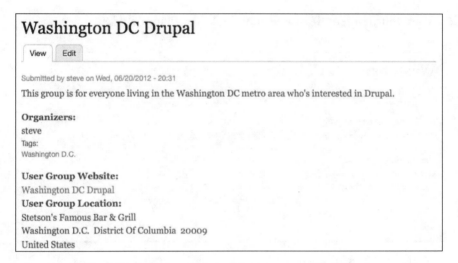

Figure 6.63 Content created via your User Groups content type

As a final touch, improve the display of the fields:

1. Go to Structure, Content types, and click Manage Display for the User Groups content type.

2. Set all the Labels to Inline, except for Description, which should remain set to Hidden.

3. Click the gear icon next to Organizers, and check the box that says Link label to the referenced entity. Click Update.

4. Use the crosses on the left of the screen; reorganize the fields so that they match, as shown in Figure 6.64.

5. Click Save.

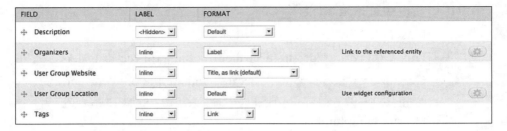

Figure 6.64 The Manage Display screen for your User Groups content type

6. Visit your content. It should now look like Figure 6.65.

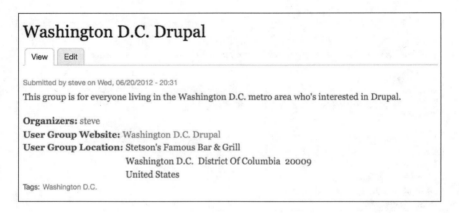

Figure 6.65 The modified version of content created
via your User Groups content type

Now you have one more task to complete your User Groups:

7. Go and find your own local User Group. You might be in North America, Europe, Asia, Africa, or Australasia, but there is a good chance you'll find a Drupal User Group meeting near you. You can use a search engine or look on http://groups.drupal.org. Find the website, location, and information for your local user group and add it to your site.

Taxonomy Explained

Out of all the fields available in Drupal, one is more frequently used, misused, explained, and misunderstood than any other: Taxonomy.

Taxonomy is Drupal's way of organizing content.

Without realizing it, you've actually been using Taxonomy already. Whenever you have used Tags, you have used Taxonomy.

Because Taxonomy is so important, we're going to explain it in more detail than any other field. We show you how Tags works and then show you how to build your own Taxonomies to organize your content.

Understanding the Term Reference Field: Terms

To start, do as follows:

1. Go to Structure Taxonomy.

   You'll see that Tags and Forums are listed on the page. Notice that these are in the column called Vocabulary Name. In Drupal, both Tags and Forums are examples of what Drupal calls Vocabularies.

2. Click List Terms next to Tags, as shown in Figure 6.66.

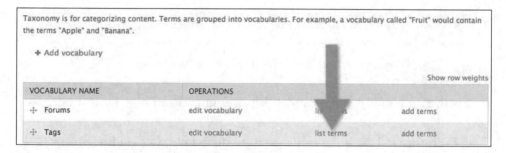

Figure 6.66 The List Terms link for the Tags Vocabulary

3. You now see a list of all the terms you've added to the site, as shown in Figure 6.67.

As you can see, all those keywords and phrases that you've added are called Terms in Drupal. That explains the name of the field type you've used through this chapter: Term Reference. The Term Reference field enables people to enter terms and for you to show them on the page.

NAME	OPERATIONS
✛ Atlanta	edit
✛ Community	edit
✛ Drupal	edit
✛ DrupalCon	edit
✛ Drupalville	edit
✛ Europe	edit
✛ Groups	edit
✛ Introduction	edit
✛ Large Projects	edit
✛ logo	edit
✛ modules	edit
✛ Munich	edit
✛ Training	edit
✛ Washington D.C.	edit

Figure 6.67 All the terms listed for the Tags Vocabulary

So, there are four definitions that help you understand how Drupal categorizes content:

- **Taxonomy:** This is the name given to the whole system of organizing content in Drupal.
    - **Vocabulary:** This is the name given to a group of terms.
- **Terms:** These are the keywords and phrases that actually categorize your content.
- **Term Reference field:** This is how your terms are connected to your content.

Let's see an example of how this can work with your content types.

You can improve your Companies content type. You can allow your companies to categorize themselves according to which language they speak.

Here's what you need to set up:

- **Vocabulary:** Languages
- **Terms:** English, Spanish, German, French, Chinese, and so on.

- **Term Reference field:** The field will be called Languages Spoken and attached to your Companies content type.

Figure 6.68 shows an overview of that categorization.

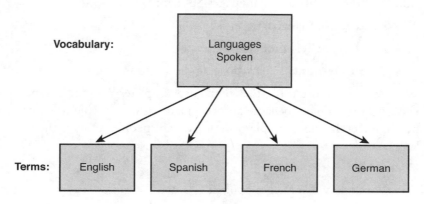

Figure 6.68 The Languages Vocabulary with specific terms

Step 1: Create the Vocabulary

1. Click Structures on the black menu bar.
2. Click Taxonomy.
3. Click Add Vocabulary.
4. Name: Languages Spoken.
5. Click Save.

Step 2: Add the Terms

1. Click Add terms next to Languages Spoken:
   - Name: English
2. Click Save:
   - Name: Spanish.
3. Click Save:
   - Name: German.
4. Click Save.

Repeat for several more languages.

Step 3: Add the Term Reference Field

1. Go to Structure, Content types, and then click manage fields next to Companies.

2. Add the New Field label: Languages Spoken:

   - **Field name:** languages_spoken
   - **Field type:** Term reference.
   - **Form element:** Check boxes/radio buttons.

   Why do you choose this rather than autocomplete? You don't want to choose autocomplete because autocomplete enables people to enter their own choices. In this example, you don't want people to enter their own languages.

3. Click Save:

   - Vocabulary: Languages Spoken

4. Click Save Field Settings:

   - Number of values: Unlimited.

5. Click Save Settings.

Step 4: Use the Term Reference Field

Go to Find Content and click Edit next to any of the companies you've added. You can now choose to add the languages spoken by that company.

So that's the process that you can use for categorizing content in Drupal. However, Taxonomy can be much more flexible than you've seen so far.

Arranging Terms in a Simple Hierarchy

You can add terms to your Events content type. These enable Event organizers to show what topics will be covered during an event. Notice this time that you organize your terms into a hierarchy. The organization of the terms is also shown in Figure 6.69:

- **Vocabulary:** What topics will be covered?
- **Terms:** Community:
  - Learning Drupal
  - Contributing to Drupal
  - Running a User Group

- **Design:**
  - Building themes
  - Building photo galleries
  - Making Drupal mobile-ready
- **Coding:**
  - Building modules
  - Security
  - Integrating Drupal with other software
- **Term Reference field:** The field will be called What Topics Will Be Covered? and attached to your Events content type.

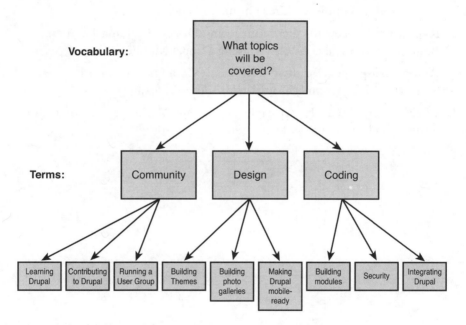

Figure 6.69 The What Topics Will Be Covered? Vocabulary with specific terms

Step 1: Create the Vocabulary

1. Click Structures on the black menu bar.
2. Click Taxonomy.

3. Click Add Vocabulary:

    ■ Name: What Topics Will Be Covered?

4. Shorten the machine_readable name.

5. Click Save.

Step 2: Add the Terms

1. Click Add Terms next to What Topics Will Be Covered?

    ■ **Name:** Community and then click Save.

    ■ **Name:** Learning Drupal and click Save.

    ■ **Name:** Contributing to Drupal and click Save.

    ■ **Name:** Running a User Group and click Save.

2. Repeat that process for these four terms: Design, Building Themes, Building Photo Galleries, and Making Drupal Mobile-Ready.

3. Repeat that process for these four terms: Coding, Building Modules, Security, and Integrating Drupal with Other Software.

4. Click the List tab at the top-right of the page. You'll see a list of all your terms, which should look like Figure 6.70.

Figure 6.70 The terms in your What Topics Will Be Covered? vocabulary

5. You can use the arrows next to each term to drag-and-drop each term. If this doesn't work for you, click Edit, Relations, and you can use the Parent Terms field to organize your terms. Your aim is to organize your terms to match your original plan, as shown in Figure 6.71.

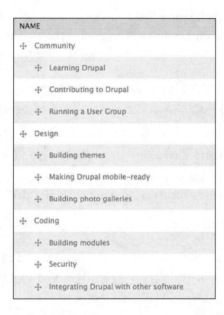

Figure 6.71 The rearranged terms in your What Topics Will Be Covered? vocabulary

Step 3: Add the Term Reference Field

1. Go to Structure, Content types, and then click Manage Fields next to Events.

2. Add New Field label: **What Topics Will Be Covered?**
   - **Field name:** events_topics_covered
   - **Field type:** Term reference.
   - **Form element:** Check boxes/radio buttons.

3. Click Save:
   - Vocabulary: What Topics Will Be Covered?

4. Click Save field settings:

  - Number of values: Unlimited.

5. Click Save Settings.

Step 4: Use the Term Reference Field

Go to Find content and click edit next to any of the events you've added. You can now choose to add the topics covered by that event.

Arranging Terms in a Complex Hierarchy

So far, you've seen three ways in which terms can be organized:

- **Tags:** The terms are completely unorganized with no hierarchy.
- **Languages Spoken:** The terms are ordered with no hierarchy.
- **What Topics Will Be Covered?:** The terms are ordered and in a simple hierarchy where many terms are organized under parent terms.

There is a fourth option: You can have a complex hierarchy where one term has multiple parents.

Now you can see an example of how this might work. Both Building Themes and Making Drupal Mobile-Ready are under two parent terms:

- **Vocabulary:** What Topics Will Be Covered?
- **Terms:** Community:
  - Learning Drupal
  - Contributing to Drupal
  - Running a User Group
  - **Design:**
    - Building themes
    - Building photo galleries
    - Making Drupal mobile-ready
  - **Coding:**
    - Building modules
    - Building themes
    - Making Drupal mobile-ready
    - Security
    - Integrating Drupal with other software

Now see how you can organize terms in this way:

1. Go to Structure, Taxonomy.

2. Click list terms next to What Topics Will Be Covered?

3. Click Edit next to Building themes.

4. Click Relations.

5. Using your cursor, you can select more than one parent term, as shown in Figure 6.72. Depending on the type of computer you use, you may also need to touch a key, such as Shift or Command. In the example shown in Figure 6.72, we're selecting both Design and Coding.

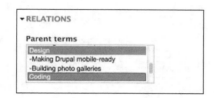

Figure 6.72 Choosing the parent terms for a particular term

6. Click Save.

   You can see that Building Themes is now underneath two terms, as shown in Figure 6.73.

7. Repeat that process for Making Drupal mobile-ready.

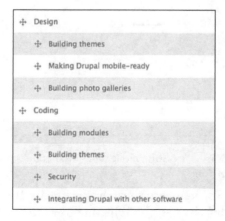

Figure 6.73 A complex hierarchy of terms

The only disadvantage with this complex hierarchy is that the drag-and-drop feature will not work any longer. You must rearrange all the terms by clicking Edit, Relations, and selecting a parent.

What's Next?

Now see what your Drupalville site looks like at the end of this chapter. It should look similar to Figure 6.74.

Figure 6.74   Your Drupalville site at the end of this chapter

Don't worry if your site doesn't match this exactly. If you understand the concepts covered in this chapter, you'll be fine to move on to Chapter 7, "Drupal Modules Explained."

Chapters 5 and 6 show you how content works in Drupal. However, most websites don't just have content, they also have features. In Chapter 7, you move beyond content and add more features to your site. You add social bookmarks, contact forms, sitemaps, and more.

You add those features by adding more modules. In this chapter, you installed several modules using the FITS workflow. In the next chapter, you add many more.

7

Drupal Modules Explained

If you've used a mobile phone in the last few years, you can understand modules. Modules in Drupal are like the apps on a phone. Modules are the source of all the features on our Drupal sites.

We've already seen modules in Chapter 5, "Drupal Content Explained," and Chapter 6, "Drupal Fields Explained." In Chapter 5, you went to the Modules page on your site and turned on four core modules: Blog, Book, Forum, and Poll. In Chapter 6, you went a step further. By using the FITS workflow, you added modules from Drupal.org to your site.

- Find

- Install

- Turn on

- Set up

In this chapter, you use modules to add many more features.

At the end of this chapter, you should be able to use modules to add these features:

- Links that enable visitors to share your content on social sites

- Links that enable visitors to print content or email it to friends

- Links that enable visitors to bookmark content

- Ratings so that visitors can vote on content

- More flexible URL patterns

- Forms so that visitors can contact you

- A text editor so that you can format your content.

You also see how to research and evaluate modules on Drupal.org.

Adding Modules Explained

After Chapters 5 and 6, you have nine content types. The plan is to add six features to one or more of your content types. Table 7.1 lists the content types and which features will be set up for each.

This chapter's introduction described the features you're going to add. Here is a list of the modules you can use for each feature:

- **AddtoAny:** Social sharing links that enable visitors to share your content on sites such as Facebook and Twitter
- **Printer, email, and PDF Versions:** Links that enable visitors to print content or email it to friends
- **Flag:** Links that enable authenticated users to bookmark content
- **Fivestar Ratings:** So visitors can vote on content
- **Pathauto:** More flexible URL patterns
- **Webform:** Forms so that visitors can contact you
- **WYSIWYG:** A text editor so that you can format your content

Sharing Drupal Content

Have you ever visited a web page and thought, "This would be a great page to share on Facebook or Twitter"? In this section, you can make it easy for your visitors to share your content.

The Share Buttons (AddToAny) by Lockerz module (AddtoAny module for short) is one of the modules that provides this feature.

Use the FITS workflow to find, install, turn on, and set up this module.

Step 1: Find the Module

1. Go to http://drupal.org/project/addtoany.
2. Copy the tar.gz link for the Drupal 7 version of this module.

Step 2: Install the Module

1. Go to your site.
2. Click Modules on the black menu bar.
3. Click Install New Module.
4. Paste the link from Drupal.org into the Install from URL field.
5. Click Install.
6. Click Enable Newly Added Modules.

Table 7.1 The Features You Can Add to Your Content Types

Content Types	Basic Article	Blog Page	Book Entry	Page	Companies	Events	Forum Topic	Poll	Sites	User Groups
Social Sharing	Yes	Yes	Yes	Yes	Yes	Yes	Yes	Yes	Yes	Yes
Printer, email and PDF	Yes	No	Yes	Yes	Yes	Yes	No	No	Yes	Yes
Bookmarks	Yes	Yes	Yes	Yes	Yes	Yes	Yes	No	Yes	Yes
Rating	Yes	No	Yes	Yes	No	Yes	No	No	Yes	No
URL Improvements	Yes	Yes	Yes	Yes	Yes	Yes	Yes	Yes	Yes	Yes
Contact Forms	No	No	No	No	No	Yes	No	No	No	No
Text Editor	Yes	Yes	Yes	Yes	Yes	Yes	Yes	Yes	Yes	Yes

Step 3: Turn On the Module

1. Scroll down your module list and check the box next to AddtoAny.

2. Click Save Configuration.

Step 4: Set Up the Module

The setup process for modules varies from one module to the next.

With some modules, such as Blog and Poll, all you need to do is turn them on. That was true of the modules in Chapter 5.

With other modules, such as Links and Date, you need to create fields to put them into action. That was true of the modules in Chapter 6.

Some other modules have one or more configuration pages that need to be managed and saved before the module will work.

For the AddtoAny Share buttons to appear, you need to manage and save the module's settings. Do that now.

You can find the configuration page in two ways:

- Click Configure next to the module on the Module page.

- Click Configuration on the black menu bar and find the entry for the module.

Now use the second of those two ways, because the black menu bar is always available no matter where you are in your site:

1. Click Configuration on the black menu bar.

2. In the right column, under the System block, locate and click AddtoAny, as shown in Figure 7.1.

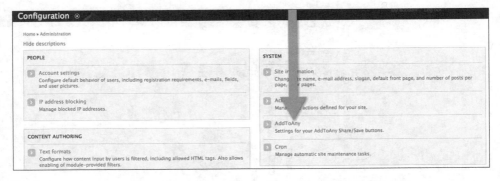

Figure 7.1   The link to access the AddtoAny module's configuration area

3. Click Placement to view the options, as shown in Figure 7.2.

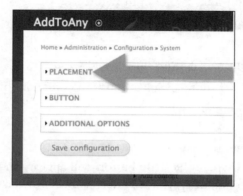

Figure 7.2   Links inside the AddtoAny module's configuration area

4. Observe the list of content types, as shown in Figure 7.3.

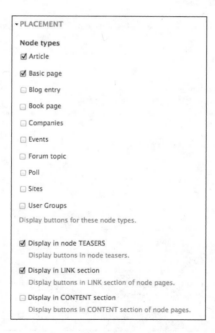

Figure 7.3   Choosing which content types have the AddtoAny module

5. Check the box for every content type.

6. Click the Button link, as shown in Figure 7.2.

   In this area, you choose from several existing images or you can add your own image.

7. Click the Additional Options link, as shown in Figure 7.2.

8. Observe this is for more advanced, custom configuration.

9. Click Save Configuration.

Step 5: See the Results

There are two places where the share button will appear: on the full view of a page created with a content type and on teaser lists. Now take a look:

1. Click the home icon in the top-left corner on the black menu bar.

2. The pages in the teaser list now show the Share button (see Figure 7.4).

Figure 7.4   The AddtoAny module placed on your content teasers

3. Click one of the page titles.

4. Observe the Share button, as shown in Figure 7.5.

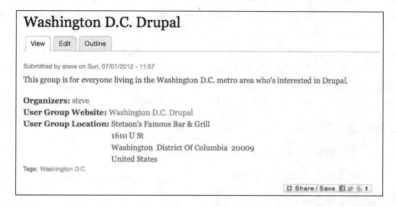

Figure 7.5   The AddtoAny module placed on your full content display

5. Hover over the AddtoAny button. You can see the sharing options available, as shown in Figure 7.6.

Figure 7.6   The social bookmarking options provided by the AddtoAny module

Printing Drupal Content

Have you ever printed a webpage and wished you could just print the article on that page versus all the ads, menus, and such that surround the article? Well, you can provide that feature to your site visitors with the module called Printer, email, and PDF versions.

This feature is particularly useful with the Book page content type. Recall that your plan is to have a user manual with multiple related pages connected in an outline. This module allows your visitors to print the entire book to one page or any subsection in the book to one page. Now see how you can do this.

Step 1: Find the Module

1. Go to http://drupal.org/project/print.
2. Copy the tar.gz link for the Drupal 7 version of this module.

Step 2: Install the Module

1. Go to your site.
2. Click Modules on the Administration menu.
3. Click Install New Module.
4. Paste the link from Drupal.org into the Install from URL field.
5. Click Install.
6. Click Enable Newly Added Modules.

Step 3: Turn on the Module

Similar to some modules you saw in Chapter 6, this module actually comes with three modules: Printer-Friendly Page (Required), PDF Version, and Send by Email:

1. Scroll down your module list and check the box next to Printer-Friendly Pages and Send by Email. You can skip PDF Version for now because it can be difficult to set up on many servers.
2. Click Save Configuration.

Step 4: Set Up the Module

Unlike the AddtoAny module, you don't need to go to the module's configuration screen before you see the results of this module. But, there are setup options available to you, so take a look. There are two places where you can configure this module:

- Printer, Email, and PDF Versions module configuration page
- Each content type's configuration page

Print, Email, and PDF Module Configuration Page

Although you don't have to set anything on this page, it is worth reviewing your options:

1. Click Configuration on the black menu bar.
2. Click Printer, Email, and PDF Versions link in the User Interface block on the right, as shown in Figure 7.7.

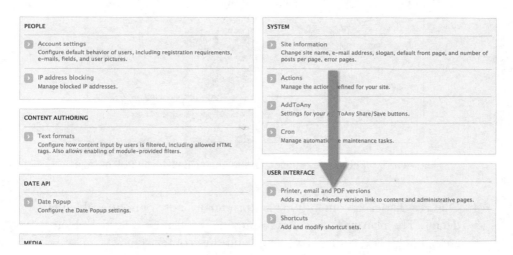

Figure 7.7   The link to access the Printer, Email, and PDF module's configuration area

There are two options in here that you might want to change:

- **Printer-friendly page link:** Controls where on the content the links are shown
- **Link style:** Controls whether visitors see text links or image links

Content Type Configuration Pages

1. Click Structure; then click Content Types.
2. Click Edit for any content type.

3. Scroll down and click the Printer, Email, and PDF Versions tab, as shown in Figure 7.8.

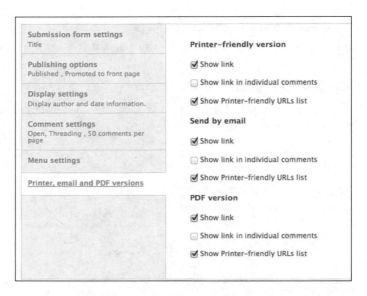

Figure 7.8   The display options for the Printer, Email, and PDF module

4. Observe that each content type has printer-friendly options enabled by default. The plan in Table 7.1 is to provide this feature on article, blog entry, book page, companies, events, and sites content types.

5. Edit these content types and uncheck all the Printer, Email, and PDF Versions boxes: Basic Page, Forum Topic, and Poll.

Step 5: See the Results

1. To see the Printer-Friendly options, go to one of the many pages you have already created and observe the link, as shown in Figure 7.9.

2. Click Printer-Friendly Version, and you'll see the screen, shown in Figure 7.10.

3. Click Send by Email, and you'll see the screen shown in Figure 7.11.

Figure 7.9   The Print, Email, and PDF module visible on your site's content

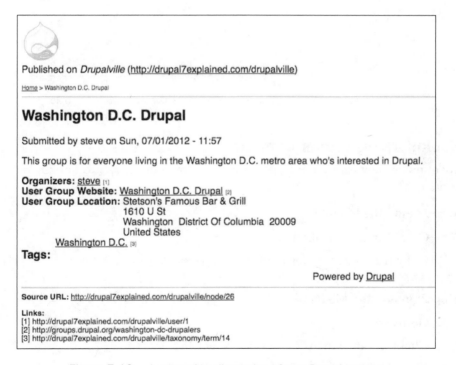

Figure 7.10   A printer-friendly version of your Drupal content

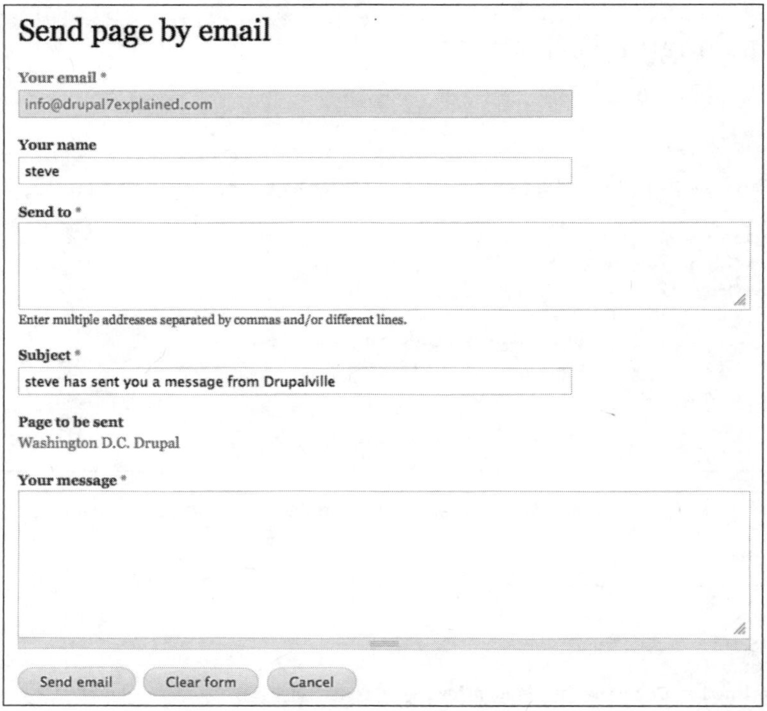

Send page by email

Your email *

info@drupal7explained.com

Your name

steve

Send to *

Enter multiple addresses separated by commas and/or different lines.

Subject *

steve has sent you a message from Drupalville

Page to be sent
Washington D.C. Drupal

Your message *

Send email   Clear form   Cancel

Figure 7.11   Allowing visitors to email your content to other people

Bookmarking Drupal Content

We're now going to use the Flag module to allow our visitors to bookmark content.

Step 1: Find the Module

1. Go to http://drupal.org/project/flag.
2. Copy the tar.gz link for the Drupal 7 version of this module.

Step 2: Install the Module

1. Go to your site.
2. Click Modules; then click Install New Module.
3. Paste the link into the Install from URL field and then click Install.

Step 3: Turn on the Module

Again, you see that the Flag module has more than one module that can be turned on: Flag and Flag Actions. For this activity, you need to turn on only the Flag module:

1. Scroll down; check all three boxes in the Flag area.

2. Click Save Configuration.

Step 4: Set Up the Module

Unlike some other modules, you don't have a separate configuration page for the Flag module. All of your configuration settings are specific to the flag itself:

1. Click Structures and then Flags.

2. Click Edit for the Bookmark flag, as shown in Figure 7.12.

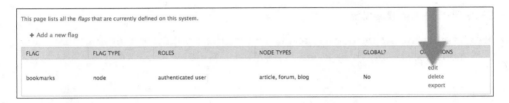

Figure 7.12   The link to edit a flag in the Flag module

3. Review the options and notes under each option.

4. Locate the Flaggable content list.

5. Observe that this is where you tell the Flag module to which content type the flag should be applied, as shown in Figure 7.13. This is a different way to link the module and the content type. With the AddtoAny module you went to the Configuration area and with the Print, Email, and PDF Versions module, you edited each content type.

6. As per your plan in Table 7.1, check all the content types except for Poll.

7. Click Submit.

Figure 7.13   Choosing which content can be used with the Flag module

Step 5: See the Results

1. Return to the homepage. You'll see that the Bookmark This links have appeared, as shown in Figure 7.14.

Figure 7.14   The Flag module visible on your content teaser

2. Click the Bookmark this link, and it will change to read Unbookmark This.

3. Click the content title, and you can see that the Bookmark This link appears, as shown in Figure 7.15.

At the moment, it's not possible to see a list of all the content you've bookmarked. That comes in Chapter 11, "Drupal Views Explained." We will add the Views module to the site and that will allow you to display all of your bookmarks.

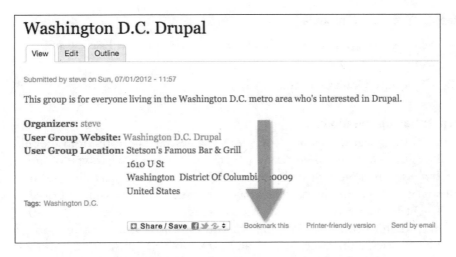

Figure 7.15   The Flag module visible on your full content display

Voting on Drupal Content

Feedback is often good to have, and one way to accomplish this is to allow your visitors to vote on the content on your site. The Fivestar module is one of the modules that provides a voting feature.

Step 1: Find the Modules

As you've seen, some modules rely on others to work. This time you need the Fivestar module but also the VotingAPI module:

1. Go to Fivestar page on Drupal.org: http://drupal.org/project/fivestar. Copy the tar.gz link for the Drupal 7 version of this module.

2. Repeat the process for the VotingAPI module: http://drupal.org/project/votingapi.

Step 2: Install the Module

1. Go to your site.

2. Click Modules; then click Install New Module.

3. Paste the link into the Install from URL field and click Install.

4. Repeat this process for the VotingAPI module.

Step 3: Turn on the Module

1. Scroll down your module list; check the boxes next to Fivestar and Voting API.

2. Click Save Configuration.

Step 4: Set Up the Module

You've noticed that the setup process for modules varies greatly from module to module. The way a module is set up depends not only on what type of module it is, but also on choices made by the module's developer. Many different developers write Drupal modules, and not all of them choose the same approach.

To get Fivestar set up, use the process used in Chapter 6.

According to your plan in Table 7.1, you can allow visitors to vote on articles, blog entries, book pages, events, and sites. Now add this voting feature to the Sites content type and then repeat the process for the other content types:

1. Click Structures; then click Content Types.

2. Click Manage fields for the Sites content type.

3. Add the new field:

   - Label: **Vote**

   - Field name: vote

   - Type of data to store: Fivestar Rating

   - Form element to edit the data: Stars (rated while viewing)

4. Click Save, Save field settings, and then Save Settings.

5. Chapter 6 showed you how to reuse fields. Use that technique to reuse this field to add ratings to Articles, Blog Entries, Book Pages, and Events.

Step 5: See the Results

1. Go to the homepage; locate one of your Sites pages in the homepage teaser list.

2. Click the page title. The voting option will be down at the bottom of the screen, as shown in Figure 7.16.

3. Click the stars, and your vote will be recorded. Drupal enables each authenticated user to vote once on each content item.

Figure 7.16   The Fivestar module visible on your content

Changing Drupals URLs

When you save content on your Drupal site, the URL for that page looks like this: /node/23.

What does this URL mean?

- Node is a word that Drupal sometimes uses when it means content.
- 23 shows that this is the 23rd content item added to your site.

However, although these URLs are logical, after you know what they mean, most sites won't find them to be user-friendly or search engine optimization (SEO)-friendly.

Default Drupal comes with a Path module that enables you to manually define the URL you would like for your content, but this requires that you manually set it up whenever you create content.

The Pathauto module provides a way to automatically create URLs according the pattern you decide. Pathauto relies on the Token module, so you'll install that also.

Step 1: Find the Module

1. Go to http://drupal.org/project/pathauto.
2. Copy the tar.gz link for the Drupal 7 version of this module.

Step 2: Install the Module

1. Click Modules; then click Install New Module.
2. Paste the link into the Install from URL field, and then click Install.
3. Repeat Step 1 and Step 2 for the Token module: http://drupal.org/project/token.

Step 3: Turn on the Module

1. Check the box next to Pathauto and Token.
2. Click Save Configuration.

Step 4: Set Up the Module

1. Click Configuration.
2. Click URL aliases in the Search and Metadata block.
3. Observe the five tabs across the top-right of the screen, as shown in Figure 7.17.
4. Click the Patterns tab.
5. By default, Pathauto creates a pattern for all your URLs. That pattern is content/[node:title], as shown in Figure 7.18. With this pattern, your About Us page would have the URL /content/about-us. Remember that node is the word that Drupal sometimes uses to refer to content, so *node title* means the title of your content.
6. Click Replacement Patterns at the bottom of the Content Paths block. You now see a list of tokens, as shown in Figure 7.19. As you gain more experience with Drupal, you'll see tokens in many places. They are provided by the Token module and enable you to easily create automatic patterns for all sorts of things on your site.

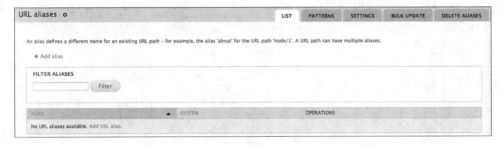

Figure 7.17   The Pathauto module's configuration area

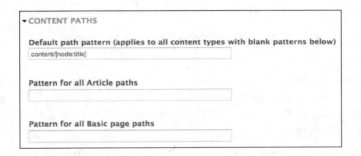

Figure 7.18   The default URL patterns provided by the Pathauto module

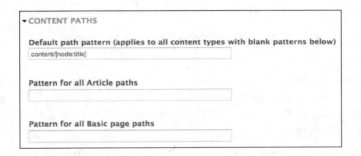

Figure 7.19   A list of types of token inside the Pathauto module

For example, click Nodes and you see a list of options, as shown in Figure 7.20. These tokens provide a variety of ways in which the URL for a content item can be created.

NAME	TOKEN	DESCRIPTION
		Click a token to insert it into the field you've last clicked.
Current date		Tokens related to the current date and time.
Current page		Tokens related to the current page request.
Current user		Tokens related to the currently logged in user.
Nodes		Tokens related to individual content items, or "nodes".
Author	[node:author]	The author of the node.
Body	[node:body:?]	The main body text of the node. The following properties may be appended t (Summary), format (Text format)
Book	[node:book]	The book page associated with the node.
Bookmarks flag count	[node:flag-bookmarks-count]	Total flag count for flag Bookmarks
Bookmarks flag link	[node:flag-bookmarks-link]	Flag/unflag link for Bookmarks
Comment count	[node:comment-count]	The number of comments posted on a node.

Figure 7.20   A list of tokens inside the Pathauto module

7. The default pattern content/[node:title] is not terrible, but we're going to try to provide some more relevant and descriptive URLs. Here are some example URL patterns to try. When you enter them, your screen should look like Figure 7.21.

We are inserting the word /resources/ into some patterns for a reason: Later in this book we will create landing pages for several content types. Those landing pages will be located at URLs such as /articles/, /companies/ and /events/. By adding the word /resources/, we make sure those URLs will still be available.

Here are the patterns to create for your URLs:

- **Article:** resources/articles/[node:title]
- **Basic page:** [node:menu-link:parent]/[node:menu-link]
- **Blog:** blogs/[node:author]/[node:title]
- **Book:** [node:book:parent]/[node:book]
- **Companies:** resources/companies/[node:title]
- **Events:** events/[node:title]
- **Forum:** forums/[node:taxonomy_forums]/[node:title]
- **Poll:** polls/[node:title]
- **Sites:** resources/sites/[node:title]
- **User Groups:** resources/user-groups/[node:title]

Figure 7.21   New, recommended URL patterns for your URLs

If you make a mistake with your URL patterns or just want to try something different, you can delete and re-create the URLs, as follows:

1. Click the Bulk Update tab in the top-right corner.

2. Check all the boxes and click Update.

3. Click the Delete Aliases tab in the top-right corner.

4. Check All aliases and click Delete Aliases Now!

Step 5: See the Results

Go to your homepage and click one of the titles in the teaser area. You see the new URL in the browser bar.

Using Pathauto, you can also manually create the URL for any page, as follows:

1. Click the Edit tab for any content item.

2. Scroll down, and you'll see a URL path settings box where you can modify the URL (see Figure 7.22).

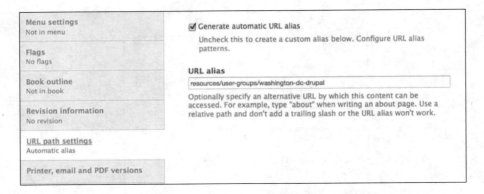

Figure 7.22   Customizing URLs for individual content items

Creating a Form

Almost everyone needs to allow their visitors to contact them easily. The Webform module is a convenient way to collect information from your visitors. You can use Webform to create a contact form, registration forms, survey forms, and more.

For your Drupalville site, create a contact form.

Step 1: Find the Module

1. Go to http://drupal.org/project/webform.

2. Copy the tar.gz link for the Drupal 7 version of this module.

Step 2: Install the Module

1. Go to your site, click Modules, and click Install New Module.

2. Paste the link into the Install from URL field; then click Install.

3. Click Enable Newly Added Modules.

Step 3: Turn on the Module

1. Scroll down your module list and check the box next to Webform.

2. Click Save Configuration.

Step 4: Set Up the Module

1. Click Add Content.

2. Click Webform.

3. Title: Contact Us

4. Menu Settings: Check the Provide a Menu link box.

5. Comment Settings: Closed.

6. Click Save.

7. You'll now see the Webform interface, as shown in Figure 7.23. This is where you can build your form. This is similar to the process you used to add fields in Chapter 6, although Webform is simpler and more limited than Drupal's fields.

Figure 7.23   A blank form in the Webform module

8. Start by collecting the name of people contacting you. Enter Name for the Label and choose Textfield for the Type, as shown in Figure 7.24.

Figure 7.24   Adding a textfield component to a Webform form

9. Click Add.

10. Keep the default settings, but you can review your options before you click Save Component.

11. Enter E-mail for the Label and choose E-mail for the Type, as shown in Figure 7.25.

12. Click Add and then Save Component.

13. Enter Message for the Label and choose Textarea for the Type.

14. Click Add and then Save component.

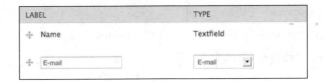

Figure 7.25   Adding an email component to a Webform form

You can modify the settings for your Contact Form by clicking small tabs in the top-right corner, as shown in Figure 7.26.

Figure 7.26   The Form settings link inside the Webform module

Click each of those sublinks to see the settings they offer:

1. Click Form components, and you'll be on the screen where you can add more fields to your form.

2. Click E-mails, and you can choose where messages from the form will be sent.

3. Click Form settings. Here you can write a thank-you message to people submitting your form and modify other settings.

4. Click View, and you see the form live on your site, as shown in Figure 7.27.

Now, test the form:

1. Enter a name, email, and message.

2. Click Submit.

3. You'll see a thank-you message. Click Go Back to the Form.

4. Click the Results tab.

5. You'll see a list of the submissions made via the form. You'll also see other options, including Analysis, Table, Download, and Clear in the top-right corner, as shown in Figure 7.28.

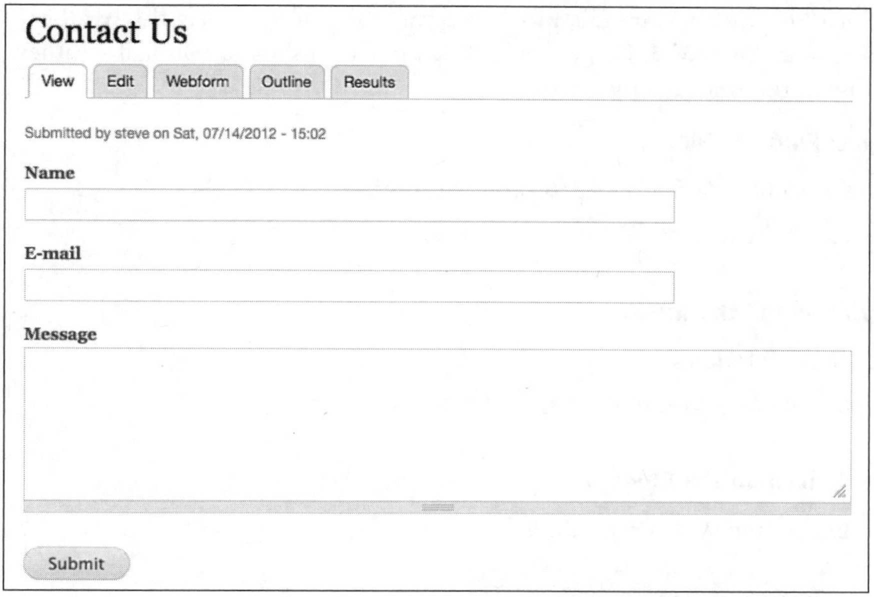

Contact Us
View
Edit
Webform
Outline
Results
Submitted by steve on Sat, 07/14/2012 - 15:02
Name
E-mail
Message
Submit

Figure 7.27 A completed Webform published on your site

Home » Contact Us
Submissions
Analysis
Table
Download
Clear
Showing all results.
#
SUBMITTED
USER
IP ADDRESS
OPERATIONS
1
07/14/2012 - 15:30
steve
74.176.188.213
View
Edit
Delete

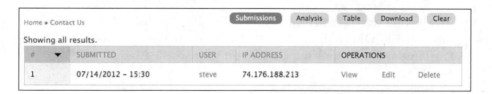

Figure 7.28 Recorded submissions to a form created with Webform

Showing Weather

Throughout this book, there are times when we're going to give you a gentle, short introduction to something we'll deal with in more depth later. This is one of those times.

You work with blocks in Chapter 10, "Drupal Blocks Explained." Blocks are accurately named. They are small blocks of content or information that often appear in the sidebar of your site. Some modules work by creating blocks. Now we're going to look at two examples that visually illustrate exactly what blocks are.

First, the Weather module provides a way for you to display the weather from around the world. This module uses a block to show a regional weather forecast in the sidebar of your site.

Step 1: Find the Module

1. Go to http://drupal.org/project/weather.
2. Copy the download link.

Step 2: Install the Module

1. Go to Modules.
2. Install New Module and install Weather.

Step 3: Turn on the Module

1. Enable the Weather module.

Step 4: Set Up the Module

1. Click Configuration.
2. Locate Weather in the User Interface block and click the link.
3. You'll see a screen similar to Figure 7.29. Observe that you have three options: Add Display, Edit Default Display, and Create a Directory to hold any custom images you want to use on your weather blocks.

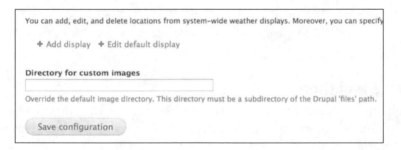

Figure 7.29   The configuration area for the weather module

4. Click Add Display.
5. Observe your options and click Save.

6. Click Add location to this display, as shown in Figure 7.30.

Figure 7.30   Adding a new location to the Weather module

7. Select a country.

8. Select a place.

9. Select an alternative name for the selected place. This enables you to give the place a more human-readable name. For example, I selected GA - Atlanta, De Kalb-Peachtree Airport for the Place, but simply wrote Atlanta in here.

10. Your finished screen will look like Figure 7.31.

Figure 7.31   Choosing the details for the new location in the Weather module

11. Click Save.

12. Save the configuration.

Step 5: See the Results

1. Go to Structure and then Blocks.

2. Scroll down the area marked Disabled at the bottom of the page.

3. Find the row with the title Weather: System-Wide Display (#1), as shown in Figure 7.32.

Figure 7.32   Finding the Weather block in the Blocks screen

4. In the Weather: System-Wide Display (#1) Row, choose Sidebar first from the large drop-down, as shown in Figure 7.33.

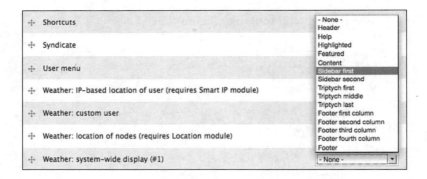

Figure 7.33   Placing the Weather block into your site's sidebar

5. Click Save Blocks.

6. Click the Home icon in the top-left corner of your screen, and you see that the Weather block is now live on your site, as shown in Figure 7.34. Notice that there is also a link called Weather in the Navigation area. That was automatically created by the Weather module and enables people to search for weather in their own area.

Figure 7.34   The Weather module published on your site inside a block

Showing Maps

When you installed the Address field module, you took the first step to display a map on your site. The Address Field Static Map module works with the Address field module. Each time you create an event page on the site and include an address, a block appears with a map and a marker showing the location of the event.

Now install and set up the map.

Step 1: Find the Module

1. Go to http://drupal.org/project/addressfield_staticmap.

2. Copy the download link.

Step 2: Install the Module

1. Go to Modules; then install the new module and Address Field Static Map.

Step 3: Turn on the Module

1. Enable the Address Field Static Map module.

Step 4: Set Up the Module

1. Click Configure on the black menu bar.

2. Locate Address Field Static Map Block in the System block and click the link. Enter these settings:

   - Address Field: field_address

   - Image Size: 170x170

   - Click the Get Directions link and check the box that says Display Get Directions.

3. Click Save Configuration.

4. Go to Structure and then Blocks.

5. Scroll down the area marked Disabled at the bottom of the page.

6. Find the row with the title Address Field Static Map.

7. In the Address Field Static Map row, choose Sidebar first from the large drop-down, as shown in Figure 7.35.

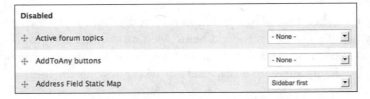

Figure 7.35   Placing the Address Field Static Map block into your site's sidebar

8. Click Save Blocks.

9. Click the Home icon in the top-left corner of your screen. You'll notice that the Map is not showing yet. This is because it shows only when there is an address field on the content. Visit one of your User Group pages and you'll see the map in the left sidebar, as shown in Figure 7.36.

Figure 7.36   The Address Field Static Map module published
on your site inside a block

Text Editors for Drupal Explained

Most people writing content for websites want a text editor. They want to add bold, italic, underline, and other formatting to their text. They also want to create tables and insert images.

There are two problems with doing that in Drupal:

- Drupal 7 does not install with a point-and-click text editor by default. Drupal's developers know this is a problem and will probably include an editor in Drupal 8.

- Installing a text editor is more difficult than installing a normal module.

This section tries to overcome those two problems. You see how to install a text editor, or to give it another name, a WYSIWYG (What You See Is What You Get) editor.

Step 1: Install the WYSIWYG Module

Use the FITS workflow to install the WYSIWYG module:

1. Go to http://drupal.org/project/wysiwyg and copy the link.

2. Go to Modules; then Install new module and install WYSIWYG.

3. Enable the WYSIWYG module.

Step 2: Upload the TinyMCE Files

Now upload the files for the editor. You need to access your Drupal site's file structure. This exercise shows you how to upload the TinyMCE files. This exercise also gives you an introduction to Drupal's folder structure, and you'll learn some important lessons for managing a Drupal site:

1. Click Configuration.

2. Click WYSIWYG Profiles in the Content Authoring block. You'll see a list of text editors that you could use together with Drupal, as shown in Figure 7.37.

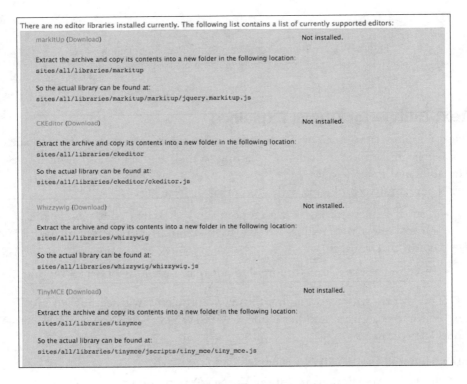

There are no editor libraries installed currently. The following list contains a list of currently supported editors:

markItUp (Download)   Not installed.

Extract the archive and copy its contents into a new folder in the following location:
sites/all/libraries/markitup

So the actual library can be found at:
sites/all/libraries/markitup/markitup/jquery.markitup.js

CKEditor (Download)   Not installed.

Extract the archive and copy its contents into a new folder in the following location:
sites/all/libraries/ckeditor

So the actual library can be found at:
sites/all/libraries/ckeditor/ckeditor.js

Whizzywig (Download)   Not installed.

Extract the archive and copy its contents into a new folder in the following location:
sites/all/libraries/whizzywig

So the actual library can be found at:
sites/all/libraries/whizzywig/whizzywig.js

TinyMCE (Download)   Not installed.

Extract the archive and copy its contents into a new folder in the following location:
sites/all/libraries/tinymce

So the actual library can be found at:
sites/all/libraries/tinymce/jscripts/tiny_mce/tiny_mce.js

Figure 7.37   The WYSIWYG Profiles Configuration area

In addition to suggesting editors, Drupal gives brief instructions for uploading each one. For example, try to install an editor called TinyMCE. Figure 7.38 shows that Drupal provides a download link and also tells you where to upload the files.

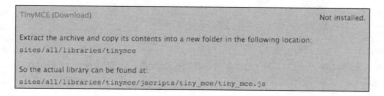

Figure 7.38   Installation instructions for the TinyMCE editor

3. Click the Download link next to TinyMCE, and you'll be taken to a
   screen like the one in Figure 7.39. Click the Download button for
   TinyMCE 3 (Please note that at the time of writing, the WYSIWYG
   module does not support TinyMCE 4.).

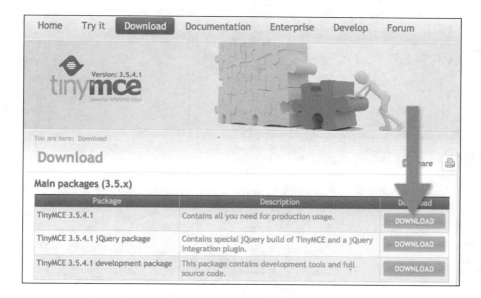

Figure 7.39   Download link for the TinyMCE editor

4. A file downloads to your computer. The file has a name similar to
   tinymce_3.5.4.zip. Click this file to extract it. You'll see a folder called
   /tinymce/. Open this folder and check that the contents look like
   Figure 7.40.

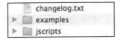

Figure 7.40   The contents of the downloaded /tinymce/ folder

5. Now you need to log in and access your Drupal files. In Chapter 3, "Drupal Installations Explained," you needed a login to install Drupal. You either had a login to your hosting Control Panel or you had a direct FTP login to your sites files. Whichever login you had, you need it again now. If you're stuck, ask the person who hosts your website.

6. Log in to your Drupal site's files. You'll be in the correct place when you see files and folders that look like Figure 7.41.

Figure 7.41   The files and folders of your Drupal site

There is one mistake that is easy to make at this point. If you upload a module or related files, you might expect to upload your module to the /modules/ directory. Actually, you need to upload the files to the /sites/ folder. There are two reasons for this:

- **Updating:** The /modules/ folder is only for Drupal's default modules. Every time you update your Drupal site, the /modules/ folder is overwritten and all changes are lost.

■ **Multisites:** The /sites/ folder enables you to run multiple Drupal websites from just one set of files. Everything you upload to the /sites/ folder can be made available to all those websites. Actually setting up and using multisites is out of the scope of this book, but you can find more information at http://Drupal7Explained.com/Chapter7.

As a reminder, Figure 7.42 shows where you'll upload all of your files.

Figure 7.42   The /sites/ folder of your Drupal site

7. Click the /sites/ folder.

8. Click the /default/ folder. The folder is called /default/ because, if you were using multisites, everything in here is only available to your default site, which is the one you're working on now.

9. Click the /sites/default/files/ folder. You'll now see all the images that you've uploaded in this book so far, as shown in Figure 7.43.

10. Click the /all/ folder. The folder is called /all/ because if you were using multisites, everything in here would be available to all your sites.

11. Click the /modules/ folder. You'll now see all the modules that you've uploaded in this book so far, as shown in Figure 7.44.

Figure 7.43   The current content of the /sites/default/files/
folder in your Drupal site

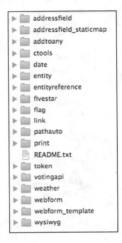

Figure 7.44   The current content of the /sites/all/modules/
folder in your Drupal site

As you can see, everything that you've uploaded to the site has gone into the /sites/ folder. If you upload modules or anything else to your site, make sure they go into the /sites/ folder. Now that we've explained how to avoid a common error, finish installing your text editor:

1. The original instructions in Figure 7.38 asked you to upload the TinyMCE folder to /sites/all/libraries/tinymce/. At the moment, you don't have a folder called /libraries/, so you need to create it. Click up one level and create a directory called /libraries/ in the sites/all directory, as shown in Figure 7.45.

2. Upload the /tinymce/ folder to sites/all/libraries/.

Figure 7.45   Creating a new /libraries/ folder

3. Check to see if the following directory/file naming structure is in place: sites/all/libraries/tinymce/, as shown in Figure 7.46.

Figure 7.46   The correct installation directory for the TinyMCE editor

4. Go back to the admin area of your Drupal site and click Configuration, Wysiwyg profiles. After a successful installation, your screen should look like Figure 7.47.

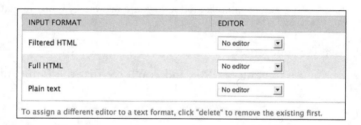

Figure 7.47   How the WYSIWYG profiles configuration area looks
if an editor is successfully installed

Step 3: Choose What Code Is Allowed

You'll notice in Figure 7.48 that there are three Wysiwyg profiles, which are designed for different purposes and allow different levels of code use.

Filtered HTML is the default option that you have been using throughout this book, so it's the one you'll modify. Now see what tags the Filtered HTML text format allows and doesn't allow:

1. Click Configuration on the black menu bar.

2. Click Text formats in the Content Authoring block.

3. Click Configure for Filtered HTML.

4. Notice that the Limit Allowed HTML tags box is checked.

5. Scroll down to the Limit Allowed HTML tags area. You'll see that the following HTML tags are permitted <a> <em> <strong> <cite> <blockquote> <code> <ul> <ol> <li> <dl> <dt> <dd>.

6. You need to add images to your content, so add <img> to this list by typing **<img>** in this space. Your screen will look like Figure 7.48.

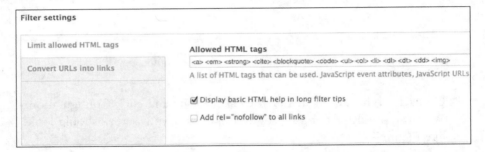

Figure 7.48   Choosing which HTML tags are allowed by a text format

7. Click Save Configuration.

8. Click Configure for Full HTML, and you'll see that the Limit Allowed HTML tags box is not checked.

9. Click Save Configuration.

10. Click Configure for Plain Text, and you'll see that the settings are exactly the same as for Full HTML, only the box Display Any HTML as Plain Text is checked.

Step 4: Choose What Buttons Are Available

Now that you know which HTML tags will work with each text format, you can enable the applicable HTML editor buttons:

1. Click Configuration.

2. Click Wysiwyg profiles in the Content Authoring block.

3. Click the drop-down next to Filtered HTML and select TinyMCE, as shown in Figure 7.49.

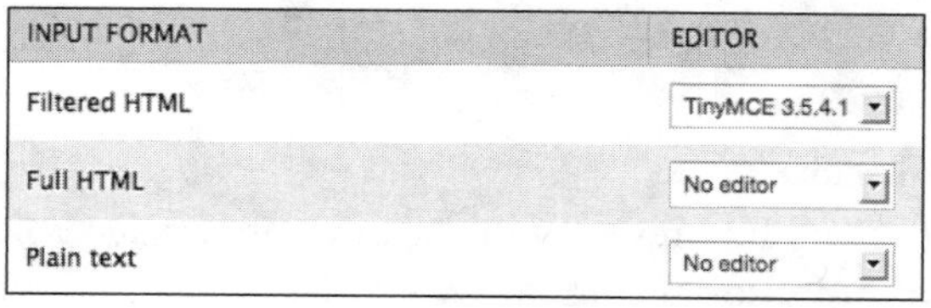

Figure 7.49   Choosing to use the TinyMCE editor with the Filtered HTML format

4. Click Save.
5. Click Edit in the Filtered HTML row.
6. Click Buttons and Plugins.
7. Check the box next to the buttons that support the HTML tags permitted by the Filtered HTML text format: Bold, Italic, Bullet list, Numbered list, Link, Blockquote, and Citationas, as shown in Figure 7.50.

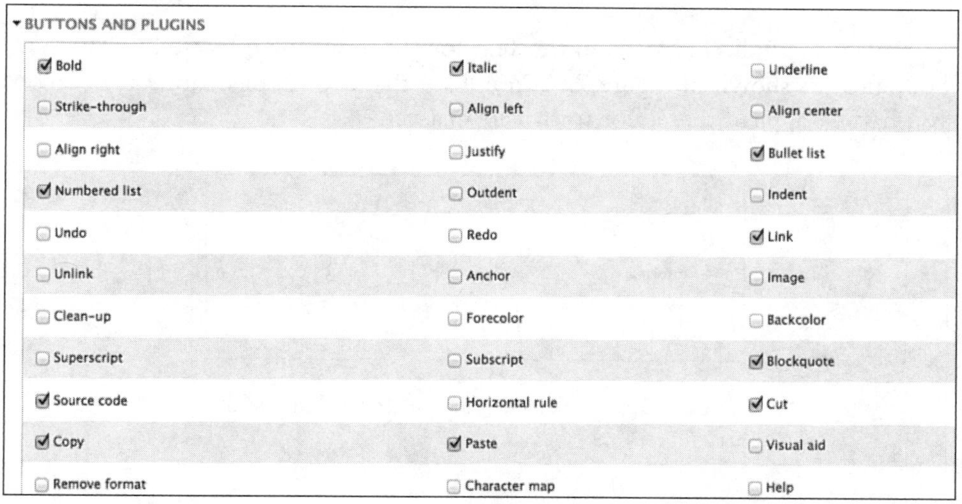

Figure 7.50   Choosing editor buttons for use with the TinyMCE editor

8. You can also safely check the boxes for these buttons because they don't produce HTML that would be stripped out by the Filtered HTML setting: Source code, Copy, Cut, Paste, Paste text, and Paste from Word.

9. Click Save.

Step 5: See the Results

The HTML Editor will be present when you create a page. Add a page using any of the content types so far, and you'll see the HTML editor buttons that appear by default, as shown in Figure 7.51.

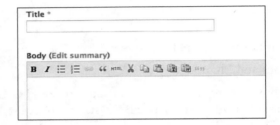

Figure 7.51   The TinyMCE editor on your content creation screen

Select the Full HTML from the Text format drop-down located below the body field, as shown in Figure 7.52. You'll see that the editor disappears because you haven't applied the editor to that format yet.

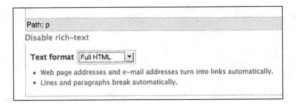

Figure 7.52   Selecting the Full HTML text format

Image Management

Now that you have better formatting for your text, also add an improved image-handling feature to your editor. You can use the IMCE module. The name is a little geeky: IMCE stands for Images for Moxie Code Editor. The phrase Moxie Code Editor has been shortened to form the MCE part of the acronyms IMCE and TinyMCE. The IMCE module allows you to upload, browse, and insert images more efficiently than you can do with the basic TinyMCE editor.

Step 1: Find the Module

1. Go to the Drupal.org page for IMCE at http://drupal.org/project/imce and copy the download link.

2. Repeat that process for the IMCE Wysiwyg bridge module: http://drupal.org/project/imce_wysiwyg.

Step 2: Install the Module

1. Go to Modules, and then Install new module and install IMCE.

2. Repeat the Installation process for the IMCE WYSIWYG Bridge module.

Step 3: Turn on the Module

1. Enable both the IMCE and IMCE WYSIWYG API Bridge modules.

Step 4: Set Up the Module

1. Click Configuration; then click IMCE in the Media block.

2. Click Add new profile, as shown in Figure 7.53.

   - Profile name: Filtered HTML

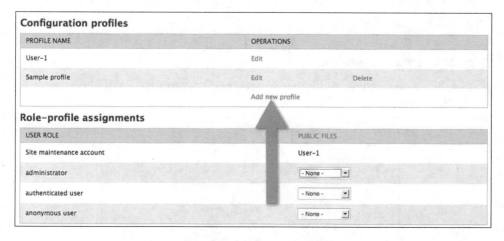

Figure 7.53   Add new profile link in the IMCE configuration area

3. Click Save Configuration.

4. Assign the new profile to the Administrator and Authenticated roles, as shown in Figure 7.54. Chapter 13, "Drupal Users Explained," covers the meaning of those roles, but briefly, the Administrator role is for people running the site, and the Authenticated role is for anyone who has an account on the site.

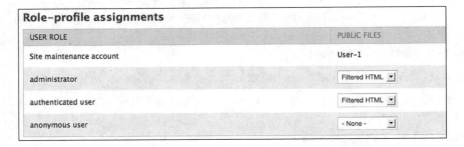

Figure 7.54   Assigning IMCE profile to different user roles

5. Click Save Configuration.

6. Click Configuration; then click Wysiwyg profiles in the Content Authoring area.

7. Click Edit in the Filtered HTML row.

8. Click Buttons and Plugins, and then check the Image and IMCE boxes.

9. Click Save.

Step 5: See the Results

1. Click Add content. You'll see that an Image button has been added, as shown in Figure 7.55.

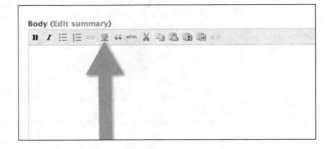

Figure 7.55   The image button in the TinyMCE editor

2. You'll now see a pop-up, as shown in Figure 7.56. If you didn't have IMCE installed, you would need to know the URL of an image to paste it in here.

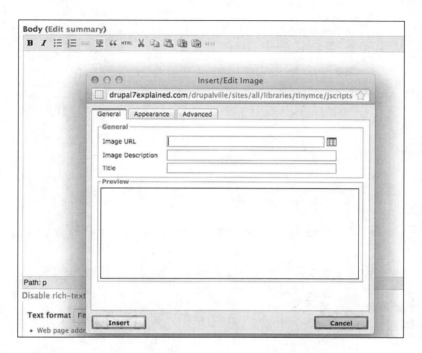

Figure 7.56   The image pop-up in the TinyMCE editor

3. Fortunately, you have IMCE, which gives you better image management. Click the IMCE button on the top-right of the pop-up, as shown in Figure 7.57.

4. You now see a larger pop-up, which enables you to browse all your current images, as shown in Figure 7.58. You can also upload new images, create thumbnails, delete or resize images, and insert images into your content.

5. To insert an image, click the filename of the image you want to use. The image then appears in the bottom half of the pop-up, as shown in Figure 7.59. Click Insert File, and you'll be back to the smaller pop-up. Click Insert, and your image will be placed inside the content.

Figure 7.57   The IMCE editor inside the image pop-up in the TinyMCE editor

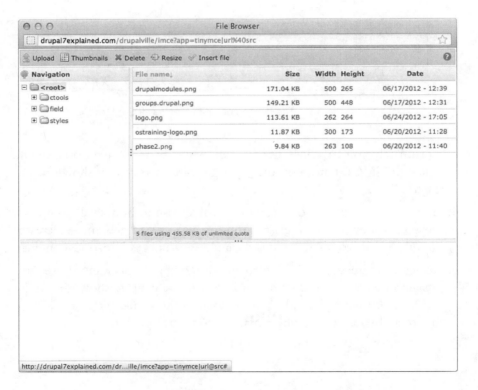

Figure 7.58   The IMCE pop-up screen

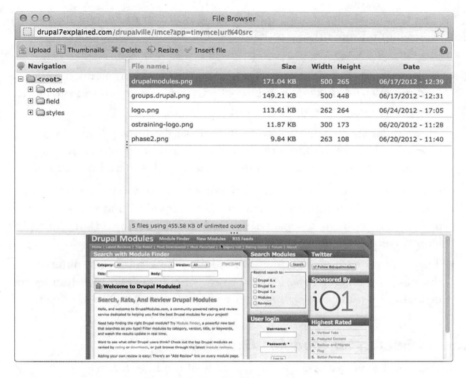

Figure 7.59   Choosing an image inside the IMCE pop-up screen

If you want to upload a new image rather than use an existing image, here's the process:

1. Click the Image button.

2. Click the IMCE button

3. Click Upload.

4. Click Browse to find the image you want to upload.

5. Click Upload.

6. After the upload finishes, click the image, Insert file, and then Insert.

Finding Modules Explained

In the first part of this chapter, we hand-picked modules for you to use. However, as you build you're own sites you're going to need to find extra modules. Here, we show you how to evaluate the modules available for Drupal and whether they are the right choice for you.

If you have used almost any other blogging platform or content management, you will find some things to be surprising and different about Drupal, including the following:

- Add modules are hosted on Drupal.org. It's never recommended to download modules from other sites. Drupal provides security checks on all the files you download from Drupal.org.

- All modules are free. Drupal companies make the money from many sources such as selling the services, training, or hosting, but there is a general feeling in the Drupal community that modules should not be sold.

- Collaboration, not competition. You won't find many modules with duplicate features. With other platforms, it's not unusual to find many solutions to the same problem. Drupal tries to encourage people working on a problem to collaborate and work on the same module.

- There are no ratings or reviews of modules. The Drupal community is thinking about adding them, but for now only http://DrupalModules.com hosts a good number of ratings and reviews about particular modules.

How to Search for Modules Explained

Now that you know that you can find all Drupal modules for free on Drupal.org, see how to find modules.

Go to http://drupal.org/project/modules and you'll see a screen like the one in Figure 7.60. As you can see there are more than 10,000 modules hosted on Drupal.org.

By default, the modules are sorted from the Most installed to the Least installed, so you can see that Views is the most commonly installed Drupal module.

If you're searching for a module, there is a detailed search box on the top of this page. You can see in Figure 7.61 that you can search in five ways. Four of these will be useful to you.

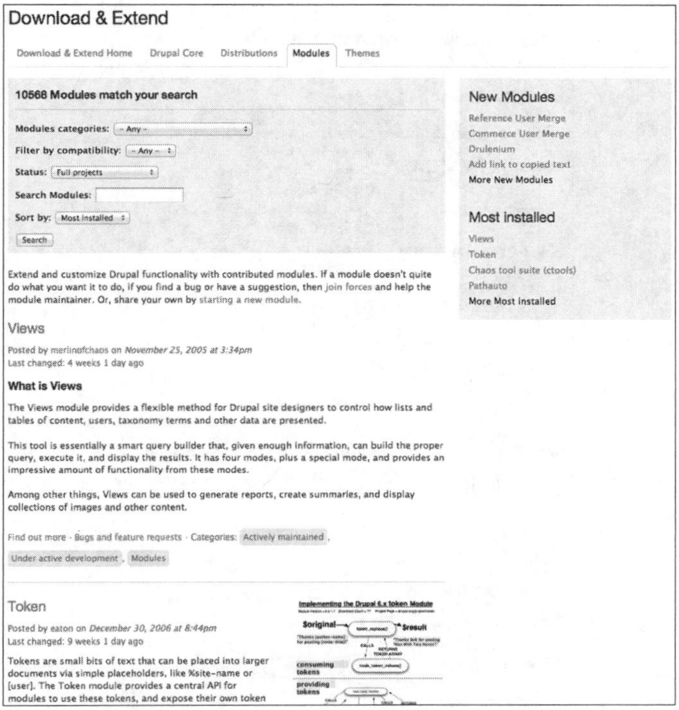

Figure 7.60   The Drupal.org modules area

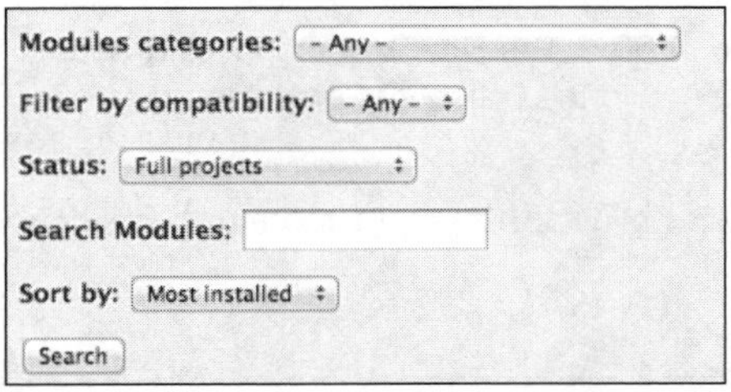

Figure 7.61   The search filters in the Drupal.org modules area

You can search by the category of module, as shown in Figure 7.62.

You can search by Drupal version to make sure that you're looking only for modules that work with Drupal 7, as shown in Figure 7.63.

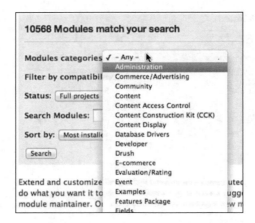

Figure 7.62   The Module categories search filter
in the Drupal.org modules area

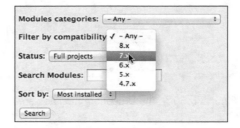

Figure 7.63   The Filter by Compatibility search filter
in the Drupal.org modules area

You can use the Search Modules field to search by keyword, as shown in
Figure 7.64.

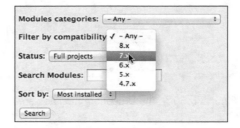

Figure 7.64   The Search Modules search filter in the Drupal.org modules area

Finally, you can choose how Drupal.org returns your results, as shown in Figure 7.65. Don't overlook this option. If you entered a keyword in the previous Search Modules field, you'll probably want to change this option to Relevancy. If you don't, you won't find the most relevant module, but only the most installed module that contains your keyword somewhere in the description.

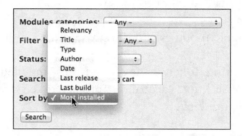

Figure 7.65   The Sort by Modules search filter in the Drupal.org modules area

Drupal now returns your search results, as shown in Figure 7.66. From here, you can click through and find out more about each module.

Figure 7.66   Search results in the Drupal.org modules area

How to Evaluate Modules Explained

Each Drupal module is different and needs to be evaluated before you use it.

There is no official stamp of approval or certification given to Drupal modules. The Drupal community aims to ensure some things about each module. It ensures that the module install and that the code is completely open source and unencrypted. Beyond that, you'll need to rely on a variety of techniques to evaluate modules.

Let's look at a couple modules and show you our recommended techniques to evaluate modules.

At the time of writing, Token is the second-most installed module, and that will be our example. Visit http://drupal.org/project/token and you'll see a screen, as shown in Figure 7.67.

Figure 7.67   The Token module's screen on Drupal.org

We encourage you to evaluate each module based on four different criteria. We call this the IRIS evaluation, and it involves the four areas of the page that you can see marked in Figure 7.68.

- **Introduction:** This area gives you an overview of all the module's key features and requirements.

- **Releases:** This area tells you if there is a module available for your Drupal version and if it is stable or perhaps only released in an alpha or beta version.

- **Information:** This area tells you if this module is actively updated and maintained, plus how many sites have installed it.

- **Sidebar:** This area shows you the people who coded the module and when they were last active. It also provides important links, such as issues users have found and documentation for the module.

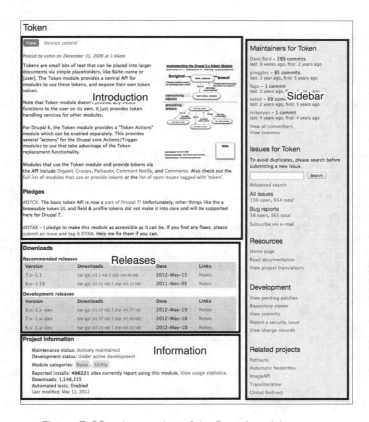

Figure 7.68   An overview of the Drupal modules screen

Area 1: Introduction

This area requires the least explanation. It provides a clear explanation of what this module does. Figure 7.69 shows the example from Token, which also has an image to help explain the module's purpose.

If the module's introduction makes it clear that this isn't what you need, end your evaluation and move on.

If the module's introduction isn't clear, you're not the first person to think that. These introductions are often geeky and contain Drupal jargon that you won't understand without more experience. If this leads to you getting stuck, we have some advice at the end of this chapter in the section, "What to Do if You're Really Stuck."

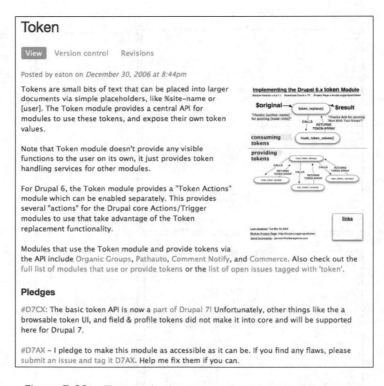

Figure 7.69   The Introduction area on Drupal.org module screens

Area 2: Releases

This area is the most important of all. If there isn't a version of the module available for your version of Drupal, stop your evaluation right here and start looking elsewhere.

Drupal.org uses a color-coded recommendation for its release, based on traffic lights:

- Modules in the green area are recommended for use on live sites.
- Modules in the yellow area need to be carefully evaluated before use.
- Modules in the red area are generally only for developers to test.

Not all modules will have a green, yellow, and red area. You can see Token's downloads in Figure 7.70.

Downloads

Recommended releases

Version	Downloads	Date	Links
7.x–1.1	tar.gz (41.5 KB) | zip (45.46 KB)	2012–May–15	Notes
6.x–1.18	tar.gz (37.31 KB) | zip (45.12 KB)	2011–Nov–03	Notes

Development releases

Version	Downloads	Date	Links
8.x–1.x–dev	tar.gz (41.67 KB) | zip (45.77 KB)	2012–May–09	Notes
7.x–1.x–dev	tar.gz (41.37 KB) | zip (45.48 KB)	2012–May–15	Notes
6.x–1.x–dev	tar.gz (37.23 KB) | zip (45.02 KB)	2012–May–09	Notes

Figure 7.70   The Token module's Releases area on Drupal.org

Figure 7.71 shows an example of all three colors from http://drupal.org/project/pathauto.

Downloads

Recommended releases

Version	Downloads	Date	Links
7.x–1.1	tar.gz (37.75 KB) | zip (42.94 KB)	2012–May–13	Notes
6.x–1.6	tar.gz (41.18 KB) | zip (46.67 KB)	2011–Oct–31	Notes

Other releases

Version	Downloads	Date	Links
6.x–2.0	tar.gz (42.78 KB) | zip (47.8 KB)	2011–Oct–31	Notes

Development releases

Version	Downloads	Date	Links
7.x–1.x–dev	tar.gz (37.76 KB) | zip (42.94 KB)	2012–May–13	Notes
6.x–2.x–dev	tar.gz (42.79 KB) | zip (47.81 KB)	2011–Dec–18	Notes
6.x–1.x–dev	tar.gz (41.17 KB) | zip (46.67 KB)	2011–Oct–30	Notes

Figure 7.71   The Pathauto module's Releases area on the Drupal.org

Area 3: Information

This area at the bottom of the page contains some useful information.

First, it tells you if the module is actively maintained and updated.

Second, it tells you if the module is frequently download or installed. The most popular Drupal modules have been downloaded more than two million times and are run on more than 400,000 websites.

Finally, it tells you when the module was last updated. If a module hasn't been updated recently, be cautious. It might mean that the module works perfectly and doesn't need updating, but it might also mean the module's coders are not providing necessary updates and fixes.

Figure 7.72 shows you the Information area for Token. This proves that Token is a module that's regularly updated and trusted by many users.

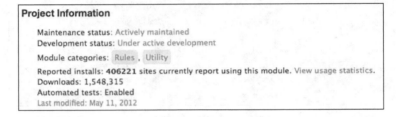

Figure 7.72   The Token module's Project Information area on Drupal.org

Figure 7.73 shows the Information area for another module. Be much more careful installing this one.

Figure 7.73   Another module's Project Information area on Drupal.org

Area 4: Sidebar

It was straightforward to explain the information contained in the first three areas on a module page. The fourth area, the sidebar, contains much more information and it is much more diverse. Figure 7.74 shows the sidebar on the Token page. Here's what's in each of the four areas:

- **Maintainers:** This is some of the most important information of all about a module. This module has five maintainers, one of whom was active 8 weeks ago. However, sometimes, this area shows only one maintainer who hasn't been active for years. Be cautious with those modules.

- **Issues:** This area provides links to all potential bugs that people have found with the module. A high number is not necessarily a bad thing because the more popular it is, the more bugs people are likely to find. At first, it won't be easy for you to get useful information from this area, but as you get more experience, you can read the list of issues and look for potential problems.

- **Resources:** This area contains key links. Perhaps the most important of all is the documentation link. Not all modules have documentation, and you should probably avoid those that don't.

- **Development:** If you're researching modules, this area might give you ideas for similar modules to evaluate.

Figure 7.74   The Token module's Sidebar area on Drupal.org

What to Do if You're Really Stuck

Sometimes, it can be hard to find the right module.

You might be stuck because you don't know the right word for what you're trying to do.

You might be stuck because none of the modules are descriptively named, so their actual functionality is not clear.

You might be stuck because the feature you need is only available by combining multiple modules, and it's not clear which modules you need.

You might be stuck because there just isn't a module available to provide the feature you need.

Regardless, you're going to get stuck at some point. Here are some suggestions for how to move forward if you're stuck while looking for a module:

- **Ask:** Log in to Drupal.org and ask about your problem: http://drupal.org/forum. The Drupal community is also active on public chats. You can find out more about joining and asking your questions at http://drupal.org/irc.

- **Search:** There's a lot more information on the web than is available on Drupal.org. Use Google or your favorite search engine to look for suggestions.

- **Use other Drupal sites:** There are sites out there, made by Drupal users, to help people find the module they need. You can find a list of these sites at http://Drupal7Explained.com/Chapter7.

Testing Modules

You must follow one golden rule, when testing a Drupal module: *Never, ever* install a Drupal module for the first time on a live site. *Always* have a second Drupal site that you use for testing, such as the one you use throughout this book.

If you need to make a copy of your own site for testing, see http://Drupal7Explained.com/Chapter7.

Why do we recommend always using a test site? Because websites are not exact or scientific. Modules that work fine on one site can fail on other sites. Some modules can cause conflict with other modules. You need to test all modules thoroughly before adding them to your live site.

Evaluating Modules

So far, you installed a good number of modules. You also saw how to research and evaluate modules.

In the final part of this chapter, we ask you find, install, and use two modules. These are the features we're looking for:

- Add an e-mail field to your content types.

- Add spam protection to your comments.

Can you find two reliable modules that provide those features?

Remember to look at each module page carefully and evaluate all four areas of the page:

- Introduction

- Releases

- Information

- Sidebar

If you get stuck, we have some recommended modules at http://Drupal7Explained.com/Chapter7.

What's Next?

In this chapter, you added features to your site by using modules. You saw that modules come in many different forms:

- Configuring modules is not always consistent from one module to the next.

- Modules can have dependencies on other modules.

- Modules can add additional functionality to a module.

- Modules can create pages and blocks.

You also saw how to evaluate and test modules before you use them on a live site.

Now we know how to add features to Drupal. Your Drupalville site should look like Figure 7.75. Don't worry if it's not exact. The important thing is that you understand the concepts behind this chapter. If you feel that you know how to search for, evaluate, install, and use modules, you're ready to move on to Chapter 8, "Drupal Menus Explained."

Figure 7.75   Your Drupalville site at the end of this chapter

So, our site now has content, fields and features. What it does not have is much organization that the visitor can see.

In Chapter 8, we'll explore our site's navigation and show you how to create and organize menus.

8

Drupal Menus Explained

Menus are a way to create navigation on your Drupal site. They are kind of a big deal. Without any menus, your visitors will be stuck on your site's homepage.

Because we are just covering the basics of how Drupal menus work, this is going to be a short chapter.

The reason we cover more advanced menu options in later chapters is because those options rely heavily on things you haven't covered yet. In Chapters 9 through 12, you discover new features that enable you to get more out of your navigation.

At the end of this chapter, you should be able to

- Understand the purpose of the four default Drupal menus.

- Add new menu links.

- Reorganize menu links.

The Four Default Drupal Menus

Start your exploration of Drupal's menu by exploring the four available menus:

1. Click Structure and then Menus. You now see the four default menus: Main menu, Management, Navigation, and User menu (see Figure 8.1).

   Now see what each menu does on your site.

2. Click list links in the Main menu row (see Figure 8.2).

   You now see four menu links, as shown in Figure 8.3.

TITLE	OPERATIONS		
Main menu The *Main* menu is used on many sites to show the major sections of the site, often in a top navigation bar.	list links	edit menu	add link
Management The *Management* menu contains links for administrative tasks.	list links	edit menu	add link
Navigation The *Navigation* menu contains links intended for site visitors. Links are added to the *Navigation* menu automatically by some modules.	list links	edit menu	add link
User menu The *User* menu contains links related to the user's account, as well as the 'Log out' link.	list links	edit menu	add link

Figure 8.1   The four default Drupal menus

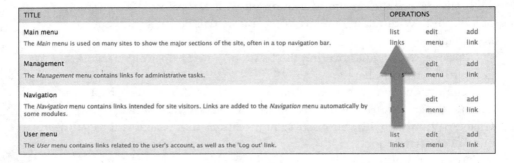

Figure 8.2   The List Links button for the Main menu

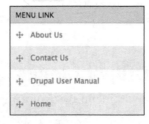

Figure 8.3   The links in the administration area for the Main menu

These links correspond to the tabs across the top of your site as in Figure 8.4. That's your Main menu.

Figure 8.4   The Main menu on your site

3. Return to Structure, Menus, and click List Links on the Management row. You now see four menu links, as shown in Figure 8.5.

Figure 8.5   The links in the administration area for the Management menu

These links correspond to the administration menus that you see after logging in, as shown in Figure 8.6. Do not modify this menu until you have more experience. Otherwise, you might find yourself without some key menu link and thus, feeling lost!

Figure 8.6   The Management menu on your site

4. Return to Structure, Menus, and click List Links on the Navigation row. You now see a list of links, as shown in Figure 8.7.

Figure 8.7   The links in the administration area for the Navigation menu

These links correspond to the menu in the sidebar of your site, as shown in Figure 8.8. These links are designed to help visitors navigate around your site. These links might not be important enough to place in the Main menu, but they are still useful to visitors.

Figure 8.8   The Navigation menu on your site

5. Return to Structure, Menus, and click List Links on the User menu row. You now see links, as shown in Figure 8.9.

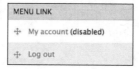

Figure 8.9   The links in the administration area for the User menu

These links correspond to the menu in the top-right of your site, as shown Figure 8.10. These links are designed to help visitors manage their account.

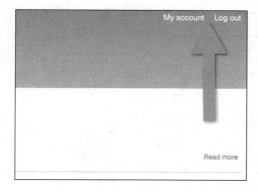

Figure 8.10   The Navigation menu on your site

Adding a New Menu Link: Site Map

In previous chapters, you added menu links from content on your site. You did that by checking the Provide a Menu Link box while you edited the content.

You now see a second way to make menu links. This method is a little more cumbersome because you need to know the URL (the path, as Drupal calls it), but you sometimes need to use it.

Chapter 7, "Drupal Modules Explained," showed you how to add modules. You combine that knowledge with what you're learning in this chapter. You install a Site Map module that automatically generates a list of all the content on your site. You then link to that site map from your Main menu. Now, we go through that process.

Step 1: Find the Module

1. Go to http://drupal.org/project/imce and copy the link.

Step 2: Turn on the Module

1. Enable the Site map module.

Step 3: Set Up the Module

1. Click Configuration and then Site map in the Search and Metadata block.

2. Check these boxes to include them in the site map:

   - **Books to include in the site map:** Drupal User Manual.
   - **Menus to include in the site map:** Main menu.
   - **Categories to include in the site map:** Check all the boxes.

3. Click Save configuration.

Step 4: Add the Menu Link

1. Click Structure and then Menus.

2. Click Add link on the Main menu row.

3. Complete the form as shown in Figure 8.11:

   - **Menu link title:** Site Map
   - **Path:** sitemap

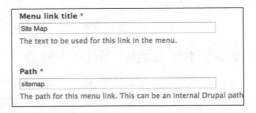

Figure 8.11 Adding the Site Map link to your Main menu

4. Click Save.

5. Return to the homepage. You see that the new menu link has become active (see Figure 8.12).

Figure 8.12 The Site map menu link added to your Main menu

Adding a New Menu Link: Blogs

Now repeat that process and add the Blogs module to your Main menu:

1. Click Structure and then Menus.

2. Click Add Link on the Main menu row.

3. Complete the form as shown in Figure 8.13:

   - Menu link title: Blogs

   - Path: blog

   - Check Show as Expanded.

> **Menu link title** *
> Blogs
> The text to be used for this link in the menu.
>
> **Path** *
> blog
> The path for this menu link. This can be an internal Drupal path such as *node/add* or an
> page.
>
> **Description**
>
> Shown when hovering over the menu link.
>
> ☑ Enabled
>   Menu links that are not enabled will not be listed in any menu.
>
> ☑ Show as expanded
>   If selected and this menu link has children, the menu will always appear expanded.

Figure 8.13 Adding the Blogs link to your Main menu

Note that you need this in Chapter 9, "Drupal Themes Explained," when you enable a drop-down Main menu.

4. Click Save.

5. Return to the homepage, and you see that the new menu link has become active (see Figure 8.14).

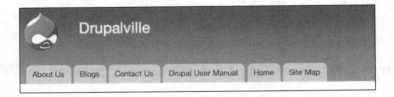

Figure 8.14 The Blogs menu link added to your Main menu

Adding a New Menu Link: Forums

Repeat this process one more time, and add Forums to your Main menu:

1. Click Structure, Menus, and then click Add Link on the Main menu row.

2. Complete the form as shown in Figure 8.15:

    - **Menu Link Title:** Forums
    - **Path:** forum

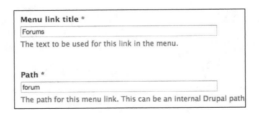

Figure 8.15 Adding the Forums menu link to your Main menu

3. Check Show as Expanded.

4. Save.

5. Return to the homepage. You can see that the new menu link has become active.

Finding the URL for a New Menu Link

By now you've seen that the method in this chapter is more difficult to use than the method used earlier in this book. In the earlier method, you only needed to check the Provide a Menu Link box while you edited the content. With this new method, you need to know the URL. Finding the URL can be difficult.

However, some pages on your site don't offer a Provide a Menu Link box, and you need to use this new method.

How can you find the URL of a page? There are three ways: Use the module name, the Pathauto module, or the Search module.

Using the Module Name

In the previous examples, the URL exactly matched the name of the module. The Site Map module's URL is /sitemap/, the Blog module's URL is /blog/, and the Forum module's URL is /forum/.

Using the Pathauto Module

One way to find the URL is with the Pathauto module:

1. Go to Configuration and then URL Aliases. You are now inside the Pathauto module. You can enter part of the URL that you're looking for into the Filter Aliases box.

2. Click Filter, and you see information about the URLs on your site, as shown in Figure 8.16. On the left side, you can see the new URLs created by Pathauto. On the right side, you see the old URLs created by the Drupal core.

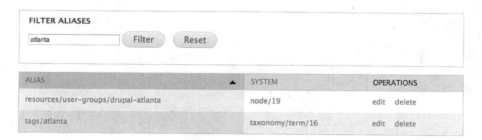

Figure 8.16 Searching for a URL in the Pathauto module

Using the Search Module

On your site's homepage, you have a search block on the left sidebar. Do the following:

1. Type information on the content you're looking for into that search box, as shown in Figure 8.17.

Figure 8.17 Using the search block

2. Click the magnifying glass icon in the search block.

   You can now see search results presented on your site, as shown in Figure 8.18. You can click the title for each search result and look up in the browser bar to find the URL.

Figure 8.18 Search results

Reorganizing Menu Links

You've now seen two ways to create menu links:

- Check the Provide a Menu Link box while creating or editing content.
- Go to Structure, Menus, and click Add Link.

However, you still have a problem with your menu links. As you can see in Figure 8.19, they're not ordered as you would expect on a website. For example, the Home menu link should be the first tab on the left, but instead, it has wandered off to the right side. This is because the menus are organized alphabetically.

Figure 8.19 Your current Main menu links, as seen from the visitor area

Now see how to reorganize your menu links:

1. Go to Structure, Menus, and click List Links on the Main menu row.
2. Select the cross next to the Home menu links, as shown in Figure 8.20.

Figure 8.20 Your current Main menu links, as seen from the administrator area.

3. Use the cross to drag-and-drop the link into a different order, as shown in Figure 8.21.
4. Repeat the previous process by making Contact Us into the second-to-last menu link.

Figure 8.21 Your Home link in a new order

5. Repeat the previous process by making About Us into the third-to-last menu link.

   When you finish, your menu links will look like Figure 8.22.

Figure 8.22 Your Main menu links in a new order, as seen from the visitor area

6. Click Save Configuration.

   Visit the homepage of your site. You see that your Main menu links have been reorganized, as shown in Figure 8.23.

Figure 8.23 Your Main menu links in a new order, as seen from the visitor area

Reorganizing Menu Links Using Weight

If the previous drag-and-drop solution doesn't work for you, for any reason, there is an alternative called Weight.

The concept behind Weight is

- Menu links are assigned a number between −50 and 50.

- Negative numbers from −50 to −1 are "light."

- Positive numbers from 1 to 50 are "heavy."

- Menu links start with a weight of 0, by default.

- If a menu link has a light number, such as −50, it rises to the top of the menu.

- If a menu link has a heavy number, such as 50, it sinks to the bottom of the menu.

Weight is a fairly cumbersome system that has been largely replaced by drag-and-drop. However, you see Weight in several difference places inside Drupal, so it's useful to know how it works.

Here is an alternative approach to reorganizing menus:

1. Go to Structure, Menus, and click List Links on the Main menu row.

2. Click Edit on the Home row. You can now see a screen like the one shown in Figure 8.24.

3. Change the Weight option from −1 to −10.

4. Click Save.

That guarantees that the Home link will be the first link that visitors see. You can repeat that process for other links, too:

1. Click Edit on the Site Map row.

2. Change the Weight option to 10.

3. Click Save.

4. Click edit in the Contact Us row.

5. Change the Weight option to 9.

   6.Click Save.

7. Click Edit in the About Us row.

8. Change the Weight option to 8.

9. Click Save.

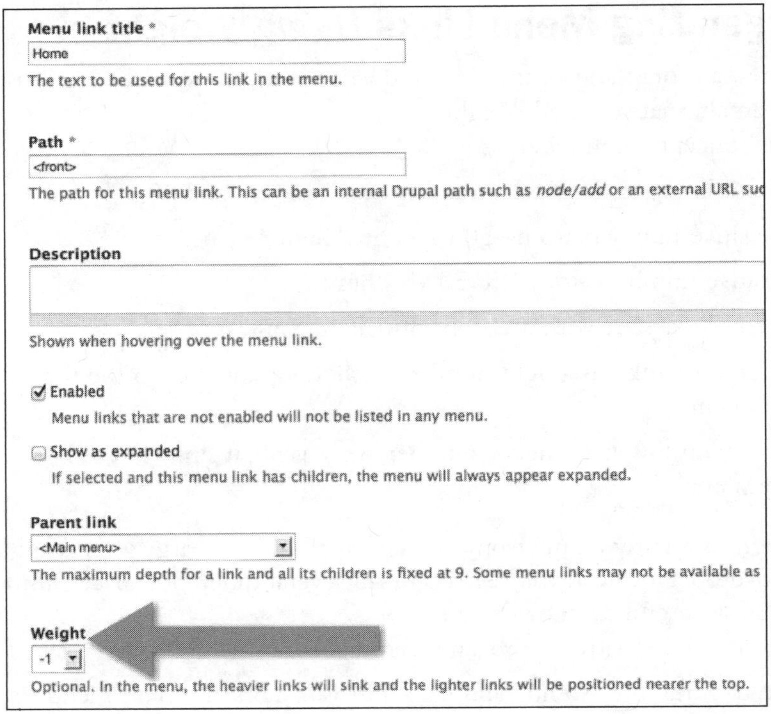

Figure 8.24 The Weight option on the editing screen for the Home menu link

When you finish, your menu links will be ordered exactly as they were in Figures 8.22 and 8.23.

This was an example of how Weight works in Drupal. You can also see Weight in other Drupal screens, but drag-and-drop will almost always be a better and easier option. Actually, you can now see one thing that drag-and-drop can do but Weight cannot: Create parent and child links.

Creating Parent and Child Menu Links

A parent and child link is a common combination that you see on most websites.

What is a parent link and what is a child link? The parent link is a menu link that you will always see on a screen. A child link is a menu link that appears only when you click or hover over a parent link.

Probably the most common type of parent and child link is the drop-down menu. If you hover over a menu link, other links appear underneath. You can see an example from http://www.acquia.com in Figure 8.25. Solutions is the parent link. If you hover over the Solutions link, four child links appear: Solutions for Marketers, Government Solutions, Education Solutions, and Publishing Solutions.

Figure 8.25 Parent and child links on Acquia.com

However, you can have parent and child links appear in different ways. For example, on http://www.amazon.com, the menus slide out horizontally instead of vertically, as shown in Figure 8.26. If you hover over the Audible Audiobooks link, six child links appear: Audible Membership, Audible Audiobooks & More, Bestsellers, New & Notable, Listener Favorites, and Whispersync for Voice.

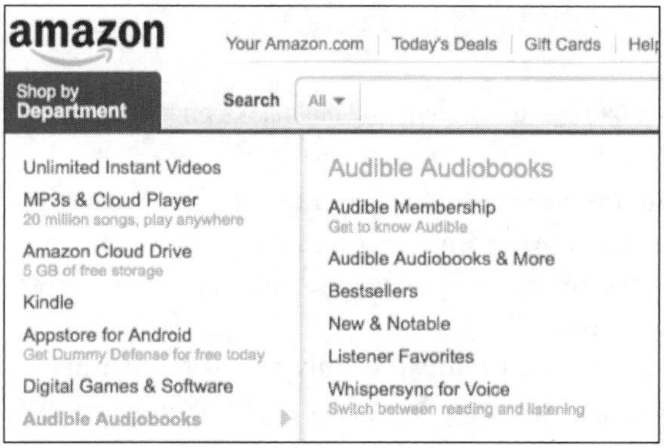

Figure 8.26 Parent and child links on Amazon.com

It's also common to see parent and child links that don't fly out. Many parent and child links simply expand to reveal more links underneath. For example, if you go to http://www.wikipedia.org and visit the main Wikipedia homepage for your language, you can see parent and child menus on the left side of the page, as shown in Figure 8.27. You can see the small arrows next to each parent link, which indicate that child links are underneath.

Figure 8.27 Parent and child links on Wikipedia.org

Now that you are clear on what parent and child menu links are, you can see how to create them. A reminder: You're going to organize the links into a parent and child relationship. How they actually appear to your visitors will be controlled by the theme.

Until you change your theme, the only menu that shows parent and child links is on the Navigation menu. So, you use the Navigation menu for all these examples:

1. Go to Structure, Menus, and click List Links on the Navigation row.

2. Check the boxes next to Blogs and My Blog.

3. Click Save Configuration.

4. Visit your homepage and click the Blogs parent link on the Navigation menu.

You'll be taken to a new page, and the My Blog child link now appears underneath, as shown in Figure 8.28.

Figure 8.28 Parent and child Blog links

That parent and child setup was already done for you. Now do a parent and child setup of your own:

1. Go to Structure, Menus, and click List Links on the Navigation row.

2. Check the boxes next to Compose Tips.

3. Select the cross next to Compose Tips and drag-and-drop that menu link so that it appears next to the My Blog menu link, as shown in Figure 8.29. You need to drag the link to the right to make it into a child link.

Figure 8.29 Setting up Compose Tips as a child link

If you cannot manage to use the drag-and-drop, you can create the same parent and child setup by doing this:

1. Click Edit on the Compose Tips row.

2. Scroll down to the Parent link area.

3. Choose Blogs from the list.

4. Click Save.

This Parent link area is why you choose to describe these links as parent and child links. You want to use the same terminology as Drupal.

Now practice what you've learned before and earlier in this chapter. Create a list of subforums under your Forums Menu link.

First, you need to the find the URLs of your subforums. If you get stuck at this point, return to earlier in the chapter for a reminder:

1. Go to the homepage of your site, and click Forums on the Navigation menu.

2. Click the Drupal link in the Forum area.

3. Look for the URL / path of the page. Don't forget to remove the URL of the site. With your example site the URL was forums/drupal.

4. Repeat that process for the other four forums and containers. Here are the URLs you collected:

   - **Drupal:** forums/drupal
   - **Drupal Design:** forums/drupal-design
   - **Drupal Installation:** forums/drupal-installation
   - **Drupal Support:** forums/drupal-support
   - **General Discussion:** forums/general-discussion

5. Go to Structure, Menus, and click Add Link on the Navigation row.

6. Enter the following information, but modify if your site is different:

   - **Menu link title:** Drupal
   - **Path:** forums/drupal
   - **Show as Expanded:** Check this box. This means that people don't have to click to see all the child links.

7. Click Save.

8. Click Add Link in the top-left corner.

9. Repeat the previous process and add the other four forums.

Now you could have selected the Parent Link option as you were creating these links, but drag-and-drop is more fun. Besides, with drag-and-drop you can visually confirm that everything is in the right place:

1. Use drag-and-drop to reorganize the Child Menu links so that they appear, as shown in Figure 8.30.

2. Click Save Configuration.

3. Go to your homepage and click the Forums Parent link.

4. Your child menus expand, as shown in Figure 8.31.

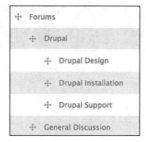

Figure 8.30 Forum parent and child links, as they appear
in the administrator area

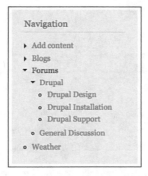

Figure 8.31 Forum parent and child links, as they appear in the visitor area

What's Next?

As mentioned in the introduction to this chapter, this chapter focused on teaching you the essential basics of how to use menus in Drupal.

Your Drupalville site should look like Figure 8.32. Don't worry if it's not exact. The important thing is that you understand the concepts behind this chapter. If you feel that you know how to manage menus and menu links, you're ready to move on to Chapter 9.

This chapter is a useful foundation for much that follows. Here's an overview of how you'll see menus again in future chapters:

- **Chapter 9:** Drop-down menus. You see drop-downs in Chapter 9 when you cover themes. That's because themes control whether you can have drop-down menus.

Figure 8.32 Your Drupalville site at the end of this chapter

- **Chapter 10:** Placing menus around your site. In Chapter 10, "Drupal Blocks Explained," you cover blocks. You've seen blocks already, but in Chapter 10 you'll see how to use blocks to place menus in more positions on your site.

- **Chapter 11:** Lists, tables, and grids of content. In Chapter 11, "Drupal Views Explained," you cover the Views module. That enables you to link to lists, tables, or grids to specific content. For example, you could create a page that lists only your Events.

- **Chapter 12:** Landing pages. In Chapter 12, "Drupal Layout Modules Explained," you cover the Panels module. That enables you to link to custom landing pages that bring together all different parts of your Drupal site.

If you're ready, turn to Chapter 9 and explore themes. For many people, themes are the fun and exciting part of building your Drupal site.

Drupal Themes Explained

Up until now, your Drupal site has had a blue-and-white design. This is because you've been using a theme called Bartik whose default settings are blue and white.

Themes are responsible for controlling both your site's design and layout. This chapter shows you how to change your theme and thus, change your site's design and layout.

At the end of this chapter, you should be able to

- Distinguish between the administrative theme and the site theme.
- Install a theme from Drupal.org.
- Turn on and set up a theme.
- Configure a theme that utilizes modules to provide features.

Bartik Explained

Start your exploration of themes by looking at the themes that come with Drupal by default. Click the Appearance link on the black admin bar, and you see a screen that looks like Figure 9.1.

Drupal comes with two themes enabled:

- **Bartik** is the default theme that your visitors see when they visit your site.
- **Seven** is the administration theme that you see when you use any of the administration screens.

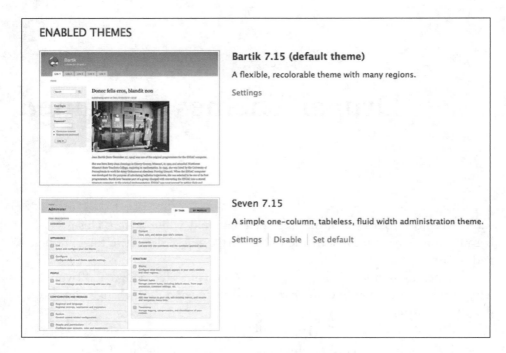

Figure 9.1   The two default Drupal themes: Bartik and Seven

Below Bartik and Seven are the currently disabled themes: Garland and Stark, which are shown in Figure 9.2. You use these two themes for demonstration purposes in this chapter, but it's highly unlikely that you'll ever use either in real life. Garland is a legacy theme from Drupal 6 and has been replaced with Bartik. Stark is an example theme that is mainly useful to experts who are comfortable with HTML and CSS.

At the bottom of the Appearance screen is the drop-down option shown in Figure 9.3. Don't touch this option. We've often talked to people who thought that this option was the way to change their site's theme. It's not. This is the option to change your administration theme, and we don't recommend you do that until you are more experienced.

Theme Settings

You don't have to replace Bartik to change the look and feel of your site. Bartik has settings that enable you to customize your site's look and feel without changing any code. Now let's see how that's done. Click Settings in the Bartik theme area, as shown in Figure 9.4.

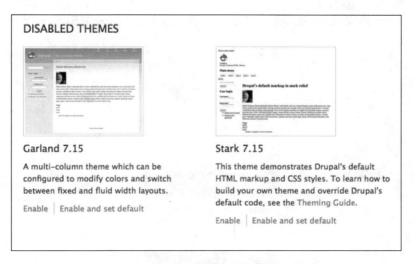

DISABLED THEMES

Garland 7.15

A multi-column theme which can be configured to modify colors and switch between fixed and fluid width layouts.

Enable | Enable and set default

Stark 7.15

This theme demonstrates Drupal's default HTML markup and CSS styles. To learn how to build your own theme and override Drupal's default code, see the Theming Guide.

Enable | Enable and set default

Figure 9.2   The two disabled Drupal themes: Garland and Stark

ADMINISTRATION THEME

Administration theme

Seven ▾

Choose "Default theme" to always use the same theme as the rest of the site.

☑ Use the administration theme when editing or creating content

Save configuration

Figure 9.3   The option for choosing your site's administration theme

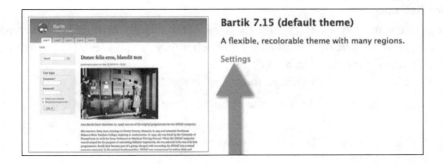

Bartik 7.15 (default theme)

A flexible, recolorable theme with many regions.

Settings

Figure 9.4   The Settings link for Bartik

You now see the settings available for Bartik (see Figure 9.5).

Figure 9.5   The settings for Bartik

Color Scheme

The first setting you see in Figure 9.5 is the color scheme setting. So, if you prefer red, green, yellow, or some other color scheme, you can use this option to change from Drupal blue to a color of your choosing.

Now, let's see how to change the color of the Bartik theme:

1. Select a color scheme from the color set drop-down, as shown in Figure 9.6.

2. Scroll down and you can see a preview of the color scheme you selected, as shown in Figure 9.7.

3. If you like the new color scheme, scroll to the bottom of the screen and click Save Configuration.

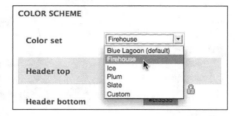

Figure 9.6   The color set options for Bartik

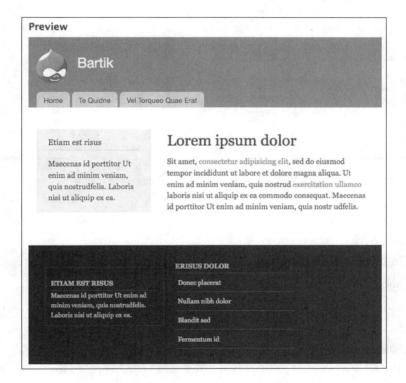

Figure 9.7   A preview of a color scheme used with Bartik

4. Go to your homepage and see the change.

5. Click on Appearance and then Settings for Bartik to return to the color scheme feature.

6. Experiment by manually changing one of the color codes by clicking in the color field of your choice and moving the color selector wheel, as shown in Figure 9.8.

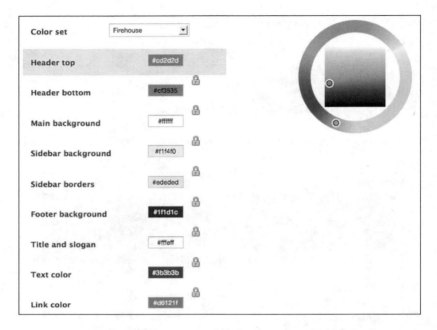

Figure 9.8   The color wheel and options in Bartik

7. If you like the new color scheme, scroll to the bottom of the screen and click Save Configuration.

8. Go to your homepage and see the change.

Repeat this as many times as you like. Remember that you can always return to the Drupal blue by selecting Blue Lagoon (Default) from the Color set drop-down.

Toggle Display

Below the Color Scheme settings is another area called Toggle Display, as shown in Figure 9.9.

The Toggle Display options show the features that the theme supports. Some themes support hundreds of features and some themes support none. A theme's features rely entirely on the designer of the theme.

Now experiment with one of the features, as follows:

1. Make sure the Site Slogan check box is checked.

2. Scroll to the bottom and click Save Configuration.

3. Click Configuration on the black menu bar.

4. Click Site Information.

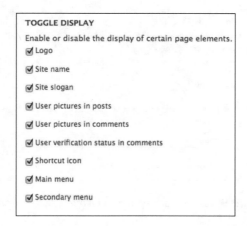

Figure 9.9   The Toggle Display settings for Bartik

5. Type this short slogan in the Slogan field: **Drupal Rocks!**

6. Click Save Configuration.

7. Return to the homepage and see the slogan appear under the name of your site, as shown in Figure 9.10.

Figure 9.10   Your Drupal site with a slogan displaying

Logo Image Settings

Now, let's see how to replace the logo for the Bartik theme:

1. Click Appearance and then Settings for Bartik.

2. Uncheck the Use the Default Logo Box.

   You now have the option to upload your own logo, as shown in Figure 9.11. You're welcome to use your own image, but we also have one that you can use at http://drupal7explained.com/chapter9.

3. Click Save Configuration.

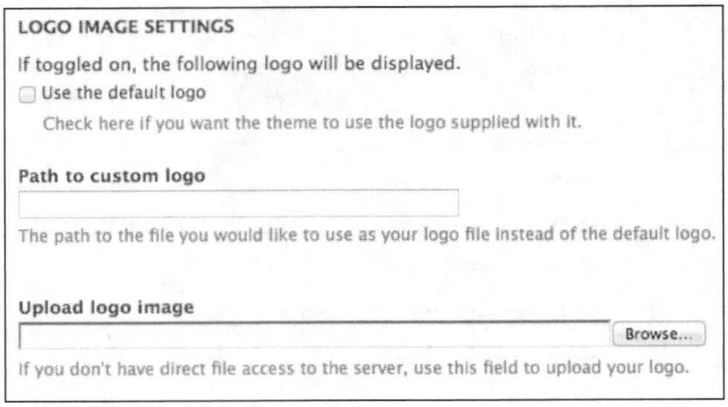

LOGO IMAGE SETTINGS

If toggled on, the following logo will be displayed.

☐ Use the default logo

Check here if you want the theme to use the logo supplied with it.

Path to custom logo

[   ]

The path to the file you would like to use as your logo file instead of the default logo.

Upload logo image

[   ] [Browse...]

If you don't have direct file access to the server, use this field to upload your logo.

Figure 9.11   Uploading a new logo to use with Bartik

Visit the front of your homepage, and it should look like Figure 9.12.

Figure 9.12   Site with completed new logo

Enabling Themes Explained

In this activity, you switch from the Bartik theme to each of the other default themes that come with Drupal.

The process of switching between themes is simple at this stage of your site building. However, after your site is built, switching between themes might take a lot more effort.

For now, practice switching between themes.

Set Garland to Default

Use Garland instead of Bartik for your site's theme:

1. Go to Appearance.
2. Click Enable, and set default next to Garland, as shown in Figure 9.13. If you click only the Enable button, you can use the Garland theme in certain situations, but it won't be the default theme for the site.

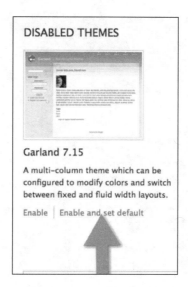

Figure 9.13   The Enable and set default button for Garland

You see a message across the top of the screen saying Garland is now the default theme.

Go to your homepage and see the new theme, as shown in Figure 9.14. You can notice several changes, including that the Main menu is located in the top-right corner of the header. You also see that the logo you uploaded for Bartik has not been automatically applied to Garland.

Set Stark to Default

Repeat that process for Stark. The Stark theme lives up to its name by providing the minimum amount of code required to display a Drupal webpage:

1. Go to Appearance.
2. Click Enable and set the default next to Stark.
3 Go to your homepage and see the new theme, as shown in Figure 9.15.

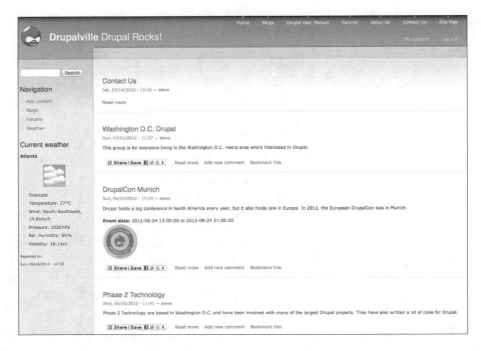

Figure 9.14 Your site with Garland as the default theme

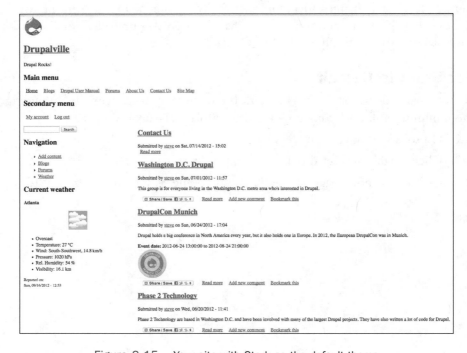

Figure 9.15 Your site with Stark as the default theme

Installing Themes Explained

Now that you've seen the default Drupal themes, install some new themes.

Start by looking at a theme called Danland, which provides an image slideshow unlike any of the default themes.

The process to install a theme is similar to the process you used when installing a module. You use the FITS workflow. Here's how the FITS workflow operates for themes:

1. Find the theme.
2. Install the theme.
3. Turn on the theme.
4. Set up the theme.

Installing the Danland Theme

Try this workflow with the Danland theme.

Find the Theme

1. Go to http://drupal.org/project/danland.
2. Copy the tar.gz link for the Drupal 7 version of this theme.

Install the Theme

1. Go to your site.
2. Click Appearance on the black menu bar.
3. Click Install New Theme.
4. Paste the link into the Install from URL field.
5. Click Install.
6. Click Enable Newly Added Themes.

Turn On the Theme

1. Scroll down and locate the Danland theme.
2. Click Enable and Set Default.

Set Up the Theme

1. Click Settings for the Danland theme.
2. Observe that Danland comes with many of the same basic settings that you saw in Bartik, Garland, and Stark.

Now visit your homepage and you see Danland live on your site, as shown in Figure 9.16.

Figure 9.16   Your site with Danland as the default theme

You'll notice that there is a large slideshow across the homepage of your site. This slideshow appears only on the homepage, but the designers of Danland realized that not every user of the theme might want such a large slideshow. If you click Appearance, you see that there is also a version of this theme called Danblog. If you enable Danblog instead of Danland, the only difference you see is that the slideshow has disappeared.

Installing the Zero Point Theme

Now install another theme. Zero Point is just one theme, but it comes with several options providing flexibility. These options include color schemes, sidebar layouts, block styling, and more. Our apologies in advance: The designer of this theme sometimes refers to it as Zero Point and sometimes as 0 Point.

Install Zero Point and see what it has to offer.

Find the Theme

1. Go to http://drupal.org/project/zeropoint.
2. Copy the tar.gz link for the Drupal 7 version of this theme.

Install the Theme

1. Go to your site.
2. Click Appearance on the black menu bar.
3. Click Install new theme.
4. Paste the link into the Install from URL field.
5. Click Install.
6. Click Enable Newly Added Themes.

Turn On the Theme

1. Scroll down and locate the 0 Point theme.
2. Click Enable and Set Default.

Set Up the Theme

1. Click Settings for the 0 Point theme. (Notice the name change from Zero to 0.)
2. Observe that Zero Point comes with many of the same basic settings that you saw in Bartik, Garland, Stark, and Danland.
3. Observe that Zero Point also has Layout Settings, Breadcrumb, Search Results, and Theme Development areas.
4. Go to your homepage, and you can see that your site looks like Figure 9.17.

Installing the Company Theme

The Danland and Zero Point themes you have explored so far enable a drop-down menu, but both require some configuration. Now look at a theme called Company, which enables you to start using a drop-down menu almost immediately after installation. In the Company theme, you need to configure only your menu.

Figure 9.17   Your site with Zero Point as the default theme

Find the Theme

1. Go to http://drupal.org/project/company.
2. Copy the tar.gz link for the Drupal 7 version of this theme.

Install the Theme

1. Go to your site and click Appearance.
2. Click Install New Theme.
3. Paste the link into the Install from URL field and then click Install.
4. Click Enable Newly Added Themes.

Turn On the Theme

1. Scroll down and locate the Company theme.
2. Click Enable and Set Default.

Set Up the Theme

1. Click Settings for the Company theme
2. Scroll down to find the Company Theme Settings and observe this theme has a slideshow.
3. Uncheck the Show Slideshow box.
4. Click Save Configuration.

Go to the homepage, and you can see the new theme live on your site. The Company theme has not only changed the design of the site, but also the layout. The left column has now moved to the right side of the screen (see Figure 9.18.)

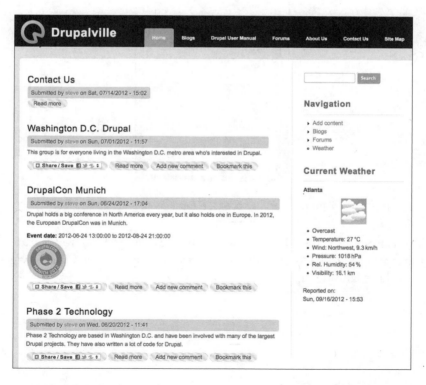

Figure 9.18   Your site with Company as the default theme

Setting Up the Drop-Down Menu

Now set up the drop-down menu for your site. As you do this, we'll remind you of what you did in Chapter 8, "Drupal Menus Explained," and introduce you to a new feature of menus: moving links from one menu to another:

1. Go to Structure and then Menus.
2. Click list links on the Navigation row.
3. Look for the parent and child links that you created in Chapter 8. You're going to move the child links to the Main menu.
4. Click Edit next to the Drupal child link.
5. Scroll down to the Parent link option. Choose Forums, which is at the top of the option area, just under <Main Menu>, as shown in Figure 9.19.
6. Click Save.

Figure 9.19   Choosing a new Parent menu link

You can now see the Main menu, as shown in Figure 9.20. Your Drupal child link and the three links underneath now have moved from the Navigation menu to this Main menu.

Figure 9.20   Child menu links moved from the Navigation
menu to the Main menu

Repeat that process and move the General Discussion link to the Main menu:

1. Go to Structure and then Menus.
2. Click List Links on the Navigation row.
3. Click Edit next to the General Discussion child link.
4. Scroll down to the Parent link option. Choose Forums, which is at the top of the option area just under <Main Menu>.
5. Click Save.

You are now at the part of drop-down menus that is often confusing to Drupal beginners: whether menus expand automatically or not. Go to your homepage and see your drop-down menus in action. On the homepage, you can see the drop-down menus don't work, as shown in Figure 9.21.

Figure 9.21   The Main menu on your homepage

However, if you click the Forums tab, the child menu links become visible, as shown in Figure 9.22.

Figure 9.22   The Main menu on your Forums page

Even now, your child links under Drupal aren't visible. It won't be until you click the Drupal link that all three child links will become visible, as shown in Figure 9.23.

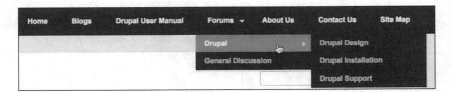

Figure 9.23   The Main menu on your Drupal Forums page

Why is this happening? By default, Drupal's menus are set up to match the needs of text menus. To use an example you've already seen, this behavior made perfect sense when you were using it with the Navigation menu. However, the same behavior seems abnormal with drop-down menus where you expect all the links to be visible on all pages.

How do you change this behavior? You need to check one box in the settings for each menu:

1. Go to Structure and then Menus.
2. Click List Links on the Main menu row.
3. Click Edit next to the Forums link.
4. Check the Show as Expanded box.
5. Click Save.
6. Check the Show as Expanded box for the Drupal and General Discussion links.
7. Click Save and go to see your menu in action.

Subthemes Explained

The themes you have installed and tested so far have been fairly straightforward, each one offering a different design, a different layout, and some different features.

You now look at the Sky theme, which is an example of a more complicated theme. The Sky theme is a subtheme, which means that it relies on another theme to work. The Sky theme requires a base theme called Adaptive Theme to work correctly.

Find a Theme

1. Go to the Drupal.org page for the Sky theme: http://drupal.org/project/sky. Copy the tar.gz link for the Drupal 7 version of this theme.

2. Repeat the process for Adaptive Theme: http://drupal.org/project/adaptivetheme.

Install the Theme

1. Go to your site and then click Appearance.

2. Click Install New Theme.

3. Paste the link into the Install from URL field and then click Install.

4. Click Enable Newly Added Themes.

5. Repeat Steps 1 and 2 for Adaptive Theme.

Turn On the Theme

1. Click Enable and set the default next to the Sky theme.

2. You do not have to enable AdaptiveTheme. It simply needs to be installed.

Set Up the Theme

1. Click Settings for the Sky theme.

2. As you can see, you now have many, many more options than you did for any previous theme. Many of these options will be useful for more experienced users but confusing for beginners. Change one of the simpler settings. Click the middle box for the Choose Sidebar Positions setting, as shown in Figure 9.24.

Go to your homepage and see how the Sky theme appears on your site, as shown in Figure 9.25.

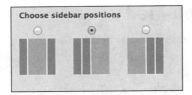

Figure 9.24   The Choose sidebar position setting for the Sky theme

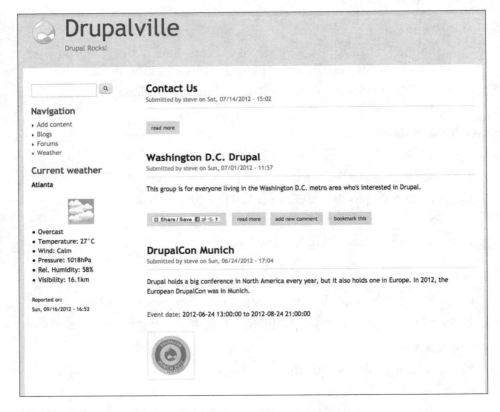

Figure 9.25   Your site with Sky as the default theme

You can notice that your Main menu is missing and that the third column, which you just chose in the settings, is not being used. Now go and fix those issues:

1. Go to Structure and then Blocks.

2. Scroll down to the Disabled area and find the Main menu block.

3. Choose Menu bar from the drop-down next to the Main menu block.

4. In the Disabled area find the Most Recent Poll Block.

5. Choose Sidebar second from the drop-down next to the Most Recent Poll Block.

6. Click Save Blocks.

Visit your homepage, and you'll now see that it looks like Figure 9.26. Notice that the drop-down menu doesn't work yet. The Sky theme, as with many things, is more complicated than most of the themes you've looked at in this chapter. You'd need to go to http://drupal.org/project/sky and view the documentation for the Sky theme to see how to set up the drop-down menu correctly.

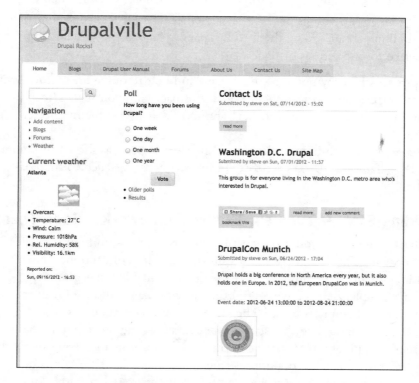

Figure 9.26   Your site with Sky as the default theme, with extra blocks published

Finding Themes Explained

Early in this chapter, you looked at the default Drupal themes: Bartik, Garland, and Stark.

Then you looked at some themes from Drupal.org: Danland, Zero Point, Company, and Sky.

All those themes that you've seen so far were chosen for you. In this part of the chapter, we'll give you some advice on how to successfully find other themes that you could use to build a site.

As we did with modules in Chapter 7, here are some important points to know about themes before you start searching:

- Most themes are hosted on Drupal.org, but not all.

- Most themes are free, but some companies sell commercial themes.

- There are no ratings or reviews of themes. The Drupal community is thinking about adding them to Drupal.org, but for now, there is no single place to find ratings or reviews.

Start searching by going to the biggest and best resource for themes, which is http://drupal.org/project/themes. Visit this page, and you see a screen like the one in Figure 9.27. Notice that there are more than 1,000 themes hosted on Drupal.org.

There is a search box on the top of the themes page, as shown in Figure 9.28. By default the themes are sorted from the Most Installed to the Least Installed.

Avoiding Starter Themes, Theme Frameworks, Base Themes

On the Themes page, you can see that Zen is the most commonly installed Drupal theme. This is a good time to introduce a note of caution: Unlike with modules, not all of the most popular themes are suitable for beginners.

For example, Zen is a wonderful theme with many advanced features, but it is not easy for beginners to use. The same is true of any theme whose description includes phrases like this: starting theme, starter theme, theme framework or base theme. A phrase like "starting theme" sounds as if its indicating that a theme is easy to use. In fact, the opposite is true.

Some of these themes can be used by beginners together with a subtheme. You saw a good example of that earlier in this chapter with Adaptive Theme, which is labeled as theme framework, and Sky, which is labeled as a subtheme.

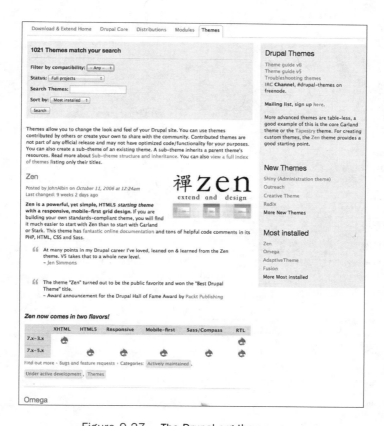

Figure 9.27   The Drupal.org themes area

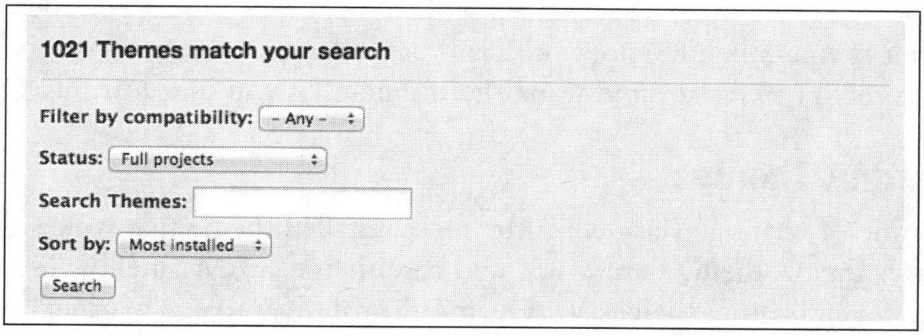

1021 Themes match your search

Filter by compatibility: – Any –

Status: Full projects

Search Themes:

Sort by: Most installed

Search

Figure 9.28   The Drupal.org themes search area

Generally, it will be obvious if you've installed one of these more complicated themes by mistake. For example, Figure 9.29 shows what happens if you
make Adaptive Theme into your site's default theme.

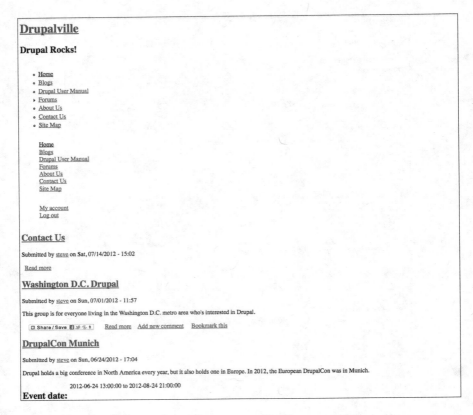

Figure 9.29   Your site with Adaptive Theme as the default theme

As you become more experienced with Drupal, you should consider exploring starter themes, theme frameworks, and base themes. However, you should walk before you run and avoid using those themes as you start learning Drupal.

Evaluating Themes

At the time of writing, Marinelli is the most installed theme that is not labeled as a starter theme, theme framework, and base theme. So, Marinelli is used as an example for evaluating themes. Visit http://drupal.org/project/marinelli, and you can see a screen as shown in Figure 9.30.

Figure 9.30   The Marinelli theme's screen on Drupal.org

We encourage you to evaluate each theme based on four different criteria, as shown in Figure 9.31. As with modules, we call this the IRIS evaluation and it involves the four areas of the page introduced in Chapter 7, "Drupal Modules Explained:"

- **Introduction:** This area gives you an overview of all the theme's key features and requirements.

- **Releases:** This area tells you if there is a release of a theme available for your Drupal version and if it is stable or perhaps only released in an alpha or beta version.

- **Information:** This area tells you if this module is actively updated and maintained, plus how many sites have installed it.

- **Sidebar:** This area shows you the people who coded the module and when they were last active. It also provides important links, such as those to issues users have found and to documentation for the module.

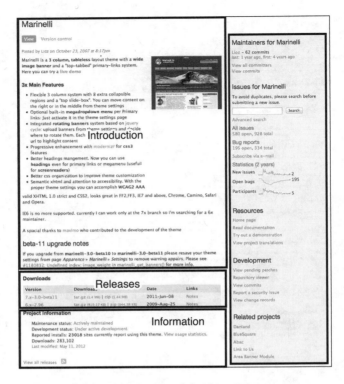

Figure 9.31   An overview of the Drupal themes screen

Area 1: Introduction

This area requires the least explanation. It provides a clear explanation of what this theme does. Figure 9.32 shows the example from Marinelli, which also has a screenshot of the theme.

For Marinelli, the first paragraph is clear and useful: "Marinelli is a 3-column, tableless layout theme with a wide image banner and a top-tabbed primary-links system." There is also a useful link to see a live demo.

The remainder of Marinelli's introduction is also fairly clear, but does contain some Drupal and design jargon that beginners won't understand.

Area 2: Releases

This area is the most important of all. If there isn't a version of the theme available for your version of Drupal, stop your evaluation right here and start looking elsewhere:

- Themes in the green area are recommended for use on live sites.
- Themes in the yellow area need to be carefully evaluated before use.
- Themes in the red area are generally only for developers to test.

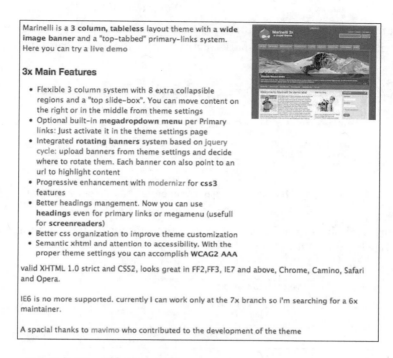

Figure 9.32   The Marinelli theme's introduction area on Drupal.org

Not all themes will have a green, yellow, and red area. You can see Marinelli's downloads in Figure 9.33.

Downloads			
Version	Downloads	Date	Links
7.x-3.0-beta11	tar.gz (1.4 MB)	zip (1.44 MB)	2011-Jun-08	Notes
6.x-2.96	tar.gz (819.17 KB)	zip (844.38 KB)	2009-Aug-25	Notes

Figure 9.33   The Marinelli theme's releases area on Drupal.org

Area 3: Information

This area at the bottom of the page, contains some useful information. First, it tells you if the theme is being actively maintained and updated. Second, it tells you if the theme is frequently download or installed.

Finally, it tells you when the theme was last updated. If a theme hasn't been updated recently, be cautious. It might mean that the theme works perfectly and doesn't need updating, but it might also mean the theme's coders are not providing necessary updates and fixes.

Figure 9.34 shows you the Information area for Marinelli. This proves that Marinelli is a theme that is fairly regularly updated and is trusted by a lot of users.

Project Information

Maintenance status: Actively maintained
Development status: Under active development
Reported installs: **23018** sites currently report using this theme. View usage statistics.
Downloads: 283,102
Last modified: May 11, 2012

Figure 9.34   The Marinelli theme's information area on Drupal.org

Figure 9.35 shows the Information area for another theme. Be more cautious about installing this one.

Project Information

Maintenance status: Unknown
Development status: Unknown
Downloads: 311
Last modified: April 13, 2007

Figure 9.35   Another theme's information area on Drupal.org

Area 4: Sidebar

It was straightforward to explain the information contained in the first three areas on a module page. The fourth area, the sidebar, contains more information and is more diverse. Figure 9.36 shows the sidebar on the Marinelli page. Here's what in each of the four areas:

- **Maintainers:** This is some of the most important information of all about a theme. Marinelli has only one maintainer, who was active one year ago. This is not necessarily a negative sign, but it is worth noting.

- **Issues:** This area provides links to all potential bugs that people have found with the theme. A high number is not necessarily a bad thing, because the more popular it is, the more bugs people are likely to find. At first, it won't be easy for you to get useful information from this area, but as you get more experience, you can read the list of issues and look for potential problems.

- **Resources:** This area contains key links. Perhaps the most important of all is the documentation link. Not all themes have documentation, but you should probably avoid those that don't.

- **Development:** If you're researching themes, this area might give you ideas for similar themes to evaluate.

Figure 9.36   The Marinelli theme's sidebar area on Drupal.org

Commercial Themes

Unlike modules, not all themes are available on Drupal.org and not all themes are free. There are some companies that sell themes commercially.

For a commercial theme, you can expect to pay between $15 and $300. For that price, you might also expect a more polished, professional design and support from the theme's developers.

However, if you're coming from another content management system or blogging platform, you might be surprised at how few companies sell themes. In total, there are probably not more than a dozen commercial Drupal theme companies.

There are some large theme companies that sell designs for Drupal and for many platforms. These sites are typically marketplaces that attract thousands of different designers. One example of these marketplace sites is Theme Forest. You can find its Drupal themes at http://www.themeforest.net/category/ cms-themes/drupal. Its list of Drupal themes is shown in Figure 9.37. It has more than 40 themes and most are priced between $15 and $50.

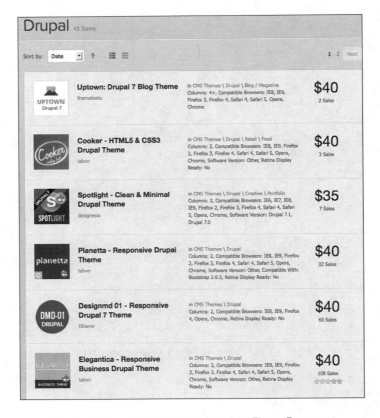

Figure 9.37   Drupal themes listed on ThemeForest.net

Another popular marketplace site is Template Monster. You can find its Drupal themes at http://www.templatemonster.com/drupal-themes.php. Its list of Drupal themes is shown in Figure 9.38. It has just hundreds of themes, and most are priced between $50 and $70.

There are also companies that specialize in creating only Drupal themes. After looking at Drupal.org, you may recognize the names of some of these companies. Many of these companies place free themes on Drupal.org as a way to give back to the Drupal community and as a form of advertising.

Figure 9.38   Drupal themes listed on TemplateMonster.com

Sooper Themes sells only Drupal themes. You can find its designs at http://www.sooperthemes.com. Its list of Drupal themes is shown in Figure 9.39. They have more than a dozen themes, and you can buy access to all of them for prices ranging from $64 to $450.

Adaptive Themes are Drupal specialists, and we used their work earlier with the Sky theme. You can find its designs at http://www.adaptivethemes.com. Its list of Drupal themes is shown in Figure 9.40. It has approximately ten themes, and you can buy access to all of them for $65.

Theme Shark has one of the larger selections of Drupal themes. You can find its designs at http://www.themeshark.com. Its list of Drupal themes is shown in Figure 9.41. It has more than 30 themes, and you can buy access to all of them for between $59 and $299.

Figure 9.39   Drupal themes listed on SooperThemes.com

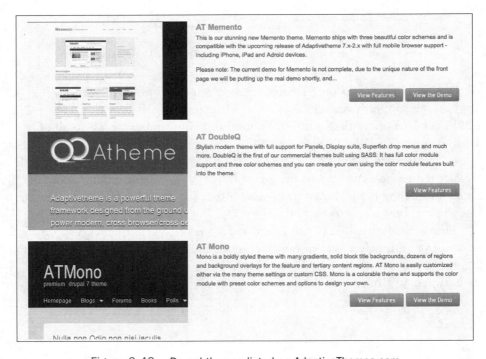

Figure 9.40   Drupal themes listed on AdaptiveThemes.com

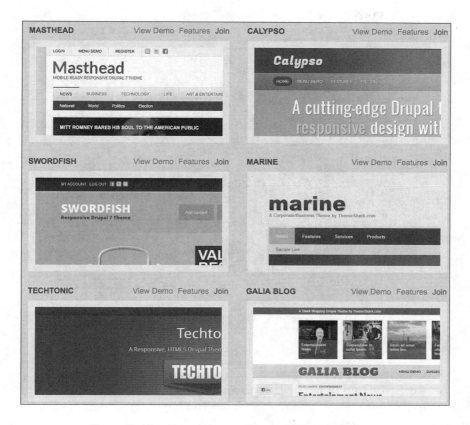

Figure 9.41   Drupal themes listed on ThemeShark.com

Artisteer

So far, you have looked at two ways to get Drupal themes: free themes from Drupal.org and commercial themes.

There is a third option available for people who want to design their own themes. Artisteer is desktop software that can create themes without requiring any coding. After installing Artisteer on your desktop, you can click buttons to change layouts, colors, menus, fonts and more. You can import images to use as headers and backgrounds. An example of the theme creation process is shown in Figure 9.42.

When your design is complete, you can export your design as a complete Drupal theme. The theme can then be imported by going to Appearance; then Install new theme and by choosing the option to upload directly from your local computer.

Figure 9.42   Creating a Drupal theme with Artisteer

Artisteer won't produce the most beautiful underlying code, but it will produce workable, customized themes for people without a great deal of time or money.

Artisteer costs $130 and is available from http://www.artisteer.com. There is a free trial version that enables you to try all the features.

A Final Note on How Themes Get Built

In this chapter, you've seen three ways to find a Drupal theme for your site:

- Free themes from Drupal.org
- Commercial themes
- Artisteer

In the Drupal community, using free themes is by far the most popular option.

It is rare to see a theme built from scratch. Nearly every Drupal project starts with an existing theme and brings in a designer to make modifications. Even the most prestigious Drupal projects tend to start with a theme from Drupal.org. Using an existing theme has many benefits:

- The code behind popular existing themes has been heavily road-tested.
- Many themes already come with features such as mobile-compatibility.
- Drupal themes can be complicated to build from scratch.
- Reusing existing code saves time and money.

It is beyond the scope of this book to teach you how to recode existing Drupal themes. However, for your first Drupal sites, you can find a suitable design from Drupal.org, a commercial theme site, or Artisteer.

Installing the Final Theme for Your Site

To end this chapter, install a theme to use to actually build your Drupaville site. Install a new theme, modify the settings, and enable a drop-down menu.

First, install the Marinelli theme that you evaluated earlier. Use the FITS workflow:

1. Go to http://drupal.org/project/marinelli and copy the tar.gz link for the Drupal 7 version of this theme.

2. To install, go to your site, click Appearance, and then Install New Theme. Paste the link into the Install from URL field, and then click Install.

3. To turn it on, locate the Marinelli theme. Click Enable and Set Default. Click Settings for Marinelli. Here's what you will to modify:

   - **Logo Image Settings:** Uncheck Use the Default Logo. Upload the drupalville-logo-small.png image from http://drupal7explained.com/chapter7.

   - **Layout Settings:** Choose Content in the middle for Layout Type. This returns your site to a traditional three-column design with the content in the middle of the screen.

   - **Primary Menu Settings:** Choose Mega Drop-Down as the option for Which Kind of Primary Links Do You Want to Use? This enables the drop-drown menu.

   - **Banner Management.** Open Banner Configuration and choose Drupal region (advertise) for Do You Want to Use Marinelli Banners or a Classic Drupal Region? This removes the large slideshow from the homepage.

4. Click Save Configuration.

By following the FITS workflow, you now have a site that looks like Figure 9.43.

Figure 9.43   Your Drupal site with Marinelli as the default theme

As with any new theme, there will always be adjustments to make. For example, your parent and child links don't fit perfectly into the new menu. As shown in Figure 9.44, the phrase General Discussion is too long for the menu.

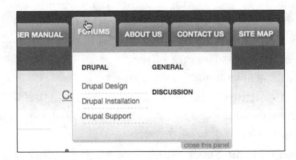

Figure 9.44   Parent and child menu links in the Marinelli theme

You can make this adjustment by thinking back to Chapter 8:

1. Go to Structure and then Menus.
2. Click List Links on the Main Menu row.
3. Click Edit on the General Discussion row.
4. Change General Discussion to General.
5. Click Save.

The adjustments you make for a new theme may involve menus, but they may involve other things, too.

You may need to tweak the logo size as we did here. The drupalville-logo.png we used earlier was too large for this theme.

You may also need to move blocks around because the new theme has a different layout. How to do that will be the topic of the next chapter.

What's Next?

In this chapter, you saw how to accomplish these tasks:

- Configure Bartik, the default Drupal theme.
- Change the default theme on your site.
- Add new themes.
- Search for and evaluate new themes.

Now you know the key details about Drupal themes. At this point, your Drupalville site will look like Figure 9.45. For the first time in this book, your site now looks substantially different. Don't worry if it's not exact. The important thing is that you understand the concepts behind this chapter. If you feel that you know how to search for, evaluate, install, and use themes, then you're ready to move on to Chapter 10, "Drupal Blocks Explained."

In Chapter 10, you dig deeper into themes and how they impact your site. You focus on how themes work to control the layout of your site and how you can use blocks within that layout. By the end of the next chapter, you'll have built on the knowledge from this chapter and have a good understanding of how to manage both design and layout.

Figure 9.45   Your Drupal site at the end of this chapter

Drupal Blocks Explained

By this point in the book, blocks are not entirely new to you.

In Chapter 7, "Drupal Modules Explained," you installed modules that added blocks to your site. You published both weather and map blocks. In Chapter 9, "Drupal Themes Explained," you learned that themes control the layout of your entire site.

This chapter builds on what you've already learned and provides a comprehensive introduction to blocks.

At the end of this chapter, you should be able to

- Understand that different Drupal themes have different block regions.
- Place blocks in regions.
- Change the order of the blocks displayed.
- Control the pages that blocks appear on.
- Edit the settings of blocks.
- Add a block manually.

Theme Regions Explained

Go to Structure and then Blocks. In the top-left corner you can see a link called Demonstrate Block Regions, as shown in Figure 10.1. This provides you with a clear overview of the regions available with Marinelli.

If you want to find the same link for other enabled themes, you can choose other themes from the tabs in the top-right corner, as shown in Figure 10.2.

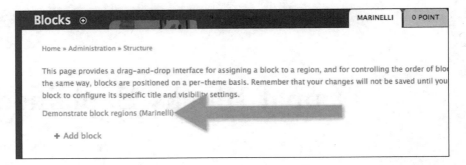

Figure 10.1   The Demonstrate Block Regions link for Marinelli

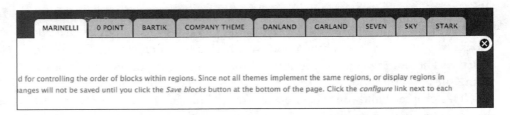

Figure 10.2   Tabs for the enabled Drupal themes

Now start with Marinelli. Click the Demonstrate Block Regions (Marinelli) link, and your screen looks like Figure 10.3. Here are some examples of what you can do with Marinelli:

- Show a block in the left column by placing it in the First Sidebar region.
- Show a block in the right column by placing it in the Second Sidebar region.
- Show a block over your main content by placing it in the Over Node or Highlight regions.
- Show a block under your main content by placing it in the Under Node region.

You haven't seen all those regions live on your site, even though you're using Marinelli. This is because many regions simply hide if they're not being used.

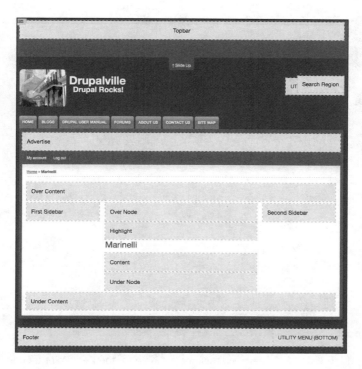

Figure 10.3   The block regions available for the Marinelli theme

Now see the block regions for another theme:

1. Click Exit Block Region Demonstration in the top-left corner, under the black admin bar.

2. Click the 0 point tab in the top-right corner.

3. Click Demonstrate Block Regions (0 Point) and you see a screen like Figure 10.4.

Notice that although the layout is actually fairly similar, almost all the region names are different when compared to Marinelli:

- The left column region is now called Sidebar First rather than First Sidebar.

- The right column region is now called Sidebar Second rather than Second Sidebar.

- The region over your main content is now called Highlighted rather than Over Node or Highlight.

- The region for your search block is called Search rather than Search Region.

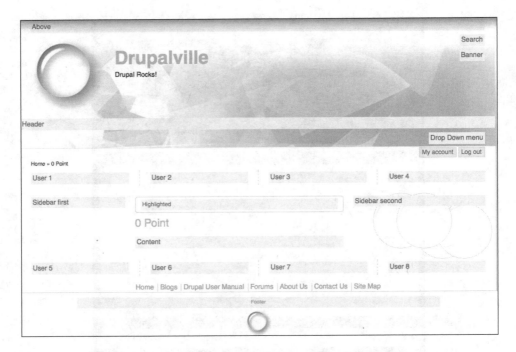

Figure 10.4   The block regions available for the Zero Point theme

There are also some small layout differences. For example, there isn't a region under your content.

Now see the block regions for a third theme:

1. Click Exit Block Region Demonstration in the top-left corner, under the black admin bar.

2. Click the Bartik tab in the top-right corner.

3. Click Demonstrate Block Regions (Bartik), and you see a screen like Figure 10.5.

Again, there are some similarities with the other themes that you've seen but also lots of differences.

Figure 10.5   The block regions available for the Bartik theme

One thing that has been consistent until now is that all the themes have had a three-column layout. Marinelli, Zero Point, and Bartik have all had both left and right columns with the main content in the center. This is not going to be true for all themes, including the next one. Now look at the Company theme's block regions:

1. Click Exit Block Region Demonstration in the top-left corner, under the black admin bar.

2. Click the Company Theme tab in the top-right corner.

3. Click Demonstrate Block Regions (Company Theme) and you see a screen like Figure 10.6.

With the Company theme, there is no left column. If you want a three-column theme, Company would simply not be an option.

Repeat the process you used for the previous four themes and look at the remaining five enabled themes.

Figure 10.7 shows the block regions for the Danland theme.

Figure 10.6   The block regions available for the Company theme

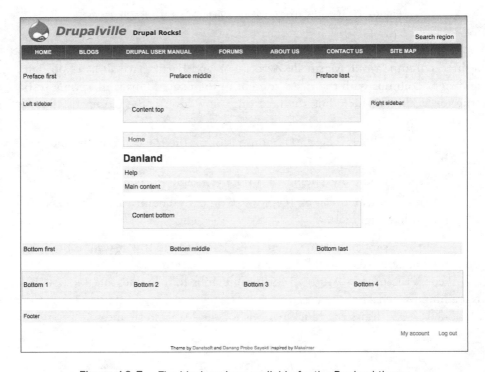

Figure 10.7   The block regions available for the Danland theme

Figure 10.8 shows the block regions for the Garland theme.

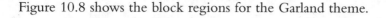

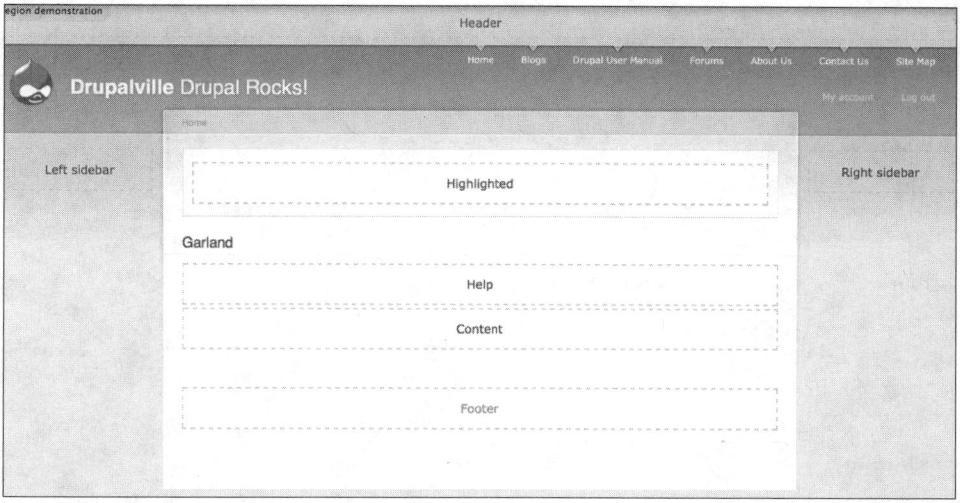

Figure 10.8   The block regions available for the Garland theme

Figure 10.9 show the block regions for the Seven theme. Remember, it is the administration theme and is not designed to show to visitors!

Figure 10.9   The block regions available for the Seven theme

Figure 10.10 shows the block regions for the Sky theme.

Finally, Figure 10.11 shows the block regions for the Stark theme.

As you can see from the tour of your enabled themes, each theme is different. You must know what regions are available to you before you choose a theme. You would need to be an advanced Drupal user to add and remove regions to a theme, so make sure that a theme has the regions it needs before you use it on your site.

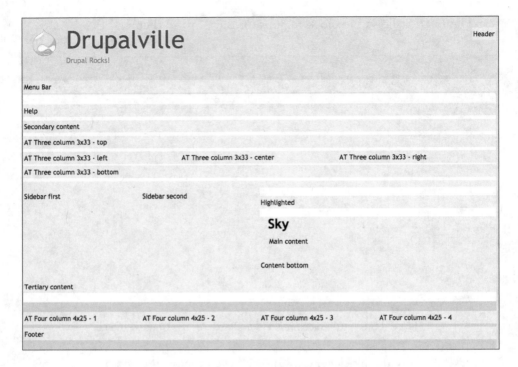

Figure 10.10   The block regions available for the Sky theme

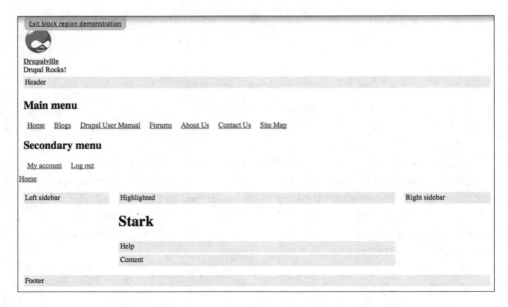

Figure 10.11   The block regions available for the Stark theme

Placing Blocks in Regions Explained

Table 10.1 lists the blocks you can allow on your site. You create more blocks in Chapter 11, "Drupal Views Explained," but for now, these are several blocks you can work with. Notice you can use the right column (called Second Sidebar in Marinelli), but not the left. This keeps the layout simple and gives you more space to work with in upcoming chapters.

Table 10.1   **The Blocks Are Going to Places into Regions of Your Site**

Blocks	Region	Page(s)
User Login	Second Sidebar	Every page
Address Field Static Map	Second Sidebar	Content with a completed address field
Most Recent Poll	Second Sidebar	Homepage
Weather	Second Sidebar	Homepage
Recent Blog Posts	Second Sidebar	Blog pages
New Forum Topics	Second Sidebar	Forum pages
Book Navigation	Second Sidebar	Book pages
Navigation	Second Sidebar	Every page
Search	Search Region	Every page

Now place all your blocks:

1. Click Structure and then Blocks.

2. Locate the User Login block.

3. In the row for the User Login block, select Second Sidebar, as shown in Figure 10.12.

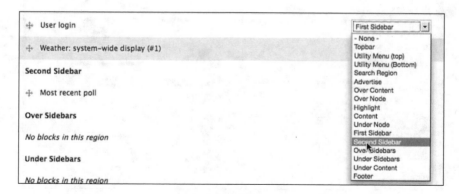

Figure 10.12   Placing the User Login block into the Second Sidebar region

4. Repeat the approve process and place these blocks into the Second Sidebar region:
   - Address Field Static Map
   - Most Recent Poll
   - Weather
   - Recent Blog Posts
   - New Forum Topics
   - Book Navigation
   - Navigation

5. Place the Search form block into the Search Region.

6. Place the Main Menu block into the –None– region.

7. Click Save Configuration.

   Visit your site's homepage. It should now look like Figure 10.13.

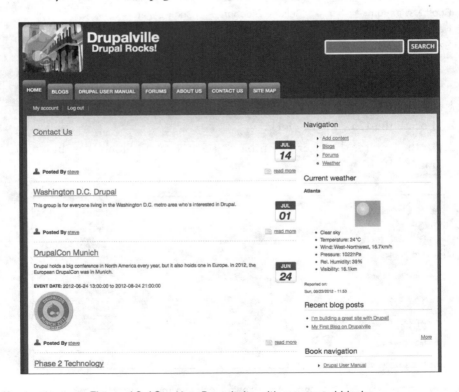

Figure 10.13   Your Drupal site with rearranged blocks

It is also possible to rearrange blocks within regions.

In Chapter 6, "Drupal Fields Explained," you rearranged the order of the fields you added. In Chapter 8, "Drupal Menus Explained," you changed the order of your menu items. The same technique used in these chapters applies to blocks as well.

Now change the order of your blocks in the right column:

1. Click Structure and then Blocks.

2. Scroll down to the Second Sidebar area.

3. Locate the crosses.

4. Rearrange the blocks so that they are in the same order as in Table 10.1. The final order should match Figure 10.14.

5. Click Save Configuration

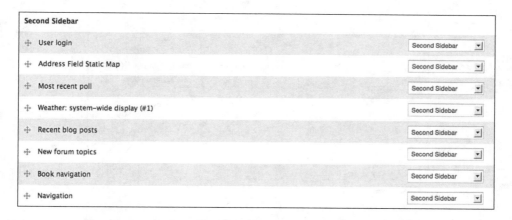

Figure 10.14   Your Second Sidebar blocks after being rearranged

Showing Blocks Under Certain Conditions Explained

So far, you have placed the blocks directly into regions, and by default the blocks have appeared on every page and for every user. However, that might not be the right choice for all sites.

Sometimes blocks need to appear only on certain pages. For example, here are some ways to make the blocks appear in a more relevant, targeted way:

- Place the Most Recent Poll block only on the homepage.
- Place the Recent Blog Posts block only on blog posts.
- Place the New Forum Topics block only on forum pages.

Here's how you place blocks only on certain pages. Start with the Most Recent Poll block:

1. Click Structure and then Blocks.
2. Locate the Most Recent Poll block.
3. Click Configure.
4. Scroll down to the Visibility settings area.
5. Click the Only the Listed Pages radio button.
6. Type **<front>** in the space provided, as shown in Figure 10.15.

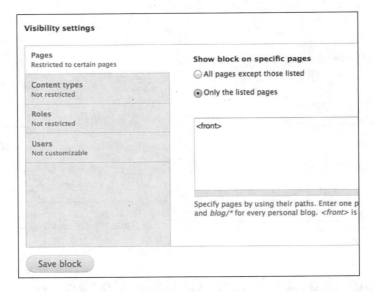

Figure 10.15   Controlling which pages a block appear on

7. Click Save Block.
8. Go to your homepage, and you see your poll block. Browse to other pages and the block will have disappeared.

Repeat that process with the Current Weather block:

1. Click Structure and then Blocks.
2. Locate the Current Weather block.

3. Click Configure.

4. Scroll down to the Visibility settings area.

5. Click the Only the Listed Pages radio button.

6. Type **<front>** in the space provided.

7. Click Save Block.

8. Go to your homepage and you see the Weather block now appears only on the homepage.

There are several other ways to control which pages blocks appear on. Often blocks are placed on different pages using URLs. Now see how that works:

1. Click Structure and then Blocks.

2. Locate the Recent Blog Posts block.

3. Click Configure.

4. Scroll down to the Visibility settings area.

5. Click the Only the Listed Pages radio button.

6. Type **blog** on one line and then **blogs★** on the next line. It should look like Figure 10.16. The asterisk (often called a wildcard) after the word "blogs" means that any pages with a URL starting in blogs will be included. This saves you from typing in the URL of every blog post.

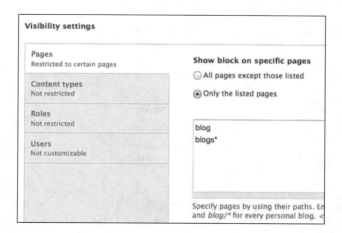

Figure 10.16   Controlling which pages the Recent Blog Posts block appears on

7. Click Save Block.

8. Go to your homepage, and you won't see the Recent Blog Posts block. Click Blogs in the Main menu and you now see the block.

Repeat the process with the New Forum Topics block:

1. Click Structure and then Blocks.

2. Click Configure next to the Recent Blog Posts block.

3. Scroll down to the Visibility settings area, and click the Only the Listed Pages radio button.

4. Type **forum** on one line and then **forums★** on the next line.

5. Click Save Block.

6. Go to your homepage and click Forums in the Main menu.

That process works when there is a distinct URL for part of your site. However, some parts of your site don't always have consistent URLs. For example, click Drupal User Manual in the Main Menu, and you can see that the URLs don't always contain a single word, such as blogs or forums. Fortunately, there is an alternative. All the Drupal User Manual pages are created by the Book module, and you can assign a block to appear only on the Book Content type:

1. Click Structure and then Blocks.

2. Click Configure next the Book Navigation block.

3. Scroll down to the Visibility settings area, and click the Content Types tab

4. Check the Book Page block, as shown in Figure 10.17.

Visibility settings

Pages Not restricted	**Show block for specific content types**
Content types Book page	☐ Article
	☐ Basic page
Roles Not restricted	☐ Blog entry
	☑ Book page
Users Not customizable	☐ Companies
	☐ Events
	☐ Forum topic
	☐ Poll
	☐ Sites
	☐ User Groups
	☐ Webform

Figure 10.17   Controlling which pages the Book Navigation block appears on

5. Click Save Block.

6. Go to your homepage and click Drupal User Manual on the Main menu. The Book Navigation block now appears only on Book pages.

There are two more options under Visibility Settings for each block: Roles and Users. These enable you to show blocks only to certain users or groups of users. However, before you can fully take advantage of these settings, you need to know more about Drupal users and groups of users. You find out more about Roles and Users in Chapter 13, "Drupal Users Explained".

Editing Blocks Explained

In the previous chapter, you often needed to make adjustments after enabling a new theme. The same is true after enabling blocks or putting them into a new region.

Here are some ways to make adjustments to a block.

Block Settings

Now look at your Most Recent Poll block, as shown in Figure 10.18.

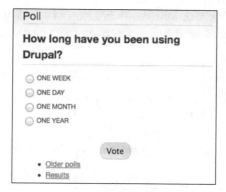

Figure 10.18   The Most Recent Poll block

There are at least two things you could improve about the display of this block:

- The Poll label is unnecessary because most people will know what it is.
- The title of the poll is too long for this region.

First, fix the label and see a quick way to edit blocks:

1. Hover your cursor over the top-right corner of the block.

2. You see a cog appear in the top-right corner and a dotted line appear around the block, as shown in Figure 10.19.

Figure 10.19   A quick way to edit the Most Recent Poll block

3. Click the cog and the words Configure Block will appear, as shown in Figure 10.20. Click Configure Block. This is a quick way to get to the settings for the block without clicking Structure, Blocks, and then Configure.

Figure 10.20   The Configure Block link for the Most Recent Poll block

First, let's remove the Poll label:

1. In the Block Title field, enter **\<none\>**, as shown in Figure 10.21.

Figure 10.21   Removing the block title for the Most Recent Poll block

2. Click Save Block.

3. Click Find Content on the admin menu bar.

4. In the filters at the top of the page, set Type to Poll, as shown in Figure 10.22. Click Filter. This results in only your Poll content showing and makes your poll easy to find.

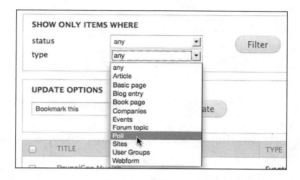

Figure 10.22   Filtering the content on your site

5. Click Edit in the row for How Long Have You Been Using Drupal?

6. Change the Question to How Long Have You Used Drupal?

7. Click Save.

8. Go to your homepage, and your Most Recent Poll block should now look like Figure 10.23. It is cleaner and more visually pleasing than before you made those two adjustments.

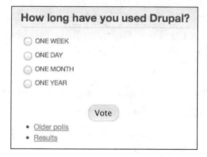

Figure 10.23   The Most Recent Poll block on your site after adjustments

Try that again with another block. Take a look at the Weather block, which should look like Figure 10.24.

Figure 10.24   The Weather block

There are at least two things you could improve about the display of this block:

- The Current weather title is not descriptive.
- The block uses Celsius but your weather is for the United States, which uses Fahrenheit.

First, change the block title:

1. Hover your cursor over the Weather block.
2. Click Configure Block in the top-right corner of the block.
3. In the Block Title field, enter **Weather at Drupalville HQ**.
4. Click Save Block.

To change the data showing on the page, you need to do something different. The How Long Have You Been Using Drupal? poll was produced by content, so you can edit it via the Find Content link. However, the Weather is produced by a module, so you need to look elsewhere to find the configuration settings.

1. Go to Modules and click Configure in the Weather row.
2. Click the System-Wide Display (#1) title.
3. In the Temperature drop-down, change Celsius to Fahrenheit, as shown in Figure 10.25.
4. Click Save.
5. Go to your homepage, and you'll see your block with the new adjustments, as shown in Figure 10.26.

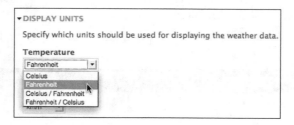

Figure 10.25   Configuring the Weather block

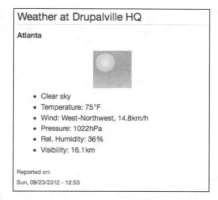

Figure 10.26   The Weather block on your site after adjustments

During these exercises, you've seen that there are some settings inside the block itself. However, the settings inside the block mainly relate to the title of the block, which region it appears in, and which pages it appears on.

If you want to make changes to the content of the block itself, you often need to go to the original source of the block's display, which might be a module or perhaps a content item.

Creating Blocks Explained

Until now, you focused on blocks that already exist. In this final part of the chapter, you see how to manually create a block. At the beginner level, creating blocks will be useful if you have a small amount of text or perhaps an image that you want to show in a block region. Use the example of a site mission statement:

1. Click Structure and then Blocks.

2. Click Add Block in the top-left corner, as shown in Figure 10.27.

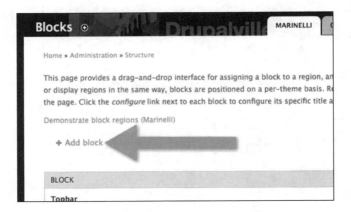

Figure 10.27   The Add Block link

3. Block title: **<none>**.

4. The Block description is what appears on the page where the blocks are listed. Type **mission block** as the description.

5. In the block body, type the site mission statement of **This site is dedicated to providing Drupal-related resources**.

6. Under Region settings, set the Marinelli (default theme) drop-down to Footer.

    Your new block should now look like Figure 10.28.

7. Save Block.

8. Click the homepage icon and see the mission block at the bottom of the page, as shown in Figure 10.29.

Block title

\<none\>

The title of the block as shown to the user. This field supports tokens.

Block description *

mission block

A brief description of your block. Used on the Blocks administration page.

Block body *

B *I* ≡ ≡ — ≡ " HTML ✂ ⬛ ⬛ ⬛ ⬛

This site is dedicated to providing Drupal-related resources

Path: p

Disable rich-text

Text format Filtered HTML ▾

• Web page addresses and e-mail addresses turn into links automatically.
• Allowed HTML tags: \<a\> \<em\> \<strong\> \<cite\> \<blockquote\> \<code\> \<u
• Lines and paragraphs break automatically.

The content of the block as shown to the user.

REGION SETTINGS

Specify in which themes and regions this block is displayed.

Marinelli (default theme)

Footer ▾

Figure 10.28   Creating the Mission block

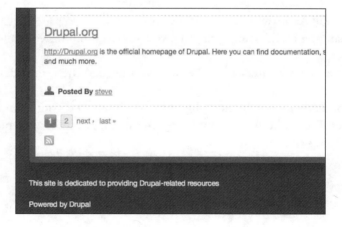

Drupal.org

http://Drupal.org is the official homepage of Drupal. Here you can find documentation, s
and much more.

👤 **Posted By** steve

1 2 next › last »

🔊

This site is dedicated to providing Drupal-related resources

Powered by Drupal

Figure 10.29   The Mission block enabled on your site

What's Next?

In this chapter, you saw that the theme you use has control of where you can place blocks. Together with Chapter 9, you hopefully now have a good understanding of how Drupal themes control both the design and layout of your site.

You now have control over your site's appearance, but some key questions remain:

- You have several companies on your site, but can you make a single page listing all those companies?
- You also have several events on your site, but how do you browse them easily?
- How do you add a photo gallery to your site?

The answer to all these questions and many more is the Views module. Views is the most important module in Drupal, and it's the first module that gets its own chapter.

At this point in the book, your site should look like Figure 10.30. As always, don't worry if your site has some small differences compared to the figure. That's OK. The goal of this book is not for you to perfectly mimic the Drupalville site. The goal of this book is to help you understand the key concepts underlying Drupal. If you understand how blocks work, you're ready to move on to the next chapter.

At this point in the book, we hope that our recommended workflow, shown in Figure 10.31, is starting to make more sense for you.

Let's quickly recap what you've done so far.

After planning and installing the site, you started building your site with content types.

You started with content types because you needed them in order to use fields.

Next you added your theme. Why did you not choose your theme as the first step? Because without any content on the site, it's very hard to picture what your site is going to look like.

Figure 10.30   Your Drupal site at the end of Chapter 10

Then you added blocks. You added blocks after the theme because the theme dictates where your regions will be. Without a theme you don't know what your regions are and where you can place blocks.

As we continue through the book, we'll introduce you to the rest of the steps in this Drupal workflow. Each step in the workflow proceeds logically from the previous step.

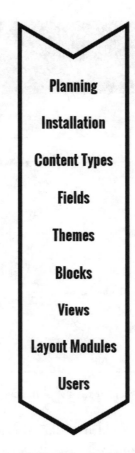

Figure 10.31   Our Drupal workflow

11

Drupal Views Explained

Views is the most popular module in Drupal. It's estimated that more than 75 percent of Drupal sites use Views. In fact, Views is so close to being an indispensable module that it will become part of Drupal 8.

So, why is Views so popular?

Because Views enables you to do many things that you can't do with default Drupal. Here are some examples:

- **Display:** Views enables you to create your own pages, blocks, RSS feeds, and more.
- **Format:** With default Drupal, you can display content only in a blog format, as with your current homepage. Views enables you to format information in tables, grids, lists, slideshows, calendars, and much more.
- **Fields:** With Views, you can display only the fields that you want. You can show, hide, reorder, and change the display of fields as you choose.
- **Filter:** With default Drupal, it's hard to select only certain content to show. For example, you can't choose to show only content from a single content type. Views enables you to filter based on content type, taxonomy terms, publication date, or many other criteria.
- **Sort:** With default Drupal, you can sort content only by showing the most recently published content first. Views enables you to sort alphabetically, by popularity, by author name, or by any criteria you choose.

So far in this book, you've added a lot of information to your site. In Chapters 5, "Drupal Content Explained," and Chapter 6, "Drupal Fields Explained," you spent time creating content types and fields. In Chapter 7, "Drupal Modules Explained," you added modules such as Bookmarks and Fivestar ratings.

Now that you have all that content, you can use Views to present it to your site's visitors in ways that are interesting and useful for them.

At the end of this chapter, you should be able to

- Create blocks and pages using Views.
- Create calendars and slideshows with Views.
- Learn to create views by thinking of the Display, Format, Fields, Filter, and Sort features that were just mentioned.
- Use modules to help you expand the features of Views.

Plan

You can use Views to create much of your site's structure. Here's an overview of all the blocks and pages that you can use Views to create.

You can use Views to create the following blocks:

- New Articles
- New Sites
- New Companies
- New User Groups
- Archived Blogs
- Upcoming Events
- Slideshow

You can also use Views to create the following pages:

- Resources landing page
- Articles sublanding page
- User Groups sublanding page
- Sites sublanding page
- Companies sublanding page
- Events landing page

Views is a popular module, but it can also be a lot to learn. You start slowly by creating some blocks, creating some pages, and then moving on and creating some more exciting displays using slideshows and calendars.

Installing the Views Modules

In Chapter 7, you installed Drupal modules using the FITS workflow: Find, Install, Turn On, and Set Up. It's time to put those skills to use again:

1. Find the following modules:
   - **Views:** http://drupal.org/project/views
   - **Devel:** http://drupal.org/project/devel

2. Install those two modules.

3. Turn on the following modules:
   - Devel
   - Devel generate
   - Views
   - Views UI

4. Now you set up the modules. In the following section, you set up the Devel module and then Views.

Generating Sample Content Explained

The Devel module provides a quick way to generate sample content that you can use to test your Views blocks and pages. Now create some content quickly and easily so you can see your Views come to life:

1. Click Configure on the black menu bar.

2. Locate the Development links on the right side of the screen, as shown in Figure 11.1.

3. Click Generate content. You see a new screen and at the top are the options shown in Figure 11.2. Make sure that all the boxes are checked.

4. Increase the number of nodes to generate from 50 to 1000.

5. Check the box labeled Add a URL Alias for Each Node.

6. Click Generate.

7. You'll see a progress bar across the screen. When the progress bar is finished, you'll see a message across the top of the screen saying that the content was generated successfully. Visit the front of your site, and you'll see lots of dummy content, as shown in Figure 11.3. The content is all in Latin.

Figure 11.1   The Devel configuration options

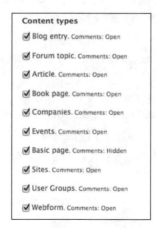

Figure 11.2   The Generate content options screen

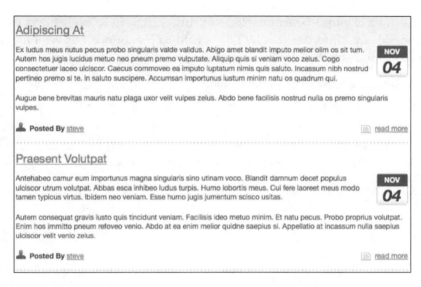

Figure 11.3   Dummy content on your Drupal site

Creating Blocks with Views Explained

In the following activities, you create five blocks. Each time you create a block, you introduce new options available to you in Views and Drupal. You create the following blocks:

- **New User Groups:** Basic listing of content titles
- **New Sites:** Basic listing of content titles
- **New Articles:** Basic listing of content titles plus post date
- **New Companies:** Basic listing of content titles plus an image with a custom style

New User Groups Block

When creating a view, there are five things to plan, which were mentioned in the introduction to this chapter: Display, Format, Fields, Filter, and Sort. Here are our choices for the User Groups Block:

- **Display:** Block
- **Format:** HTML list
- **Fields:** Title
- **Filter:** User Groups content type
- **Sort:** Newest first

Note: We like to use memorable acronyms, such as FITS, to help people remember easily. Unfortunately, DFFFS is hard to pronounce, but we'll use it again to remind you of these five options.

Step 1: Create a New User Groups Block

1. Click Structures and then Views.
2. Click Add New View. You see a screen that looks like Figure 11.4. This is the first of the two main Views screens. This screen is for creating views. There's also another screen for editing views that you see later.

Home » Administration » Structure » Views

View name *

☐ **Description**

Show [Content ▾] of type [All ▾] tagged with [○] sorted by [Newest first ▾]

☑ **Create a page**

Page title

Path
http://drupal7explained.com/drupalville/ [   ]

Display format
[Unformatted list ▾] of [teasers ▾] [with links (allow users to add comments, etc.) ▾] [without comments ▾]

Items to display
[10]

☑ Use a pager

☐ Create a menu link

☐ Include an RSS feed

☐ **Create a block**

(Save & exit)   (Continue & edit)   (Cancel)

Figure 11.4   Creating a new view

First, tackle the general settings at the top of the page, as shown in Figure 11.5:

1. View name: New User Groups.
2. Check the box for Description and type: **A block for the User groups landing page and user groups content**.
3. Select User Groups for the Type.
4. Select Sorted By Newest first.

Figure 11.5   The general settings for a new view

Now, be specific about the type of view that you want to create. Fill in the settings:

1. Uncheck the Create a Page box, as shown in Figure 11.6.

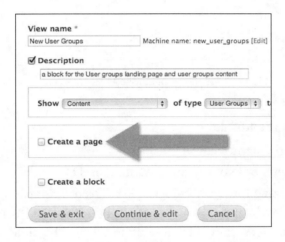

Figure 11.6   The Create a Page box in the Views settings

2. Check Create a Block. More settings appear, as shown in Figure 11.7.
    - Select HTML list from Display format.
    - Change the items per page from 5 to 10.
    - Check Use a Pager.
3. Click Save & Exit.

Step 2: Enable New User Groups Block

1. Click Structures and then Blocks.
2. Locate the block you just created. Look under the Disabled list for View: New User Groups.

3. Click Configure for This Block.

4. Place the block into the second sidebar region.

5. Set the block to show on resources/user-groups*. This will show the block on the user groups landing page and all the user groups nodes.

6. Click Save Block.

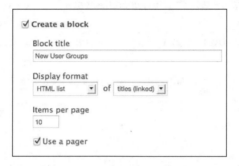

Figure 11.7   The output settings for a new view

Step 3: Observe the Results

1. Return to the homepage.

2. Use the search box to search for Washington D.C.

3. Click the listing for the Washington D.C Drupal group. You see a screen that looks like Figure 11.8 and has your new block in the right sidebar.

4. Check your block, shown in close up in Figure 11.9, and you can see that your view matches the settings you had planned:

   - **Display:** Block
   - **Format:** HTML list
   - **Fields:** Title
   - **Filter:** User Groups content type
   - **Sort:** Newest first

New Sites Block

Now repeat that process. This time you create a block showing the most recent items added to the Site content type. Here's the DFFFS plan for this view:

- **Display:** Block
- **Format:** HTML list showing five titles and a pager

- **Fields:** Title
- **Filter:** Sites content type
- **Sort:** Newest first

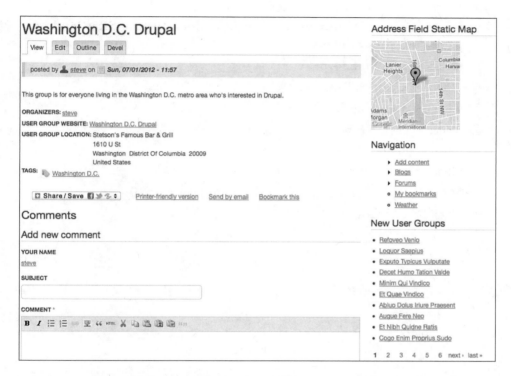

Figure 11.8   Your New User Group Groups block live on the site

Figure 11.9   A close-up of your New User Groups block

Step 1: Create New Sites Block

1. Click Structures and then Views.

2. Click Add new View.

3. View name: New Sites.

4. Check the box for Description and type: **a block for the Sites landing page and Sites content.**

5. Select Sites from the type.

6. Uncheck Create a Page.

7. Check Create a Block.

8. Select HTML list from Display format.

9. Change the items per page from 5 to 10.

10. Check Use a Pager.

11. Make sure your settings match, as shown in Figure 11.10.

12. Click Save & Exit.

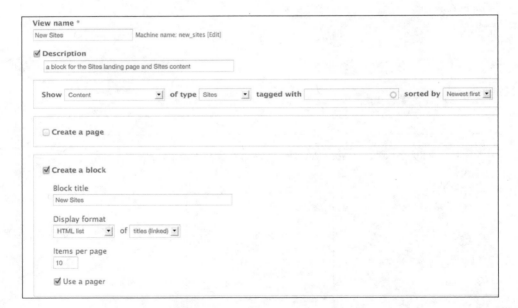

Figure 11.10   Creating the New Sites block

Step 2: Enable New Sites Block

1. Click Structures and then Blocks.

2. Locate the block you just created. Look under the Disabled list for View: New Sites.

3. Click Configure for This Block.

4. Place it in the second sidebar.

5. Set the block to Show on Resources/Sites★ to show the block on Sites Content Only.

6. Click Save Block.

Step 3: Observe the Results

1. Return to the homepage.

2. Use the search box to search for Drupal.org.

3. Click the listing for Drupal.org. You'll see a screen that looks like Figure 11.11 and has your new block in the right sidebar. This block will match the Display, Format, Fields, Filter, and Sort options that you had planned.

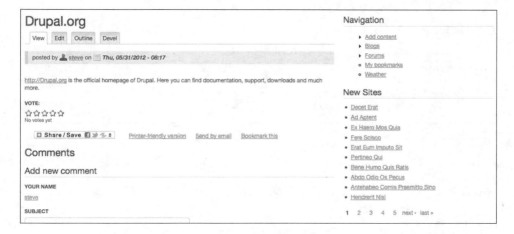

Figure 11.11   Your New Sites block live on the site

New Articles Block

Now that you created two blocks using Views, you're ready to use more of the power that Views gives you. For the first time, you won't see only the Views creation screen but also the Views editing screen.

In this task, you're going to show more than just the title of the content. Here's the DFFFS plan:

- **Display:** Block
- **Format:** HTML list

- **Fields:** Title and Post date
- **Filter:** Article content type
- **Sort:** Newest first

Step 1: Create New Articles Block

1. Click Structures and then Views.
2. Click Add New View.
3. View name: New Articles.
4. Check the box for Description and type: **a block for the article content type**.
5. Select Article from the type.
6. Uncheck Create a Page.
7. Check Create a Block.
8. Select HTML list from Display format.
9. Change the items per page from 5 to 10.
10. Check Use a Pager.
11. Make sure your settings match, as shown in Figure 11.12.

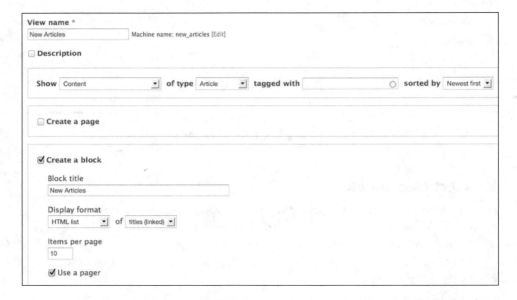

Figure 11.12   Creating your New Articles block

12. This time, don't click Save & Edit. Instead, click Continue & Edit. This takes you to the Views editing screen, which should look like Figure 11.13.

Figure 11.13   The Views editing screen

On this screen, there are four main areas that you need to be aware of:

- **Main settings:** This area contains all your DFFFS settings.

- **Extra settings:** This area contains settings that provide minor, extra tweaks to your view.

- **Advanced:** This area contains complex settings and most are well beyond the scope of this book. These settings are hidden for a reason!

- **Preview:** This area shows a preview of what your view will look like.

These four areas are marked on the screen in Figure 11.14.

As you can see, Views is an enormously powerful module with many, many settings.

This chapter focuses on areas 1, 2, and 4 (see Figure 11.14).

Figure 11.14   The four areas of the Views editing screen

Start simply by adding another field to display. Currently, the title of the article is the only field being displayed. Also add the date the article was posted:

1. Click Add next to Fields, as shown in Figure 11.15.

2. You'll now see a pop-up screen. Type **post date** in the Search box.

3. Check the box for the Content: Post Date field, as shown in Figure 11.16.

4. Click Apply (all displays) at the bottom of the pop-up.

5. Uncheck the Create a Label option.

6. Under Date Format, choose the Short Format option, as shown in Figure 11.17.

7. Click Apply (all displays) at the bottom of the pop-up.

8. Scroll down and you can see a preview of your block at the bottom of the screen.

9. Click Save in the top-right corner, as shown in Figure 11.18.

Figure 11.15   Adding a field to a view

Figure 11.16   Adding the post date field to a view

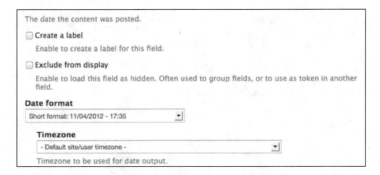

Figure 11.17   Configuring the settings for the Post Date field

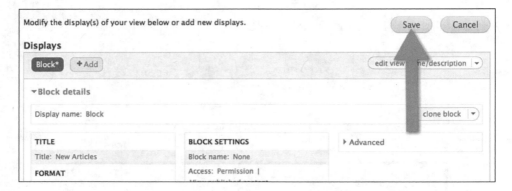

Figure 11.18   The Save button on the Views editing screen

Step 2: Enable New Articles Block

1. Click Structures and then Blocks.

2. Locate the block you just created. Look under the Disabled list for View: New Articles.

3. Click Configure for this block.

4. Place in the second sidebar.

5. Set the block to show on resources/articles★ so that the block appears on article nodes only.

6. Click Save Block.

Step 3: Observe the Results

1. Return to the homepage.

2. Use the Search box to search for your Welcome to Drupalville article.

3. Click the listing for Welcome to Drupalville. You'll see a screen like Figure 11.19 that has your new block in the right sidebar. This block matches the Display, Format, Fields, Filter, and Sort options that you had planned.

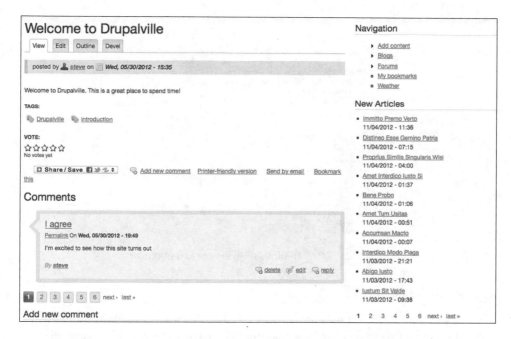

Figure 11.19   The New Articles block live on your site

New Companies View Block

For this next block, you display an image in your block. The image needs to be smaller than the default thumbnail style that comes with Drupal, so you are introduced to a new feature in Drupal: custom image styles.

Here's your DFFFS plan for this view:

- **Display:** Block
- **Format:** Unformatted list
- **Fields:** Title and Image

- **Filter:** Companies content type
- **Sort:** Random

Step 1: Create an Image Style

1. Click Configuration on the black menu bar.
2. Click Image Styles in the Media block on the left side of the page, as shown in Figure 11.20.

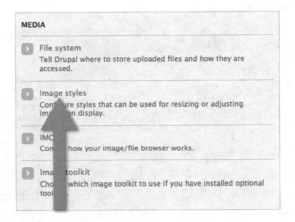

Figure 11.20   The Image Styles configuration link

3. Click Add Style.
4. Style name: scale_crop_35x35 (Note: This type of style name reminds you the type of style and the size, making it easier to know if this style will meet your needs somewhere else on the site.)
5. Click Create New Style.
6. Select Scale and Crop from the Select a New Effect drop-down, as shown in Figure 11.21.
7. Click Add.
8. Enter 35 for both Width and Height, as shown in Figure 11.22.
9. Click Add Effect.

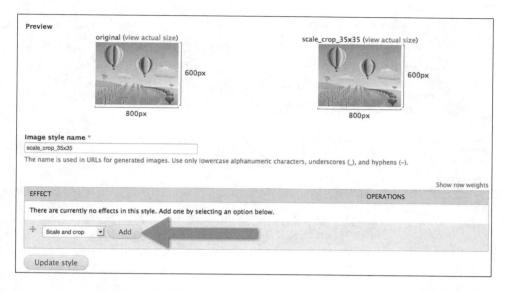

Figure 11.21   Adding a new effect to your image style

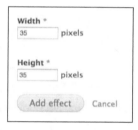

Figure 11.22   Adding a scaling effect to your image style

Step 2: Create New Companies View Block

1. Click Structures and then Views.
2. Click Add New View.
   - View name: Companies.
   - Check the box for Description and type: **a block for the companies content**.
   - Select Companies from the Type.
   - Select Unsorted from the Sort Filter.
   - Uncheck Create a Page.

- Check Create a Block.
- Select Unformatted List from Display Format.
- Check Use a Pager.

Make sure your settings match Figure 11.23.

3. Click Continue & Edit.

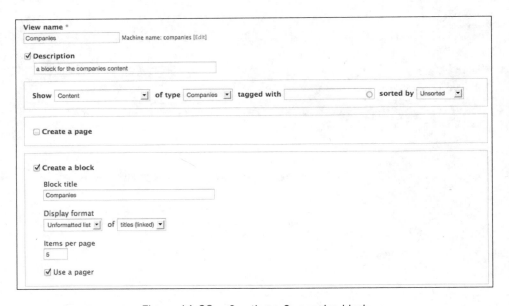

Figure 11.23   Creating a Companies block

You can now add an image field to your display using the same steps you used when adding the Post date to your New Articles block:

1. Click Add next to Fields.
2. Search for the Image field, and check the box for the Image field as shown in Figure 11.24.
3. Click Apply (all displays).
4. Uncheck the Create a Label option.
5. In the Image Style drop-down, select scale_crop_35x35, as shown in Figure 11.25.

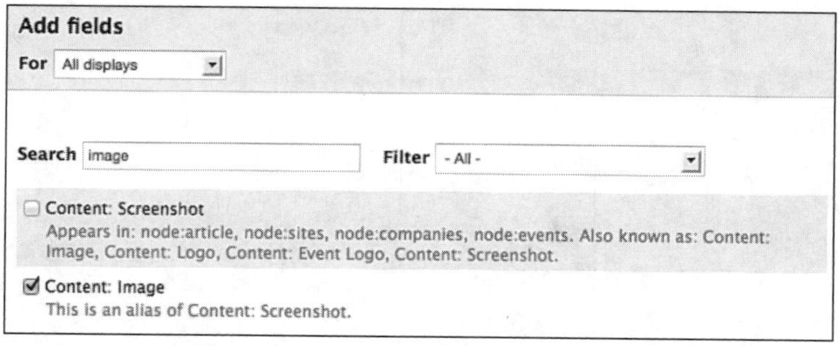

Figure 11.24   Adding an Image field to the Companies block

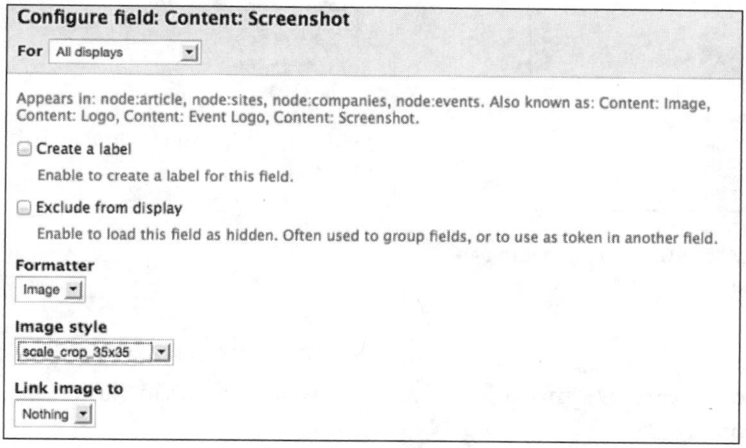

Figure 11.25   Configuring the Image field for the Companies block.

6. Click Apply (all displays).

7. Scroll down and see a preview of your content, as shown in Figure 11.26. There isn't a logo attached to Acquia because you created that content before adding the Image field to Companies.

Now that you have added the image field, let's tweak a few things starting with the field order:

1. Return to the Add button next to Fields, and click the arrow next to Add. You'll see the Rearrange option, as shown in Figure 11.27.

2. Click Rearrange.

Figure 11.26   Configuring the Image
field for the Companies block

Figure 11.27   The Rearrange button
for fields

3. You can rearrange the fields using the same Click+Hold+Drag technique used to rearrange the order of your fields and blocks in earlier chapters (see Figure 11.28).

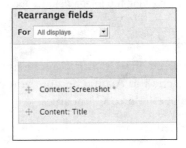

Figure 11.28   Rearranging fields using Click+Hold+Drag

4. Click Apply (All Displays).

The last change to make is to add sort criteria. You don't want to show favoritism to the companies on your site, so in this block your list order will be random:

1. Click Add next to Sort Criteria, as shown in Figure 11.29.

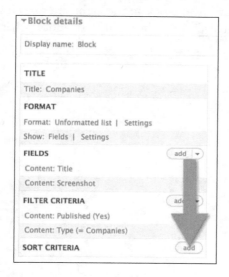

Figure 11.29   Adding a new sort criteria

2. Type **random** in the Search box.
3. Check the box next to Global: Random.
4. Click Apply (All Displays).
5. Click Apply (All Displays).
6. Click Save in the top-right corner.

Step 3: Enable Companies Block

1. Click Structures and then Blocks.
2. Locate the block you just created. Look under the Disabled list for View: Companies.
3. Click Configure for This Block.
4. Place the block into the second sidebar region.
5. Set the block to show on resources/companies* to show the block the article nodes only.
6. Save Block.

Step 4: Observe the Results

1. Return to the homepage.

2. Use the Search box to search for OSTraining.

3. Click the listing for OSTraining. You'll see a screen that looks like Figure 11.30 and has your new block in the right sidebar. This block will match the Display, Format, Fields, Filter, and Sort options that you had planned.

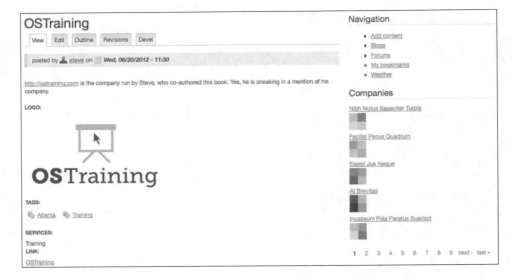

Figure 11.30   Your Companies block live on your site

Creating Pages with Views Explained

In the first part of this chapter, you created blocks. You created four blocks, one each for pages created with the Article, User Groups, Sites, and Companies content types.

In the next part of this chapter, you create landing pages for Articles, User Groups Sites, and Companies.

The process you use is similar to the process you used to create the view blocks.

On a normal site, you would probably make all these landing pages look the same. However, you're building a site for no other reason than to help you learn. You use different strategies for each page, offering you an insight into some of the options available to you in Views.

In this part of the chapter, you build four landing pages for your content types:

- **Articles landing page:** Basic page with teaser display
- **User Groups landing page:** Basic page with a table display and added fields
- **Sites landing page:** Basic page with a table display and added fields
- **Companies landing page:** Basic page with a grid display, added fields, and a new image style

You also build a page that shows all the resources you have available:

- **Resources landing page:** Basic page with a table display, added fields, and an exposed filter

Articles Landing Page

To create the Articles landing page, use the Quick Page Create feature you used to create the New Sites view block.

This is your DFFFS plan for this view:

- **Display:** Page.
- **Format:** Unformatted list of teasers showing 10 titles, a pager, and a link on a menu.
- **Fields:** None. Fields are not an option on a teaser format.
- **Filter:** Articles content type.
- **Sort:** Latest first.

Now create the view:

1. Click Structures and then Views.
2. Click Add New View.

- View name: Articles.
- Check the box for Description and type: **the articles landing page**
- Select Article from the type.
- Observe the default settings that you will be using.
- Change the Path from articles to resources/articles to match the path patterns.
- Check the box to Create a Menu Link.
- Select Main menu from the Menu drop-down.

Check that your settings match Figure 11.31.

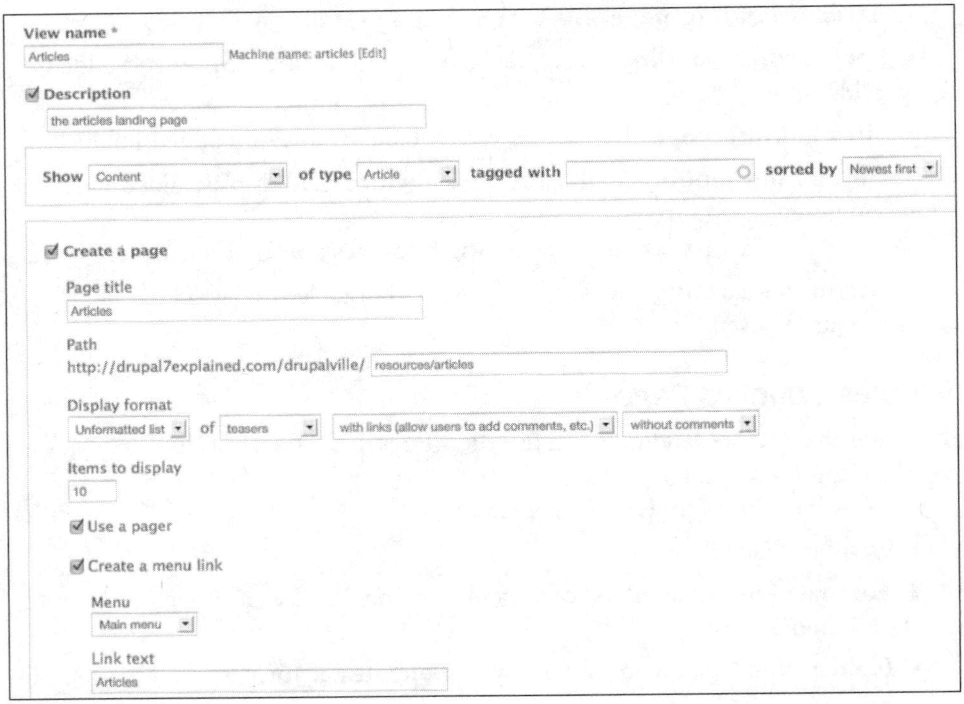

Figure 11.31   Creating your Articles landing page

3. Click Save & Exit.

   You'll be taken to the new Articles page, and it will look like Figure 11.32. Notice that there's now a menu link to this page on the Main menu.

User Groups Landing Page

For your next page, create a table display. Start as you did when creating the Articles page, but then choose a different display and add a couple fields.

This is the DFFFS plan for this view:

- **Display:** Page
- **Format:** Table, a pager, and a link on a menu
- **Fields:** Title, Post Date
- **Filter:** User Groups content type
- **Sort:** Latest first

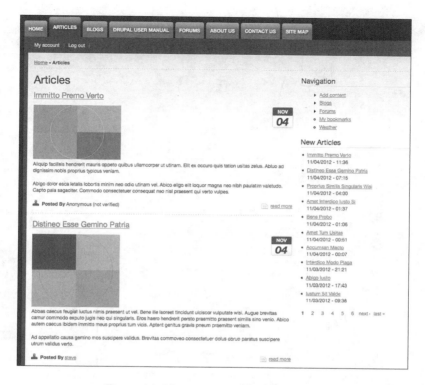

Figure 11.32   Your Articles landing page

Follow these steps:

1. Click Structure and then Views.
2. Click Add New View.
   - View name: User Groups.
   - Check the box for Description and type: **the user groups landing page**
   - Select User Groups from the Type.
   - Change the Path from user-groups to resources/user-groups to match the path patterns.
   - Select Table from the Display Format drop-down.
   - Check the box to Create a Menu Link.
   - Select Main menu from the Menu drop-down.

   Make sure that your settings match Figure 11.33.
3. Click Continue & Edit.

Figure 11.33   Creating your User Groups landing page

You need to add a field to your display: Post Date (which you added in the Articles view block):

1. Click Add next to Fields.

2. Search for the post date, and check the box for the Post Date field.

3. Click Apply (All Displays).

4. Choose Short Format under the Date Format drop-down.

5. Click Apply (All Displays).

    Check your preview. It will look like Figure 11.34.

There are several improvements you could make to this table. First, make the column titles more meaningful:

1. Click Content: Title (Title) under the Fields list.

2. Type **User Group Name** in the label field.

3. Click Apply (All Displays).

4. Click Content: Post Date (Post Date) under the Fields list.

5. Type **User Group Listing Date** in the Label field.

6. Click Apply (All Displays).

TITLE	POST DATE
Erat Immitto	11/04/2012 – 14:04
Adipiscing At	11/04/2012 – 13:52
Ibidem Populus Velit	11/04/2012 – 13:42
Praesent Volutpat	11/04/2012 – 13:36
Acsi Causa Sed	11/04/2012 – 12:48
Esse Populus	11/04/2012 – 12:40
At Immitto Similis	11/04/2012 – 12:22
Immitto Premo Verto	11/04/2012 – 11:36
Oppeto Proprius Tation Vero	11/04/2012 – 11:17
Mauris Ut	11/04/2012 – 11:14

Figure 11.34   A preview of your User Groups landing page

You also edit the Format settings so the table columns can be sorted by users:

1. Click Settings for the Table Format, as shown in Figure 11.35.

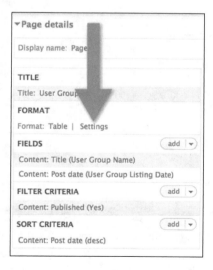

Figure 11.35   Changing the settings for the table format

2. Check the boxes under the Sortable column, as shown in Figure 11.36.

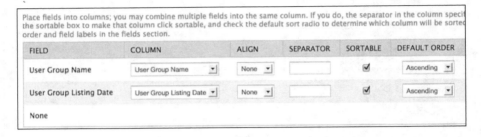

Figure 11.36   Allowing visitors to sort the table

3. Click Apply (All Displays).
4. Click Save in the top-right corner.
5. Click the View Page link in the top-right corner under the Save button.

    You'll now see your new page, as shown in Figure 11.37. You can click the User Group Name and User Group Listing Date to reorganize the table.

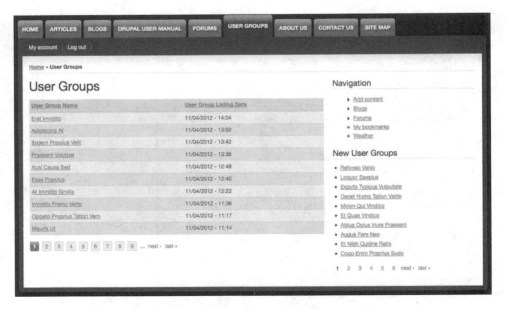

Figure 11.37   Your User Groups page live on your site

Sites Landing Page

The Sites landing page will also have a table display. This time you add two fields to the table.

Here is your DFFFS plan for this view:

- **Display:** Page
- **Format:** Table
- **Fields:** Title, Post Date, Topics
- **Filter:** User Groups content type
- **Sort:** Latest first

Now create this view:

1. Click Structures and then Views.
2. Click Add New View.
   - View name: Sites.
   - Check the box for Description and type: **the sites landing page**.
   - Select Sites from the type.
   - Change the Path from sites to resources/sites to match the path patterns.
   - Select Table from the Display format drop-down.
   - Check the box to create a Menu link.
   - Select Main menu from the Menu drop-down.

   Check that your settings look like Figure 11.38.
3. Click Continue & Edit.

You need to add two fields to your display: Post Date (which you added in the Articles view block) and Content:Topics (the username of the person who added the site page):

1. Click Add next to Fields.
2. Search for the Post Date and check the box for the Post Date field.
3. Click Apply (All Displays) twice.
4. Choose Short Format under the Date Format drop-down.
5. Click Apply (All Displays).
6. Click Add next to Fields.
7. Search for topics and check the box for the Content:Topics field.

8. Click Apply (All Displays) twice.

9. Scroll down and see a preview of your content, as shown in Figure 11.39.

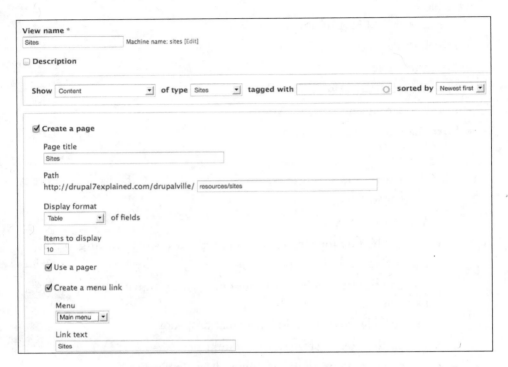

Figure 11.38   Creating the Sites page

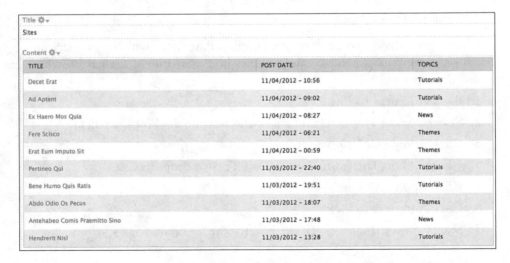

Figure 11.39   A preview of your Sites page

Now make improvements to the table. We're going to add labels and a new way of sorting the results.

First, add the labels:

1. Click Content: Post Date under the Field list.

2. Type Site Name in the Label field.

3. Click Apply (All Displays).

4. Click Content: Title under the Field list.

5. Type Site Listing Date in the Label field.

6. Click Apply (All Displays).

Now add sorting. You also split the table into several sections based on what topic the sites deal with:

1. Click Settings for the Table Format.

2. Check the Site Name and Site Listing Date boxes under the Sortable column.

3. Select Topics under Group field Nr.1, as shown in Figure 11.40.

4. Click Apply (All Displays).

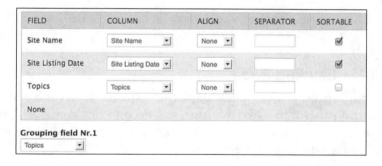

FIELD	COLUMN	ALIGN	SEPARATOR	SORTABLE
Site Name	Site Name ▾	None ▾		☑
Site Listing Date	Site Listing Date ▾	None ▾		☑
Topics	Topics ▾	None ▾		☐
None				

Grouping field Nr.1
Topics ▾

Figure 11.40   The table settings for your Sites page

5. Click Save and then click View Page.

You'll see your new Sites page, as shown in Figure 11.41.

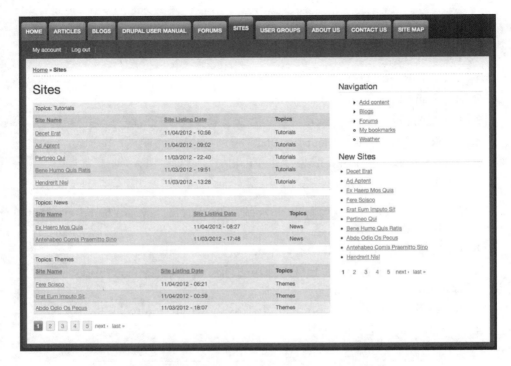

Figure 11.41   Your Sites page live on your site

Companies Landing Page

For your fourth page, you use a grid display to show the logo and company name in a grid pattern. To make this page, you need to first configure a new image style so that you will have it ready when you create the Views page.

Here is your DFFFS plan for this view:

- **Display:** Page
- **Format:** Grid
- **Fields:** Title and Logo
- **Filter:** Companies content type
- **Sort:** Title

Create an Image Style

1. Click Configuration on the black menu bar.
2. Click Image Styles in the Media block on the left side of the page.
3. Click Add Style.

4. Style name: scale_90w. (Note: This strategy will allow logos with different sizes to be the same width but be resized without becoming distorted.)

5. Select Scale from the Select a New Effect drop-down.

6. Type 90 for Width. You can leave the Height box empty.

7. Click Add Effect.

Create the View Page

1. Click Structure, Views, and then Add New View.

2. View name: Companies.

3. Machine-readable name: companies_page (Note: You already used companies here for the Companies block.)

4. Check the box for Description and type: **the companies landing page**

5. Select Companies from the Type.

6. Sort by Title.

7. Change the Path from companies to resources/companies to match the path patterns.

8. Select Grid of Fields from the Display Format drop-downs.

9. Check the box to Create a menu link.

10. Select Main menu from the Menu drop-down.

11. Click Continue & Edit.

For your grid, you need to add the image field, just like you did with the New Companies view block:

1. Click Add next to Fields.

2. Search for the image field and check the box for Field.

3. Click Apply (All Displays).

4. Uncheck the Create a Label option.

5. Scroll down to the Image style drop-down and select scale_90w.

6. Click Apply (All Displays).

Scroll down and see a preview of your content, as shown in Figure 11.42.

Figure 11.42   A preview of your Companies page

Now that you have added the image field, rearrange the field order:

1. Return to the Add button next to Fields, click the arrow next to Add, and see the Rearrange option.

2. Click Rearrange.

3. Drag the image field above the Title field using the same Click+Hold+Drag technique used to rearrange the order of your fields and blocks.

4. Click Apply (All Displays).

You have one final setting to change. You have a grid with 12 spaces, but only 10 items showing on the page:

1. In the middle of the Views editing screen, click Paged, 10 items. As shown in Figure 11.43.

2. Under Items per Page, change 10 to 12.

3. Click Apply (All Displays).

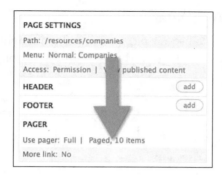

Figure 11.43   Changing the number of items on your Companies page

4. Click Save and then click the View Page link.

You'll see your Companies page live on your site, as shown in Figure 11.44.

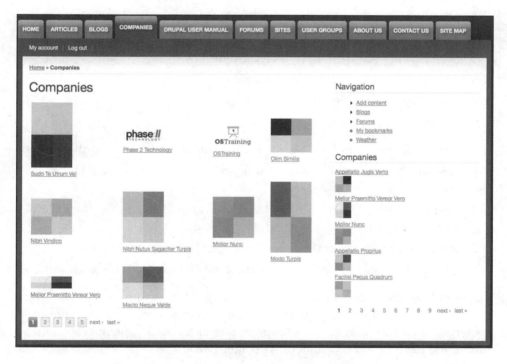

Figure 11.44   Your Companies page live on your site

Resources Landing Page

Each page you have created so far has introduced a different feature of Views. For the Resources page, you engage your site visitors by offering them the ability to filter the content.

Here's your DFFFS plan for this view:

- **Display:** Page
- **Format:** Table, a pager, and a link on a menu
- **Fields:** Title, Post Date, and Logo.
- **Filter:** Companies, Sites, Articles, and User Groups content type
- **Sort:** Newest First

Now start:

1. Click Structure, Views, and then Add New View.
2. View name: Resources.
3. Check the box for Description and type: **the resources landing page**.
4. Select All from the Type.
5. Select Table from the Display Format drop-down.
6. Check the box to Create a Menu link.
7. Select Main menu from the Menu drop-down.
8. Click Continue & Edit.

Next, using what you have already learned, modify your view in these ways:

1. Add the Image field set with the scale_crop_35x35 image style. Don't create a label.
2. Add the Post Date field. Set the Label to Listing Date and the Date Format to Short Format.
3. Rearrange the fields in the following order: Image, Title, Post Date.
4. Change the Table settings to make the Title and Listing Date fields sortable.

Now add one filter criteria twice. Confusing? Maybe. You want to limit the content that displays on the page to four content types. Then, you want the site visitors to limit the content on the page to one of the four content types. This means you need to add the content type filter twice:

1. Click Add next to Filter Criteria.
2. Search for Type and select Content: Type.
3. Click Apply (All Displays).

4. Check the boxes for Article, Companies, Sites, and User Groups, as shown in Figure 11.45.

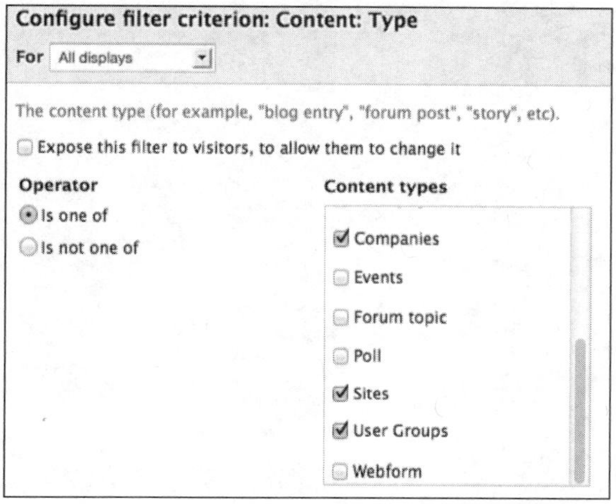

Figure 11.45   Filtering content on your Resources page

5. Click Apply (All Display).

Repeat the previous steps exactly but with two differences, both shown in Figure 11.46:

1. Check the box to expose the filter.

2. Check the box to Limit List to Selected Items.

The exposed filter isn't going to show up without a little help. You need to enable Ajax on your view:

1. Click Advanced on the right side of the page.

2. Locate the Use Ajax feature and set it to Yes, as shown in Figure 11.47.

3. Save the view and click the View Page link.

   Your Resources page will look like Figure 11.48.

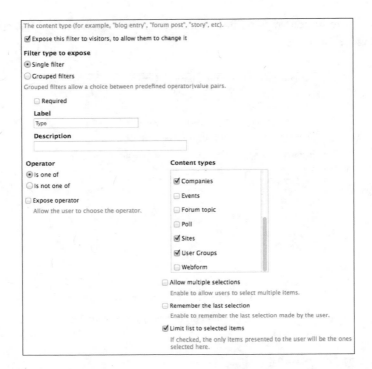

Figure 11.46   Filtering content on your Resources page but with extra boxes checked

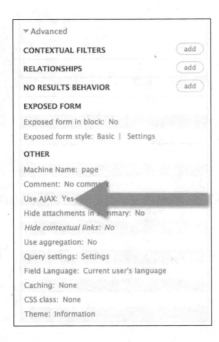

Figure 11.47   Allowing your page to use Ajax

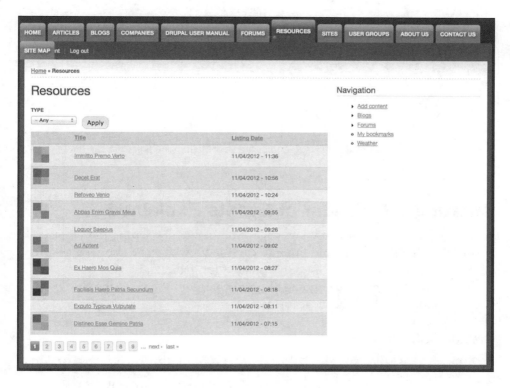

Figure 11.48   Your Resources page live on your site

Reorganizing the Main Menu

Now you have five new pages created by Views. However, there's now too many menu links on the Main menu and you need to do some reorganizing. Keep Resources as the parent link and turn Articles, Companies, Sites, and User Groups into child links:

1. Click Structures and then Menus.
2. Click List Links next to Main menu.
3. Place Articles, Companies, Sites, and User Groups under the Resources link, as shown in Figure 11.49.
4. Click Save Configuration.

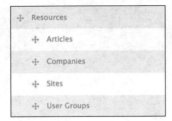

Figure 11.49   Reorganizing your Main menu links

Creating a Calendar of Events Explained

In this chapter, you've created Views pages from scratch by setting the Display, Format, Fields, Filters, Sort, and other features in Views. You've also seen a variety of formats, including HTML list, Unformatted list, Table, and Grid.

In this next activity, we're going to go further with Views. Using the Calendar module, add a Calendar format.

Install Calendar

1. Install and enable the Calendar module: http://drupal.org/project/calendar.
2. When you enable Calendar, Drupal also prompts you to enable Date Views. Click Continue to accept.

Configure the Calendar of Events Views

1. Click Structures and then Views.
2. This time, click a different link. Click Add View from Template, as shown in Figure 11.50.

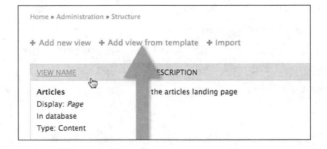

Figure 11.50   The Add View from Template link

3. Click Add next to "A calendar view of the 'field_events_date' field in the 'node' base table," as shown in Figure 11.51.

Home » Administration » Structure » Views

NAME	DESCRIPTION	OPERATION
Image Gallery	Shows all images which was uploaded on the "field_image" field	add
Calendar	A calendar view of the 'created' field in the 'comment' base table.	add
Calendar	A calendar view of the 'changed' field in the 'comment' base table.	add
Calendar	A calendar view of the 'field_events_date' field in the 'node' base table.	add
Calendar	A calendar view of the 'last_comment_timestamp' field in the 'node_comment_statistics' base table.	add
Calendar	A calendar view of the 'created' field in the 'node' base table.	add
Calendar	A calendar view of the 'changed' field in the 'node' base table.	add
Calendar	A calendar view of the 'timestamp' field in the 'print_page_counter' base table.	add
Calendar	A calendar view of the 'sent_timestamp' field in the 'print_mail_page_counter' base table.	add
Calendar	A calendar view of the 'created' field in the 'users' base table.	add
Calendar	A calendar view of the 'access' field in the 'users' base table.	add
Calendar	A calendar view of the 'login' field in the 'users' base table.	add

Figure 11.51   Creating a view using the Calendar template

4. Name the view **Events**.

5. Click Continue.

We've talked about the DFFFS settings in this chapter. You've seen that a view can have multiple fields, filter criteria, and sort criteria. This view shows that it's possible to have multiple displays. Each display is similar but has slight variations. You can see the displays along the top of the screen, as shown in Figure 11.52.

Modify the display(s) of your view below or add new displays.

Displays

Month Week Day Year Block Upcoming + Add

Figure 11.52   Different displays for the Calendar view

6. Scroll down and you see the preview for the main Month display, as shown in Figure 11.53.

7. Click the Week tab at the top of the page. Figure 11.54 shows a preview of this display.

Figure 11.53   The Month display for the Calendar view

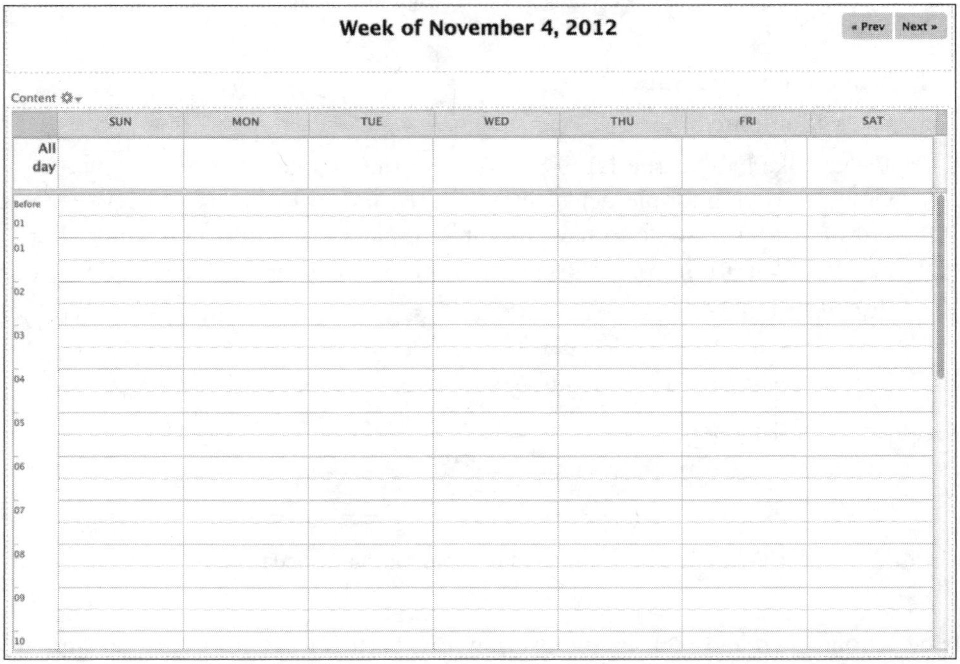

Figure 11.54   The Week display for the Calendar view

Browse through the Day, Year, and Block previews. You'll start to get an idea of how powerful and flexible Views is:

1. Return to the Month display and click the Path link in the Page settings area.

2. Change calendar-node-field-events-date/month to events/month to match the path pattern you set for Events.

3. Click Parent menu item next to Menu in the Page settings area.

4. Change Calendar to Events and Select Main Menu from the Menu drop-down.

5. Click Apply.

6. Click the tab for Week, click the Path settings, and change calendar-node-field-events-date to events/week.

7. Repeat the path change for Day and Year.

8. Click Save.

Return to the homepage and click the Events menu item available on the Main menu. You'll see the Month tab first. All the other displays are available as tabs, as shown in Figure 11.55.

Figure 11.55   The Calendar view live on your site

Add Event Blocks to Events Page

Inside the Views editing page, there were two block displays. One was literally called Block. The other was called Upcoming. Now see what they look like by configuring them:

1. Click Structure and then Blocks.
2. Locate View: Events and click Configure for that block.
3. Select the second sidebar for Marinelli (default theme).
4. Set the block to show on events★ so that the block appears on event pages only.
5. Save Block.
6. Repeat this configuration for the View: Events: Upcoming block.
7. Return to the homepage.
8. Click your Events link in the Main menu, and you see the blocks you just enabled, as show in Figure 11.56.

Figure 11.56   The Calendar events view live on your site

Cloning Views Explained

You've clicked Structure and then Views many times in this chapter. On that page, before you clicked Add New View, you might have noticed there were some views already created but not yet enabled.

These views are useful when learning different ways to configure Views. In this activity, you use an existing view to create an archive block for your Blog page, a common block on blogs.

Enable and Clone the View

1. Click Structure and then Views.
2. Click the Arrow next to Enable for the Archive View and click Clone. This is shown in Figure 11.57.

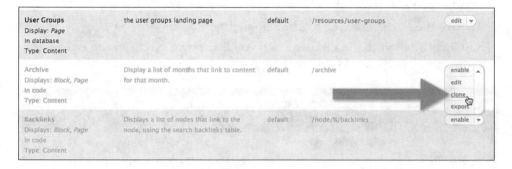

Figure 11.57   Click Clone

3. Name it **Blog Archive** and click Continue.
4. Click Add next to the Filter Criteria.
5. Search for type and select Content: Type.
6. Add and configure filters criteria.
7. Check the box for Blog Entry.
8. Click Apply.
9. Click the Block display and observe the filter was added to both the Page and Block display.
10. Return to the Page display.
11. Edit the Path under Page settings from archive to blogs/archive to keep you paths consistent.

12. Click No Menu under Page settings.

13. Choose Normal Menu Entry.

14. Enter Blog Archive as the Title.

15. Select Main menu as the Menu.

16. Click Apply and then Save in the top-right corner.

17. Go to Structure, Menus, and then List Links next to Main menu.

18. Place the Blog Archive link as a child menu link under Blogs.

Configure the Blog Archive Block

1. Go to Structure, Blocks, and click Configure next to View: Blog Archive.

2. Select the second sidebar for Marinelli (default theme).

3. On the Path tab, set the block to show only on blog*.

4. Save the block and return to the homepage.

5. Click Blogs in the Main menu and you'll see your block on the right side, as shown in Figure 11.58.

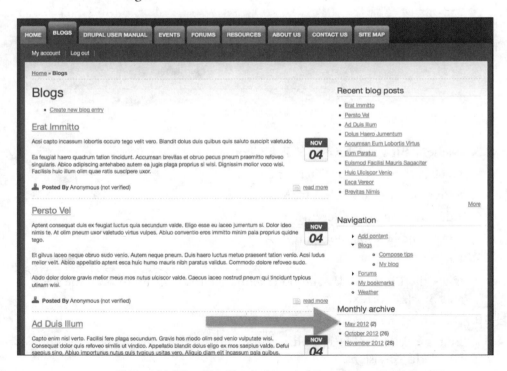

Figure 11.58   The Blog Archive view live on your site

6. Click the Blog Archive child link under Blogs, and you can see this same output in Page form.

Creating a Slideshow Explained

So far, you have displayed content in lists, tables, and even a grid. As your last task in this chapter, you create a slideshow using Views. You use a module called Views Slideshow, logically enough. You install that module but also need to upload some files via FTP.

Create an Image Style

1. Install Views Slideshow: http://drupal.org/project/views_slideshow.
2. Install Libraries: http://drupal.org/project/libraries.
3. Access your site's files as you did back in earlier chapters.
4. Browse to the /sites/all/ folder.

    You see a folder that you created earlier in the book called /libraries/.
5. Open the /libraries/ folder and create a folder called /jquery.cycle/.
6. Go to https://github.com/malsup/cycle/downloads.

    Download the jquery.cycle.all.latest.min.js file, as shown in Figure 11.59. You can spot this because it has many more downloads than any other file.

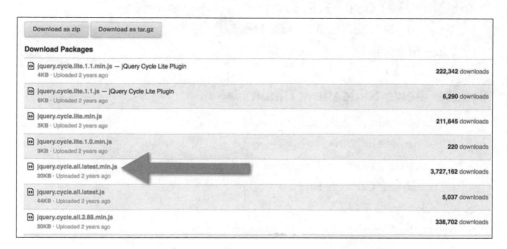

Figure 11.59   Download the JQuery cycle file

7. Rename this file to jquery.cycle.all.min.js.

8. Upload the file your /jquery.cycle/ directory.

   Check that the full path to this file is /sites/all/libraries/jquery.cycle/ jquery.cycle.all.min.js, as shown in Figure 11.60.

Figure 11.60   The location of the JQuery cycle file

9. Go the admin area of your Drupal site, and enable the Views Slideshow, Views Slideshow: Cycle and Libraries modules.

Create an Image Style

1. Click Configuration and then Image styles.

2. Click Add Style.

3. Style name: resize_650w_250h. (Note: This strategy will allow logos with different sizes to be the same width but be resized without becoming distorted.)

4. Select Scale from the Select a New Effect drop-down.

5. Type 650 for Width and 250 for Height.

6. Click Add Effect.

Create Views Slideshow Block

1. Click Structure, Views, and then Add New View.

2. View name: Slideshow.

3. Select Article Content Type from the Type drop-down.

4. Uncheck the Create a Page.

5. Check Create a Block.

6. Select the Slideshow from the Display format.

7. Click Continue & Edit.

8. Add the Image field to the display.

9. Uncheck the Create a Label box.

10. Set Image style to resize_650w_250h.

11. Set Link Image to Content.

12. Click Save.

Configure the Slideshow Block

1. Click Structures and then Blocks.

2. Locate View: Slideshow block and click Configure for that block.

3. Enter Drupal Articles Slideshow for the Block title.

4. Select the Over Node content region.

5. On the Path tab, set to show only on <front>.

6. Click Save Block.

   Return to the homepage and your slideshow will be on your homepage, as shown in Figure 11.61. The titles and images should be rotating automatically.

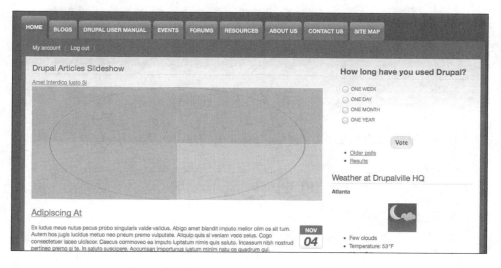

Figure 11.61   A slideshow created with Views

It is possible to think of several ways to improve this slideshow. The most obvious is that images could be designed specifically to fit in here. Neither scaling nor resizing offers a perfect solution. Scaling can lead to problems with fitting the image into the predefined height and width for the slideshow. Resizing can cause problems by squashing the image into the predefined height and width. Automatically manipulating your images can be useful, but there would be no substitute for creating images that were designed to be 650 pixels wide and 250 pixels high.

Here's what you can do if you want to go back and edit the slideshow settings:

1. Hover your mouse over the view so that the dotted line appears.

2. Click the cog in the top-right corner of the view.

3. Click Edit, as shown in Figure 11.62.

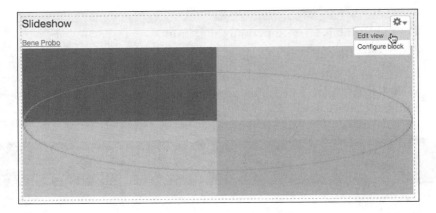

Figure 11.62   Click Edit view

4. Click the Settings link next to Slideshow, as shown in Figure 11.63.

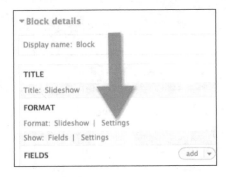

Figure 11.63   Click Settings

What's Next?

The beginning of the chapter mentioned that Views was the most popular and important module in Drupal. In this chapter, you've seen some of what Views can do. Views is so powerful and flexible that we could write an entire book on it.

However, when you start with Views, focus on the five DFFFS settings. Focus on these five decisions, and you can create many of the views that you want.

- **Display:** Do you want a page, a block, or an RSS feed?
- **Format:** Do you want a list, a grid, a table, a slideshow, or something else?
- **Fields:** Which fields do you want shown?
- **Filter:** Do you want to drill down and select only some content?
- **Sort:** How do you want to organize all the content shown?

At the end of this chapter, your site should look like Figure 11.64. As always, it's more important that you understand the lessons covered in this chapter than that your site exactly matches the image.

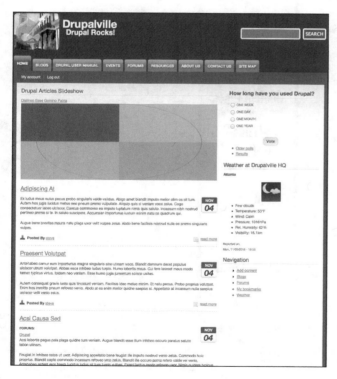

Figure 11.64   Your site at the end of this chapter

You now have only one main chapter left that will change the look of your site. In the previous chapter, you saw how to display and organize many content items.

Chapter 12, "Drupal Layout Modules Explained," talks about the layout of those individual content items. You see how to combine multiple elements such as content, blocks, and views to create a single page, such as a homepage. You can achieve both tasks by using design modules.

Before starting the next chapter, let's see how Views fits into our Drupal workflow shown in Figure 11.65:

- You had to create content types before you could use fields.
- You needed content on your site before we could successfully set up our themes and blocks.
- You had to install a theme before you could place blocks.
- You needed content before you could use Views. You also needed to have your theme before you could place the Views that we created.

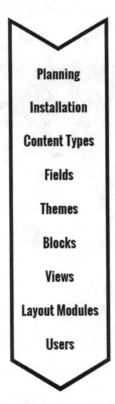

Figure 11.65   Our Drupal site workflow

Drupal Layout Modules Explained

This chapter is the end result of nearly everything covered in the book so far. This chapter covers almost everything you've seen so far, from content, fields, and modules to themes, blocks, and views. You see how to take all those elements and lay them out on the page in the way that you want.

You focus on two modules—Display Suite and Panels—which enable you to control the layout of your Drupal content. You need these modules because there is a limit to the layout options provided by themes. Display Suite enables you to accurately control the layout of individual content items. Panels enables you to combine different elements from across your site.

This chapter is the last one in which you focus on building and designing your site. After this, you focus on how to manage and maintain your site.

After reading this chapter, you should be able to

- Use Display Suite to control the layout of existing content.

- Use Panels to create new pages.

- Understand how the Drupal Workflow takes you logically, step-by-step from Chapter 5, "Drupal Content Explained," to the end of this chapter.

Display Suite Explained

The first module that you tackle in this chapter is Display Suite. What is the purpose of Display Suite? Well, look at your current content. Figure 12.1 shows a site listing. All the details on the page from the title to the comments display vertically.

Figure 12.1   An example of your Sites content type

The same is true of your other content types: They all have the same top-to-bottom layout. Figure 12.2 shows an example from your Companies content type.

In the first part of the chapter, you install Display Suite and redesign the layout of this content.

Installing Display Suite

Use the FITS workflow to get Display Suite running on your site:

1. Go to http://drupal.org/project/ds and copy the link for the Drupal 7 version of Display Suite.

2. To install, go back to your site and install Display Suite.

3. To turn on Display Suite, you need to check only the Display Suite and Display Suite UI boxes.

4. To set up, read on because that's our next step.

Figure 12.2   An example of your Companies content type

Using Display Suite

Display Suite greatly enhances the Manage Display screen that you have seen in earlier chapters:

1. Go to Structure, Content types, and then click Manage Display next to Sites.

   This screen should look exactly the same as it did in earlier chapters, except for two extra tabs at the bottom of the screen.

2. Click the Select a Layout drop-down, as shown in Figure 12.3.

   In this drop-down you can see a variety of layout options, as shown in Figure 12.4. You can choose from a variety of one to four column layouts.

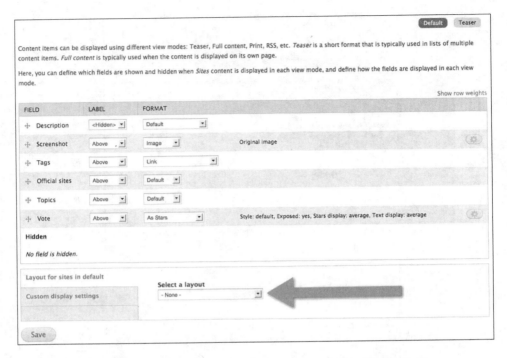

Figure 12.3   The Select a Layout options provided by Display Suite

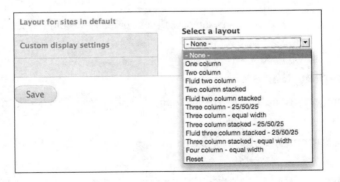

Figure 12.4   The Select a layout drop-down

3. Choose the Two Column option and you see a preview, as shown in Figure 12.5. Choose the other options one-by-one to get a preview of all the layout options.

4. Choose the Two Column option again.

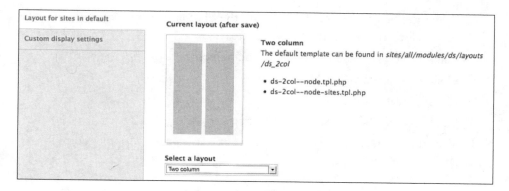

Figure 12.5   A two-column layout preview in Display Suite

5. Click Save.

You now see that the page changes substantially. One of the most important changes is that different areas have now appeared in the list of field. You can see Left, Right, and Disabled areas, as shown in Figure 12.6.

FIELD	REGION	LABEL	FORMAT		
Left					
✛ Description	Left	‹Hidden›	Default		
✛ Screenshot	Left	Above	Image	Original image	⚙
✛ Tags	Left	Above	Link #		
✛ Official sites	Left	Above	Default		
✛ Topics	Left	Above	Default		
✛ Vote	Left	Above	As Stars	Style: default, Exposed: yes, Stars display: average, Text display: average	⚙
Right					
No fields are displayed in this region					
Disabled					
✛ Post date	Disabled	‹Hidden›	Long		
✛ Submitted by	Disabled	‹Hidden›	Time ago		
✛ User picture	Disabled	‹Hidden›	Thumbnail		
✛ Author	Disabled	‹Hidden›	Author		
✛ Read more	Disabled	‹Hidden›	Default		
✛ Links	Disabled	‹Hidden›	Default		
✛ Comments	Disabled	‹Hidden›	Default		
✛ Title	Disabled	‹Hidden›	Default		

Figure 12.6   Three new areas in your manage display screen

6. Select the Screenshot field, and using the drag-and-drop feature that you've seen before, move it into the Right area.

7. Click the cog on the right side of the Screenshot row.

8. Change Image style to Medium.

9. Click Update.

10. Click Save at the bottom of your screen.

11. Visit the homepage of your site and search for DrupalModules.com. It should now look like Figure 12.7.

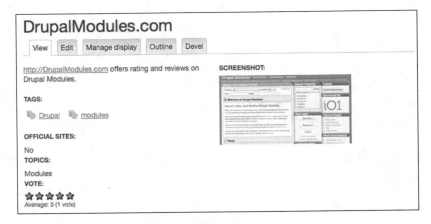

Figure 12.7   The DrupalModules.com screen, after modification by Display Suite

You can do several additional things to tidy up this page. For example, the labels take up too much space, and you're missing your comments area.

Fortunately, it's now easy to access your Display Suite options because there's a Manage Display tab over the content, as shown in Figure 12.7:

1. Click the Manage Display tab.

2. At the bottom of the screen, in the Layout for Sites in Default Area, change Two Column to Two Column Stacked.

3. Click Save.

4. Click Save again, without changing the default settings for moving fields.

5. In the Tags row, set the Label option to Inline.

6. In the Official Sites row, set the Label option to Inline.

7. In the Topics row, set the Label option to Inline.

8. In the Vote row, set the Label option to Inline.

9. In the Screenshot set the Label option to Hidden.

10. Move the Comments field out of the Disabled area and into the Footer area.

11. Check that your fields now look like Figure 12.8.

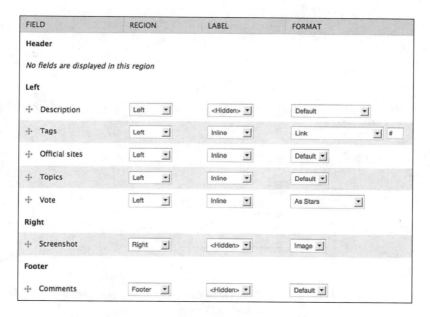

Figure 12.8   The Site content type display, modified by Display Suite

12. Click Save.

13. View your DrupalModules.com content again, which should look like Figure 12.9.

Now repeat that process with another content type:

1. Go to Structure, Content types, and then click manage display next to Companies.

2. Under Layout for companies in default, choose the Three Column Stacked – Equal Width option.

3. Click Save.

4. Move the Logo field to the Right column and hide the label.

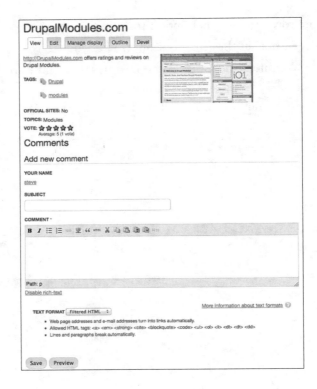

Figure 12.9   The DrupalModules.com content after being
modified by Display Suite

5. Change the Image style for the Logo field to scale_90w. Don't forget to click Update.

6. Move the Tags field to the Middle column and place the label inline.

7. Move the Services field to the Middle column and place the label inline.

8. Move the Link field to the Middle column and place the label inline.

9. Move the Languages Spoken field to the Middle column and place the label inline.

10. Move the Comments field into the Footer area.

11. Check that your fields now look like Figure 12.10.

12. Click Save.

13. View a company listing on your site, and it will look like Figure 12.11.

FIELD	REGION	LABEL	FORMAT
Header			
No fields are displayed in this region			
Left			
⊹ Description	Left ▾	<Hidden> ▾	Default ▾
Middle			
⊹ Tags	Middle ▾	Inline ▾	Link ▾ #
⊹ Services	Middle ▾	Inline ▾	Default ▾ #
⊹ Link	Middle ▾	Inline ▾	Title, as link (default) ▾
⊹ Languages Spoken	Middle ▾	Inline ▾	Link ▾ #
Right			
⊹ Logo	Right ▾	<Hidden> ▾	Image ▾
Footer			
⊹ Comments	Footer ▾	<Hidden> ▾	Default ▾

Figure 12.10   The Companies content type display, modified by Display Suite

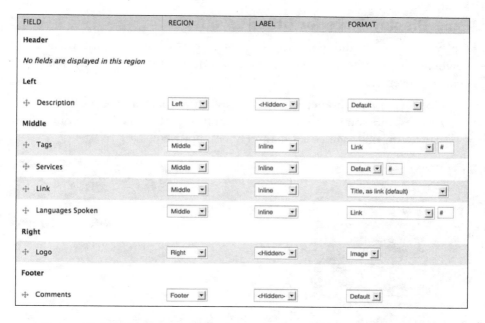

Figure 12.11   The Phase 2 Technology content, after being modified by Display Suite

Using Display Suite for Other Layouts

Display Suite can modify your normal content pages, but it can also be used elsewhere on your site. For example, you may decide that your Articles page needs improvement:

1. Go to your site's homepage, Resources in the Main menu, and then Articles, and you see a screen, as shown in Figure 12.12. The layout of the articles on this page could definitely be improved.

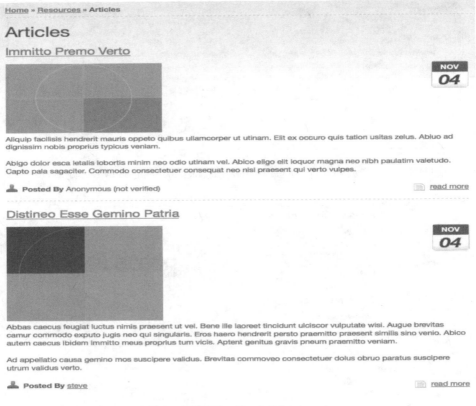

Figure 12.12   The Articles layout

2. Go to Structure, Content types, and click Manage Display next to Article.
3. Click the Teaser button in the top-right corner of the screen, as shown in Figure 12.13.
4. Under Layout for article in teaser, choose the Fluid two-column stacked option.

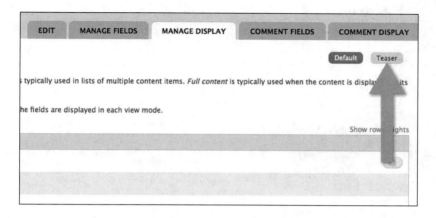

Figure 12.13   The Teaser display option

5. Click Save.

6. Change the Image style for the Logo field to scale_90w. Don't forget to click Update.

7. Move the Body field to the Right column.

8. Move the Tags field to the Disabled area.

9. Move the Title field to the Header area.

10. Move the Post Date field to the Header area.

11. Move the Read More field to the Footer area.

12. Check that your fields now look like Figure 12.14.

13. Click Save.

FIELD	REGION	LABEL	FORMAT
Header			
✛ Title	Header ▾	<Hidden> ▾	Default ▾
✛ Post date	Header ▾	<Hidden> ▾	Long ▾
Left			
✛ Image	Left ▾	<Hidden> ▾	Image ▾
Right			
✛ Body	Right ▾	<Hidden> ▾	Summary or trimmed ▾
Footer			
✛ Read more	Footer ▾	<Hidden> ▾	Default ▾

Figure 12.14   The Article content type display, modified by Display Suite

14. View the Articles page on your site. It should look like Figure 12.15.

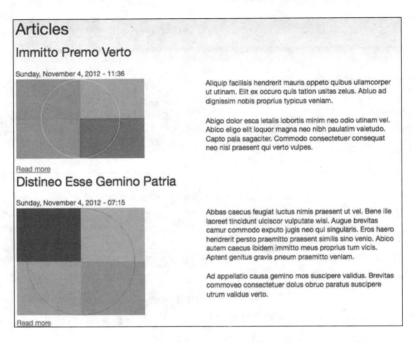

Figure 12.15   The Articles blog, modified by Display Suite

You can also modify other displays beyond the Teaser. If you're in the manage display screen, click Custom Display Settings, and you'll see that you can alter the layout of other displays, as shown in Figure 12.16.

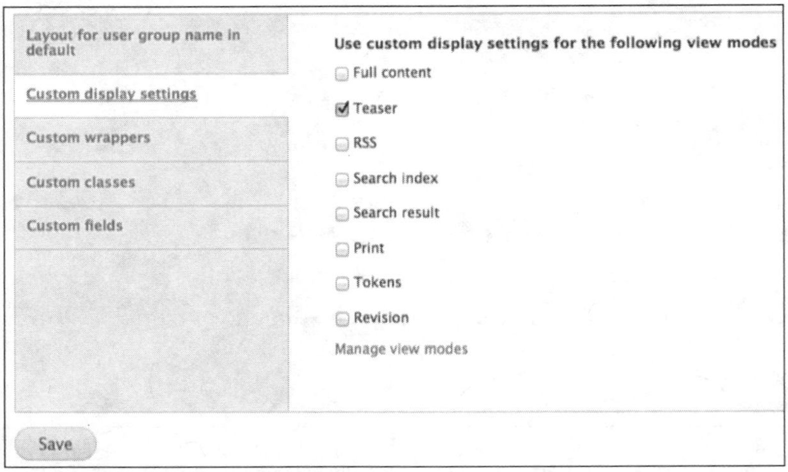

Figure 12.16   Custom display settings, provided by Display Suite

Advanced Display Suite

If Display Suite did only what we've seen so far, it would be a useful module. However, it goes much further and has many more features than are covered in this book. In this section, you get a glimpse into what else is possible with Display Suite.

Search for and find the Washington D.C. Drupal content item on your site. It currently looks like Figure 12.17.

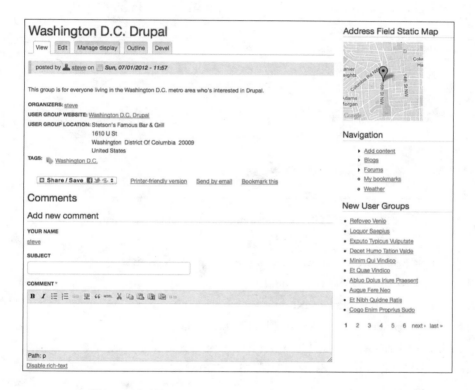

Figure 12.17   The Washington D.C. Drupal content item

You can move the map inside the main area so that it's part of the content, rather than isolated in the right column:

1. Click the Manage display tab at the top of the content.

2. Under Layout for user group name in default, choose the two-column stacked option.

3. Click Save.

4. Move the Description field to the Left column.

5. Move the Organizers field to the Left column.

6. Move the User Group Website field to the Left column.

7. Move the User Group Location field to the Right column.

8. Move the Tags field to the Disabled area.

9. Move the Comments field to the Footer area.

10. Scroll down to the Custom Fields area, as shown in Figure 12.18.

Figure 12.18   The Custom fields area in Display Suite

11. Click Add a Block field and you see a pop-up screen.

12. Enter **Map** into the Label field.

13. Under Entities, choose Node.

14. Under Block, choose Address Field Static Map.

15. Under Layout, choose Show Only Block Content.

16. Check that your fields now look like Figure 12.19.

17. Click Save.

18. Move the new Maps field into the Right column.

19. Make sure the Maps field is ordered underneath the User Group Location field.

20. Click Save.

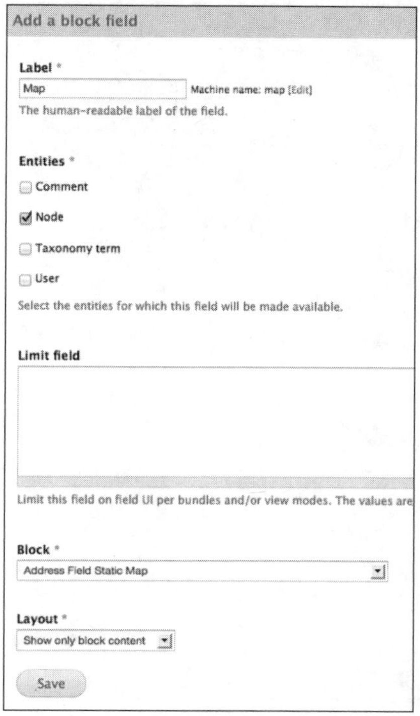

Figure 12.19   Adding a block into a Display Suite layout

21. View your Washington D.C. Drupal content again and it should look like Figure 12.20.

To finish setting up your user group content type, you can now unpublish the Address Field Static Map block:

1. Go to Structure and then Blocks.

2. Move the block to the Disabled area by selecting None.

3. Click Save blocks.

Now, see one more example from Display Suite. The beginning of this chapter mentioned that you were going to cover almost everything you've seen so for, from content, fields, and modules to themes, blocks, and views. As you go through this final Display Suite example, see if you can pinpoint all those elements from earlier in this book. Go and find the DrupalCon Munich content item. It should look like Figure 12.21.

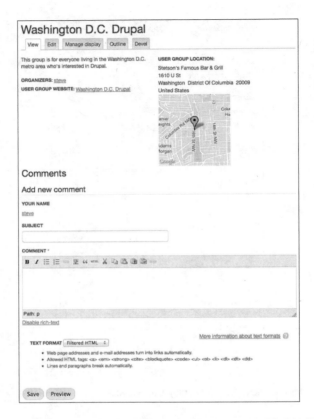

Figure 12.20   The Washington D.C. Drupal content item, modified by Display Suite

Do the following:

1. Click the Manage display tab at the top of the content.

2. Under Layout for Events in default, choose the Three-Column Stacked – Equal Width option.

3. Click Save.

4. Move the Description field to the Left column.

5. Move the Event Logo field to the Left column and hide the label.

6. Change the Image style for the Event Logo field to thumbnail. Don't forget to click Update.

7. Move the Event Price field to the Middle column.

8. Move the Event Date field to the Middle column.

9. Move the Registration field to the Middle column.

Figure 12.21   The DrupalCon Munich content item

10. Move the Sponsors field to the Middle column.

11. Click the cog in the Sponsors row, and check the box Link label to the referenced entity. Don't forget to click Update.

12. Move the Tags field to the Middle column.

13. Move the Comments field to the Footer column.

14. Move all remaining fields to the Disabled area.

Now add some more Advanced Display Suite features:

1. Go to Custom fields and click Add a block field.

2. Set the Label to Other Upcoming Events.

3. Check Node in the Entities box.

4. Choose View: Events: Upcoming in the Block option.

5. Click Save.

6. Move the Other Upcoming Events field to the Right column. Make sure that the label is set to Above.

Now repeat that process you just did to add social bookmarks to this page:

1. Go to Custom fields and click the Add a Block field.

2. Set the Label to Social Bookmarks.

3. Check Node in the Entities box.

4. Choose AddtoAny buttons in the Block option.

5. Set the Layout to Show only block content.

6. Move the Social bookmarks field to the Right column. Make sure that the label is set to Above.

7. Click Save and visit your DrupalCon Munich content item. It should look like Figure 12.22.

Figure 12.22   The DrupalCon Munich content item
after modification by Display Suite

Now see what else is available to use when you create pages with Display Suite:

1. Click Manage Display to go back to the Display Suite screen.

2. Go to Custom fields and click Add a Dynamic field.

3. Set the Label to Extras.

4. Check Node in the Entities box.

5. Click Save.

6. Move the Extras field to the Footer column.

7. Click the cog in the Extras row, and you can see an area open up, as shown in Figure 12.23.

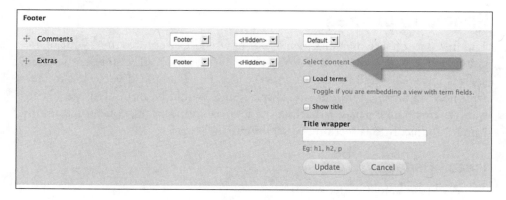

Figure 12.23   Setting up a Dynamic field

8. Click the Select content link, as shown in Figure 12.23.

9. You now see a pop-up box like the one shown in Figure 12.24.

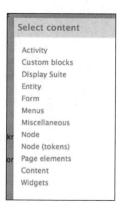

Figure 12.24   Dynamic field options

The options on the left side in Figure 12.23 contain almost everything you created in the book so far, plus much more. All these items are available to be placed into your Events pages:

1. Click through all the items in the left column, from Activity down to Widgets, to see what's available to you.

2. Experiment by adding some of these items to your content.

3. If you make a mistake with any item, you can always modify the field by clicking the cog in the Extras row and clicking Edit Content.

4. You can also manage these custom fields by going to Structure, Display Suite, and then clicking Fields in the top-right corner.

Panels Explained

The first part of this chapter showed you how you can control the layout of individual content items with Display Suite. However, Display Suite has its limits. It is not well suited for creating new pages. For example, if you want to create a new homepage for your site, Display Suite would be of limited use. If you want to create new pages, rather than redesign existing pages, you should use the Panels module. In this section, we see how Panels works.

Install Panels

To install panels, follow these steps:

1. Find the link for Panels from http://drupal.org/project/panels.

2. To install use the link to install Panels into your site.

3. To turn on, in the Panels area, check the boxes for Panel nodes, Panels, and Panels In-Place Editor. Also, in the Chaos Tools suite area, check the boxes for Page Manager and Views content panes.

4. To set up go to Structure and then Panels.

Panels User Interface

Now that you're in the main Panels screen, what you see should look like Figure 12.25.

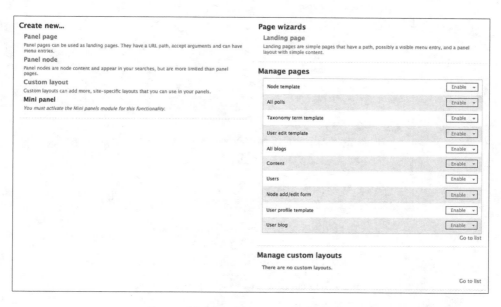

Figure 12.25   The main Panels screen

Do the following:

1. Click Panel page on the top of the left side.
2. Enter homepage for the Administrative title.
3. Enter homepage for the path.
4. Check the box that says Make This Your Site Home Page. You screen should look like Figure 12.26.
5. Click Continue.
6. Choose Columns: 2 and Two column stacked, as shown in Figure 12.27.

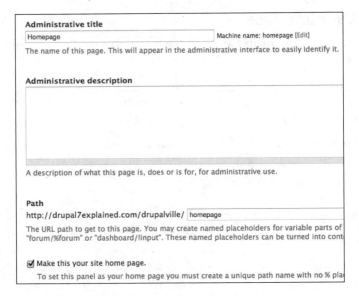

Figure 12.26   Creating a new Panel

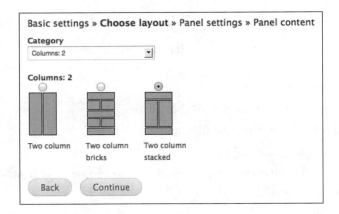

Figure 12.27   Choosing a Panels layout

7. Click Continue.

8. Click Continue again.

9. You see a screen like the one shown in Figure 12.28. Earlier, you chose a two-column stacked layout, and that's what you see now.

Basic settings » Choose layout » Panel settings » **Panel content**
▼ Display settings

Title type
[Manually set ▼]

Title
[   ]

The title of this panel. If left blank, a default title may be used. Set to No Title if you want the title to actually be blank.

⚙	Top
⚙ Left side	⚙ Right side
⚙	Bottom

(Back) (Finish)

Figure 12.28   A new potential homepage layout

Our next task with Panels is similar to one we completed earlier in this book with Display Suite. You're going to use Panels in a way that allows you select from all the content that you previously created in this book:

1. Click the cog in the top-left corner of the Top area, as shown in Figure 12.29.

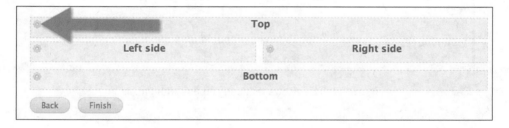

Figure 12.29   Adding content to the Top region

2. Click Add content.
3. You can now see a pop-up, as shown in Figure 12.30. This pop-up contains a list of options similar to Display Suite.
4. Click Views, and you see a screen like Figure 12.31.
5. Click Slideshow.
6. Click Continue.
7. Check the Override title box.

Figure 12.30   Content options provided by Panel

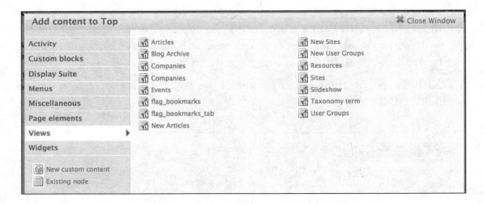

Figure 12.31   Views that you can use with Panels

8. Click Finish. You'll now see that the slideshow is in the Top region, as shown in Figure 12.32.

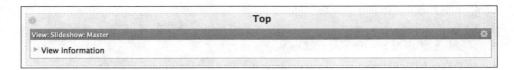

Figure 12.32   The slideshow, added to the Panels layout

9. Click the cog in the top-left corner of the Left area.

10. Click Views.

11. Click New User Groups.

12. Click Continue.

13. Click Finish.

14. Click the cog in the top-left corner of the Right area.

15. Click Views.

16. Click New Sites.

17. Click Continue.

18. Click Finish.

19. Click the cog in the top-left corner of the Bottom area.

20. Click Existing node.

21. Type **About Us** into the area named Enter the Title or NID of a Node.

22. Click Finish. Your screen will now look like Figure 12.33.

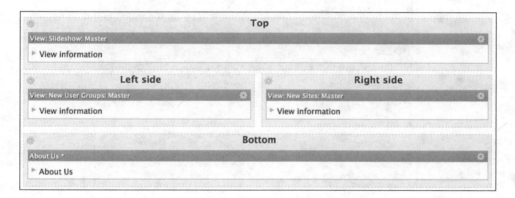

Figure 12.33   Content added to your Panels layout

23. Click Finish.

24. Set the Title type drop-down to No Title, as shown in Figure 12.34.

25. Click Update and save.

Visit your site's homepage. It should now look like Figure 12.35.

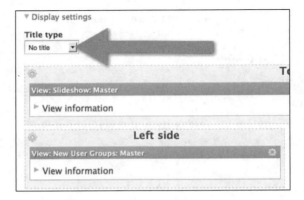

Figure 12.34   Removing the title from the Panel

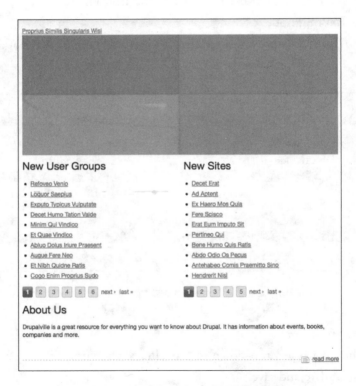

Figure 12.35   Your homepage, redesigned with Panels

If you want to make any modifications to this Panel, do what you did with Views: Hover over the homepage and click the Edit Panel in the top-right corner, as shown in Figure 12.36.

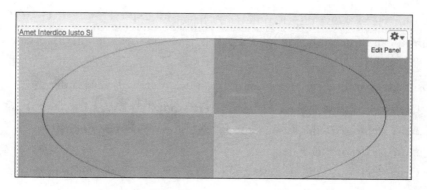

Figure 12.36   Editing the homepage panel

As with Fields, Modules, Themes, Views, and Display Suite, there is much more to Panels than covered in this book.

Panels can do everything that Display Suite did in the first part of this chapter. The main reason Display Suite is recommended for those tasks is that it's a little easier to use.

The recommendation is to use Display Suite to modify existing pages and to use Panels for creating new pages.

The Drupal Workflow Explained

What you've seen in this chapter is that layout modules, such as Display Suite, are the culmination of everything you've done so far. It's also a prefect example of the Drupal workflow that you can see in Figure 12.37.

Now think back to your DrupalCon Munich page as an example.

What did you do so that the DrupalCon Munich content item can appear as it does now?

1. **Create a content type:** Events.
2. **Add fields:** Event Logo, Event Price, Sponsors, and so on.
3. **Add a theme:** Marinelli
4. **Create views:** Upcoming Events.
5. **Use layout modules:** Display Suite.

You took all those five steps, in that particular order, to create this content item. If you tried to skip any steps or do them in a different order, it wouldn't have worked:

- You can't add fields before you've created a content type.
- You can't add content until you have the correct content types and field.

- Your views won't display unless you have content.
- You can't use layout modules if you haven't any fields, content, or views available.

To take another example: What did you do to create your homepage?

1. **Create content types:** Articles, User Groups, and Sites.
2. **Add fields:** Articles, User Groups, and Sites all needed fields.
3. **Add a theme:** Marinelli
4. **Create views:** The slideshow, plus New User Groups, and New Sites.
5. **Use layout modules:** Panels.

This is a workflow that is tailored specifically for Drupal. This workflow wouldn't apply if you built websites with other software, for example, if you build websites with Dreamweaver, WordPress, Joomla, or other software.

This does not mean that Drupal is better than these other softwares. However, this does mean that Drupal is different. Hopefully, this workflow, shown in Figure 12.37, helps you realize how Drupal is different and how you should approach using it.

Figure 12.37   The Drupal workflow

If you create your Drupal sites using this workflow, you can build better sites, quicker and with fewer mistakes and less frustration.

At the end of this chapter, your site now looks like Figure 12.38. As always, it's not important if your site doesn't match this exactly. What's important is that you understand the concepts covered.

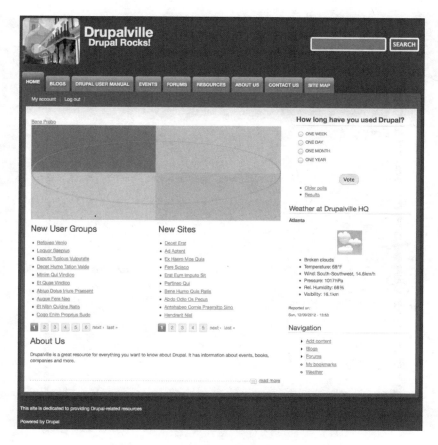

Figure 12.38   Your site at the end of this chapter

What's Next?

You completed all the visible changes to your site. However, there is one more important step in the Drupal Workflow that you haven't addressed yet: users. You have been viewing the site as administrators. What about the visitors? What about the people who view, create, and edit the content on your site?

Click Log Out in the top-right corner of your screen on the black bar. You see that your site now looks like Figure 12.39. You also see several differences between this view and the one in Figure 12.38.

In Chapter 13, "Drupal Users Explained," you see why those differences exist and how you can manage them successfully.

Figure 12.39   Your site at the end of this chapter as visitors see it

Drupal Users Explained

The first 12 chapters of this book focused on the content and features of your Drupal site. Now you look at the people who will read that content and use those features.

This chapter shows you how to control who can do what on your site. Who can create, delete, and edit content? Who can upload modules and themes? Who can modify menus and blocks?

You also see how to make user accounts more interesting. You do this by allowing users to add more information about them. Here are the things you'll be able to do after completing this chapter:

- Create roles.
- Assign permissions to roles.
- Create new users.
- Test users' accounts.
- Expand user profiles.
- Modify the registration form.

Drupal Permissions Explained

Throughout this book, you have been logged in as a site administrator. This is the most powerful user account on the site. As a site administrator you can go anywhere, do anything, and change anything. You can't remove the permissions associated with this, and this account is also difficult to delete.

However, you can probably imagine that few of your site's users can be trusted to be administrators. You will now see how to control what your users can and cannot do.

First Example

Start with the example of a Blogger. A Blogger will be a role that you can assign users to. If users are in this role, all they can do is write blog posts. There are four steps to make sure a user account is set up correctly: Roles, Permissions, Users, and Testing. Following are those four steps.

Step 1: Add a Role

1. Click People on the black menu bar and then the Permissions tab (see Figure 13.1).

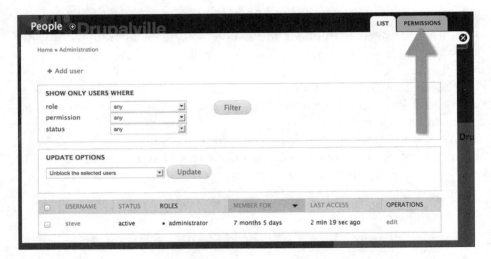

Figure 13.1   The Permissions tab

2. Click Roles, as shown in Figure 13.2.

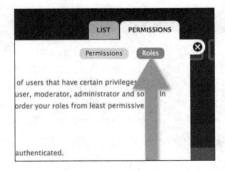

Figure 13.2   The Roles tab

You're now going to see three roles set up by default: Anonymous user, Authenticated user, and Administrator. Now take a brief look at each default role, as shown in Figure 13.3:

- **Anonymous:** Visitors to your site who are not logged into your site are considered anonymous.

- **Authenticated:** Anyone who has an account on your site and logs in is authenticated. The Authenticated role also serves as the minimum set of permissions that is given to all logged in users.

- **Administrator:** Users assigned the administrator role can do everything on the site. This is similar to the main account that you have been using throughout this book.

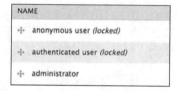

Figure 13.3   The three default user roles

Now create a fourth Role: Blogger.

3. Type **Blogger** into field under the three default roles, as shown in Figure 13.4.

4. Click Add Role.

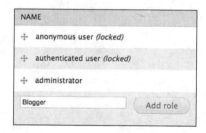

Figure 13.4   Adding a new user role

Step 2: Set Permissions

Now that the Blogger role has been created, you need to decide what users in the Blogger role can and can't do.

Click the smaller Permissions tab, as shown in Figure 13.5.

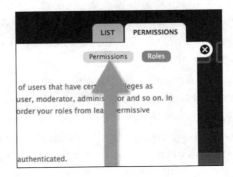

Figure 13.5   The smaller Permissions tab

You can now see a long list of check boxes with permissions for all the modules on your site, as shown in Figure 13.6.

PERMISSION	ANONYMOUS USER	AUTHENTICATED USER	ADMINISTRATOR	BLOGGER
AddToAny				
Administer addtoany	☐	☐	☑	☐
Address Field Static Map Block				
Administer Address Field Static Map Change Google Static Map and other settings for this block.	☐	☐	☑	☐
Block				
Administer blocks	☐	☐	☑	☐
Book				
Administer book outlines	☐	☐	☑	☐
Create new books	☐	☐	☑	☐
Add content and child pages to books	☐	☐	☑	☐
View printer-friendly books View a book page and all of its sub-pages as a single document for ease of printing. Can be performance heavy.	☐	☐	☑	☐
Comment				
Administer comments and comment settings	☐	☐	☑	☐
View comments	☑	☑	☑	☑

Figure 13.6   The Permissions screen

On the left side of the list, you can see all the modules and the permissions they contain. The modules are all ordered alphabetically. Across the top of the list, you see the four roles that you have set up.

The permissions for the three default roles are already set. You can also see that some permissions for the Blogger role, such as those shown in Figure 13.7, are already set. This is because the Authenticated user account serves as a minimum set of permissions. This makes it easier to ensure that all user accounts have access to at least some functionality.

Comment				
Administer comments and comment settings	☐	☐	☑	☐
View comments	☑	☑	☑	☑
Post comments	☐	☑	☑	☑
Skip comment approval	☐	☑	☑	☑
Edit own comments	☐	☐	☑	☐

Figure 13.7   Comment permissions passed from the Authenticated user role to the Blogger role

You need to allow users in the Blogger role to create Blog posts. So, scroll down until you find the Node module. Remember that Node is Drupal's geeky word for content.

At the top of the Node module area, you see some general permissions, as shown in Figure 13.8.

You should be interested in the permissions specific to content types. Scroll a little further to find the Blog entry permissions, as shown in Figure 13.9. You can see that each content type has five permissions:

- Create New Content
- Edit Own Content
- Edit Any Content
- Delete Own Content
- Delete Any Content

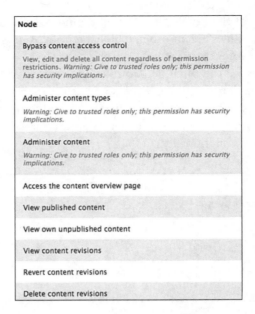

Figure 13.8   Some important Node module permissions

Figure 13.9   Permissions for the Blog entry content type

For your Bloggers, you want them to manage their own content, but not other people's content. So you allow them to create, edit, and delete their own content only as follows (shown in Figure 13.10):

- Check the Blog Entry: Create New Content Box in the Blogger Column
- Check the Blog Entry: Edit Own Content Box in the Blogger Column
- Check the Blog Entry: Delete Own Content Box in the Blogger Column
- Click Save Permissions at the Bottom of the Screen

PERMISSION	ANONYMOUS USER	AUTHENTICATED USER	ADMINISTRATOR	BLOGGER
Delete content revisions	☐	☐	☑	☐
Blog entry: Create new content	☐	☐	☐	☑
Blog entry: Edit own content	☐	☐	☐	☑
Blog entry: Edit any content	☐	☐	☐	☐
Blog entry: Delete own content	☐	☐	☐	☑
Blog entry: Delete any content	☐	☐	☐	☐

Figure 13.10   Permissions for the Blog entry content type for the Blogger role

Step 3: Create a User

Now set up an actual user account for a Blogger:

1. Click the List tab at the top of the screen.
2. Click Add user in the top-left corner.
   - **Username:** blogger
   - **E-mail address:** blogger@example.com
   - **Password:** blogger. You can set this to something more difficult if you want. Drupal warns you that this is a weak password.
   - **Roles**: Check the Blogger box.
3. Make sure your settings look like Figure 13.11.
4. Click Create New Account.

Step 4: Test the User Account

The fourth and final step is crucial. Permissions are a vital part of your site's security, and if you don't test your permissions, you could easily allow some users to do things that can compromise your site.

Following is a basic method for testing. You can use this method if you know the user's password:

1. Click logout on the black admin bar.
2. Log in via the User Login block. You can use the blogger account created in the previous Step 3.
3. Look in the Navigation block, as shown in Figure 13.12.
4. Click Add Content, and then Blog entry to go to the Create Blog entry screen, as shown in Figure 13.13.

Figure 13.11   Creating a new user account

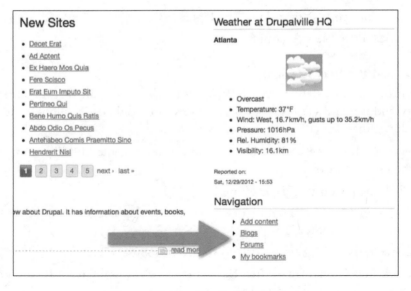

Figure 13.12   The Navigation block

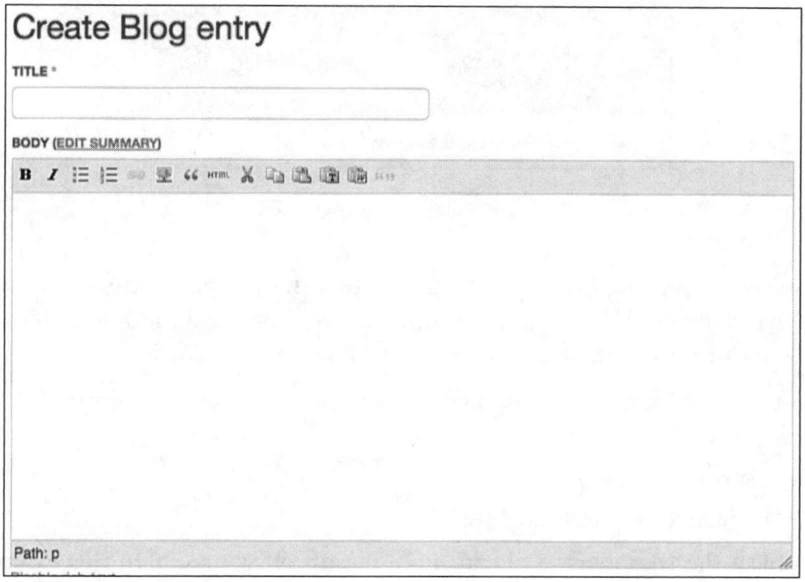

Create Blog entry

TITLE *

BODY (EDIT SUMMARY)

Path: p

Figure 13.13   The Create Blog entry screen

As you can see, the Blog entry is the only option for this user to create content. You can confirm this by looking at the expanded Navigation block, as shown in Figure 13.14.

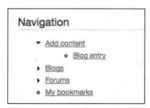

Figure 13.14   The expanded Navigation block

Notice that the black admin bar has disappeared, but logged-in users do have some simple account links under the Main menu, as shown in Figure 13.15. This is the User menu that you saw in Chapter 8, "Drupal Menus Explained."

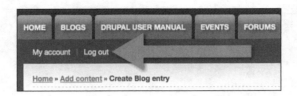

Figure 13.15   The User menu

However, there are limitations to this testing. It's neither feasible nor safe to know what your users' passwords are. Instead, you can use a module called Masquerade to easily test any user account. Here's how it works:

1. Install the Masquerade module from http://drupal.org/project/masquerade.

2. Enable the module.

3. Go to Structure and then Block.

4. Publish the Masquerade block into a region on your site. In this example, choose the Second Sidebar region.

5. Visit the front of your site, and you see the block published and showing a search box.

6. Type in the name of the user you want to test. In this example, type **blogger**, as shown in Figure 13.16.

7. Click Go.

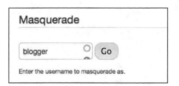

Figure 13.16   The Masquerade block

The Masquerade block now changes and shows the message that you see in Figure 13.17. Don't worry: By default, this block appears only for administrators.

You can now browse the site and see exactly what the blogger user would see. Simply click the switch back link in the Masquerade block, and you'll be back at the administrator account.

Figure 13.17   The Masquerade block in active use

Second Example

Now that you finished creating the Blogger account, go through that process once more. In this second example, create a slightly more powerful role. This role is the Company Editor. He can manage all the submissions to the Companies content type.

Step 1: Add a Role

1. Click People on the black menu bar and then on the Permissions tab.
2. Type **Company Editor** into the field under the four existing roles.
3. Click Add role.

Step 2: Set Permissions

1. Click the smaller Permissions tab.
2. Scroll down until you find the Node module.
3. Find the Companies content type permissions area.
4. Check the Companies entry: Create a new content box in the Company Editor column.
5. Check the Companies entry: Edit your own content box in the Company Editor column.
6. Check the Companies entry: Edit any content box in the Company Editor column.
7. Check the Companies entry: Delete your own content box in the Company Editor column.
8. Check the Companies entry: Delete any content box in the Company Editor column.
9. Click Save Permissions at the bottom of the screen.

Step 3: Add a User

1. Click the List tab at the top of the screen.
2. Click Add user in the top-left corner.
   - Username: **companyeditor**.
   - E-mail address: **companyeditor@example.com**.
   - Password: **companyeditor**. Again, you can set this to something more difficult if you want. Drupal warns you that this is a weak password.
   - Roles: Check the Company Editor box.
3. Click Create new account.

Step 4: Test the User Account

1. Visit the front page of your site.
2. Use the Masquerade module to see the site as the companyeditor user.
3. Go to Resources and then Companies on the Main menu.
4. Access any company listing, and you can edit or delete the listing.
5. Look in the Navigation block, and the only content you can create is in the Companies content type.

Note that Drupal takes a specific stance on security: Permissions are usually denied by default. Drupal does this to make sure that your site is as safe as possible. However, it does lead to extra clicking every time you set up a new feature. Every time you add a new content type or a new module, you need to check the permissions. Remember in early chapters when discussing the FITS workflow for adding new modules: Part of the final step in that workflow (Set Up) is to go to the People tab and set up the permissions for the module.

One common source of confusion in this regard is the Search module. You need to go to the People menu link and expressly give different roles permission to use search on your site.

Third Example

Now see one final example of user permissions, this time using more modules, instead of just the Node module.

You set up a role called Moderator. People in this role can moderate comments and forum posts. These people help to make sure that your site is a pleasant and spam-free destination.

Step 1: Add a Role

1. Click People on the black menu bar and then on the Permissions tab.
2. Type **Moderator** into the field under the five existing roles.
3. Click Add role.

Step 2: Set Permissions

1. Click the smaller Permissions tab.
2. Scroll down until you find the Comment module.
3. Check the Administer Comments and Comment Settings box in the Moderator column.
4. Scroll down until you find the Forum module.
5. Check the Administer Forums box in the Moderator column. This allows the Moderator to rearrange the forum boards if needed.
6. Scroll down until you find the Node module.
7. Check all five boxes for the Forum Topic Content Type in the Moderator column.
8. Scroll down until you find the User module.
9. Check the Administer Users box in the Moderator column. This allows the Moderator to ban users who spam or post inappropriate content.
10. Check the View User Profiles box in the Moderator column.
11. Click Save Permissions at the bottom of the screen.

Step 3: Add a User

1. Click the List tab at the top of the screen.
2. Click Add User in the top-left corner.
   - Username: **moderator**
   - E-mail address: **moderator@example.com**
   - Password: **moderator** (As before, you can set this to something more difficult if you want.)
   - Roles: Check the Moderator box.
3. Click Create new account.

Step 4: Test the User Account

1. Visit the front page of your site.

2. Use the Masquerade module to see the site as the moderator user.

3. Go to Forums on the Main menu.

4. Access any forum topic, and you can edit or delete the topic.

   If there is a comment on a topic, you can moderate it using the delete and edit links, as shown in Figure 13.18.

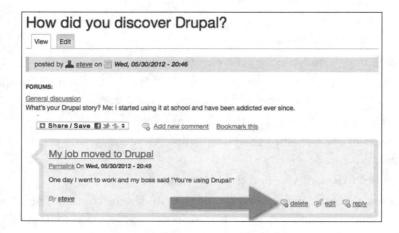

Figure 13.18   Moderating Drupal comments

5. Click any user's account name, which will be linked as shown in Figure 13.19.

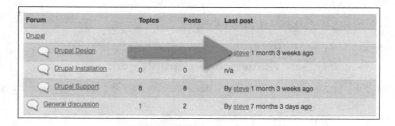

Figure 13.19   A link to a Drupal user profile

You can see the user's profile, as shown in Figure 13.20.

6. Click the Edit tab.

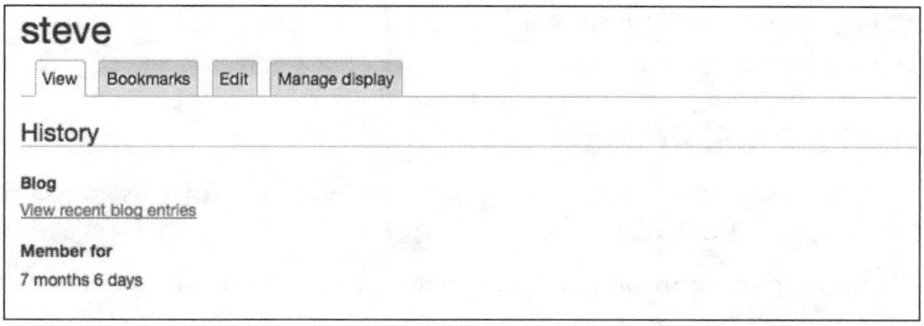

Figure 13.20   A Drupal user profile

If you think the user needs moderating, you can now set the user's status to blocked, as shown in Figure 13.21. Note: Do not try this with your own administrator account!

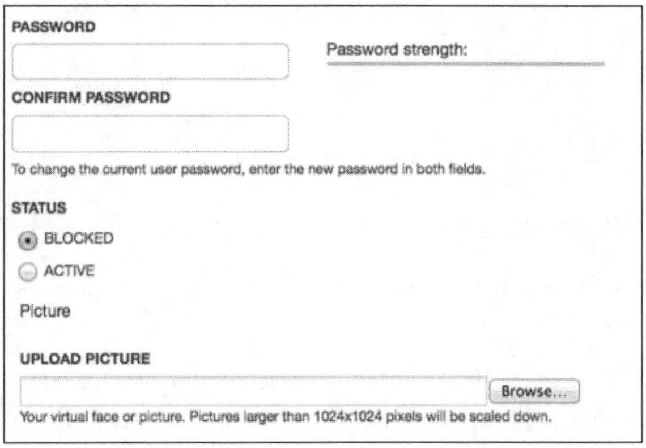

Figure 13.21   Blocking a Drupal user

Drupal User Profiles Explained

At the end of the last section, you saw a user profile on your site.

By default, a user account collects basic information about the user. Most of that information is not visible to visitors or other users on the site.

Drupal makes it easy to modify and expand this profile so that people can add useful information about themselves such as their name, address, employer, URLs, biography, and more.

Now see how to create expanded user profiles. The process is similar to adding fields to a content type.

Before you start, make sure you have used the Masquerade module to switch back to the administrator account.

Create the Profile Fields

Go ahead and add some fields to your user profiles. This allows users to provide more information about themselves:

1. Click Configuration on the black menu bar and then on Account Settings.
2. Click the Manage fields tab in the top-right corner.

   You can now see a screen, such as the one in Figure 13.22, which looks similar to the content type pages you saw earlier.

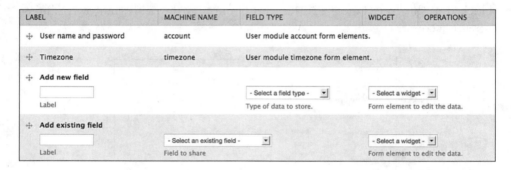

Figure 13.22   Adding fields to Drupal user profiles

3. Add the fields shown in Table 13.1. Use exactly the same process that you did in Chapter 6, "Drupal Fields Explained," when adding fields to content.

Table 13.1   **The Fields for Your Site's User Profiles**

Field Label	Machine Name	Field Type	Settings
First name	profile_first_name	Text	Required, display on user registration form
Last name	profile_last_name	Text	Required, display on user registration form
Biography	profile_bio	Long text and summary	Use default
LinkedIn URL	profile_linkedin_url	Link	Use default
Facebook URL	profile_fb_url	Link	Use default
Personal URL	profile_personal_url	Link	Use default

When you finish adding those six fields, your screen should look like Figure 13.23.

LABEL	MACHINE NAME	FIELD TYPE	WIDGET	OPERATIONS	
✛ User name and password	account	User module account form elements.			
✛ Timezone	timezone	User module timezone form element.			
✛ First Name	field_profile_first_name	Text	Text field	edit	delete
✛ Last Name	field_profile_last_name	Text	Text field	edit	delete
✛ Biography	field_profile_bio	Long text and summary	Text area with a summary	edit	delete
✛ LinkedIn URL	field_profile_linkedin_url	Link	Link	edit	delete
✛ Facebook URL	field_profile_facebook_url	Link	Link	edit	delete
✛ Personal URL	field_profile_personal_url	Link	Link	edit	delete

Figure 13.23   New fields added to Drupal user profiles

Go and see those user profile fields that you just created:

1. Visit the front page of your site.
2. Click My account on the Main menu.
3. Click the Edit tab.
4. Scroll down and you can use all the fields that you just created.

Also see how these fields appear to your site's users. For many users, this user profile editing area should look similar, but slightly different:

1. Use the Masquerade module to browse the site as the blogger user.
2. Click My account on the Main menu.
3. Click the Edit tab.

Did you notice that the fields don't show in a pop-up as they did when you were browsing the site as an administrator? This is because you haven't given the Blogger role permission to use the Overlay module. The Overlay module puts Drupal's administration area into a pop-up. This is just one of many examples of different permissions between a user in an administrator role and a lower-level role, such as a Blogger.

However, even viewing the site as a Blogger, all the user profile fields that you created are available to you, as shown in Figure 13.24. Users can also upload a profile picture of themselves—thanks to a default setting in Drupal.

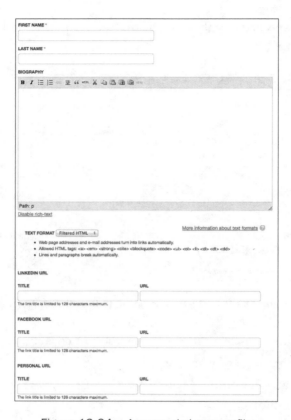

Figure 13.24   An expanded user profile

Finally, see how this appears to a new user:

1. Click Log Out on the Main menu.
2. Click Create New Account in the User Login block.

The registration screen should look like Figure 13.25. The First Name and Last Name fields show because, when creating these fields, you checked the boxes marked Display on User Registration Form. If you want to customize the emails that users receive when they register, log in as an administrator, and go to Configuration and then Account settings.

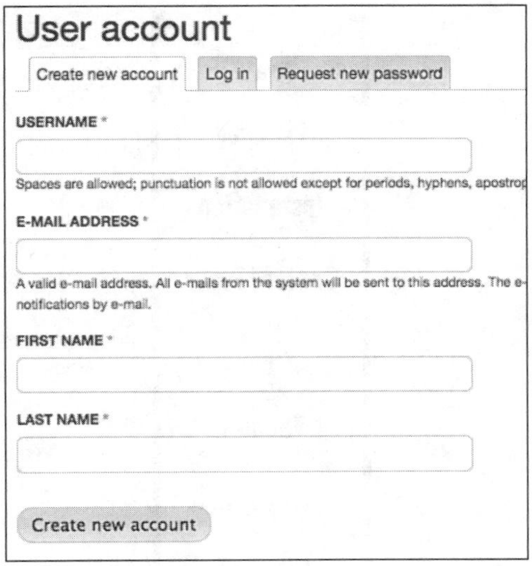

Figure 13.25   User registration form

What's Next?

At the end of this chapter, you completed your site building.

We mentioned that at the end of Chapter 12, "Drupal Layout Modules Explained," you had completed all the visible changes you were going to make to your site. However, the previous chapter was not the end of our Drupal workflow, which is shown in Figure 13.26.

User permissions are the last step in our Drupal workflow for a logical reason: it's not until every part of the site has been created that we can accurately browse the site and test the user permissions.

Now that our Drupal workflow is complete, we're going to discuss how you maintain a completed Drupal site. In the final chapter of this book, "Drupal Site Management Explained," we'll show you how to maintain and secure a Drupal site.

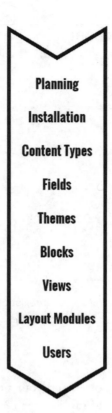

Figure 13.26   The Drupal site workflow

Drupal Site Management Explained

Are you going to be responsible for maintaining your Drupal site? If so, this chapter is for you. This chapter shows you how to keep your site safe, secure, and updated.

You might have other people taking care of these tasks for you. You might have a web design company, colleagues in the IT department, or other experienced people to help you. If that's your situation, you can happily skip this chapter.

However, if you are the person responsible for your site, you need to know how to keep your site safe and secure. Among other things, you need to know how to protect your site and update it to the latest version.

After reading this chapter, you should be able to

- Update your site.
- Update your modules and themes.
- Disable or uninstall modules and themes.
- Use additional measures to protect your site.
- Back up your site.

Updating Your Site Explained

Treat your Drupal site as you treat your car.

All cars need regular maintenance, and so do all Drupal sites. With a car, you need to pump up the tires, change the oil, change the battery, or do other fixes. With a Drupal site, you also need to apply fixes. Fortunately, many of these important fixes can be applied automatically using Drupal's update system.

Before seeing how to use Drupal's update system, you need to understand what you're updating to. Drupal's updates are based on version numbers, as described in the following section.

An Overview of Drupal Version Numbers

Chapter 1, "Drupal Explained," talked a little about Drupal's version numbers. Some of the key points mentioned were

- At the time of writing, there are three major versions of Drupal:
  - Drupal 6 was released September 2008. Millions of websites use it, and it will still be actively supported and updated by the Drupal team until Drupal 8 is released. However, there are no new plans for new features for this version.
  - Drupal 7 was released January 2011. It's the version used throughout this book.
  - Drupal 8 will be released in late 2013 or early 2014.

Now, let's get a little more specific about version numbers. There are two types of Drupal version: major versions and minor versions.

Major Versions

Major versions have large intervals between releases and always add important new features and changes to Drupal:

- **Numbering:** 5, 6, and 7 have been released, and in the future you can expect 8, 9, 10, and so on.
- **Reason for new major versions:** To add new features and improve the underlying code.
- **Importance:** Is it important to use the latest major version? It's useful but not essential. Because new major versions are released to add new features, there are no security problems if you don't upgrade. However, each major version is supported only by the Drupal team for so long; so yes, it's generally best to use the latest major version if possible.
- **Release dates.** There are no fixed release dates for major versions. However, Drupal's track record can give you an idea of how often major versions are released. After the release of Drupal 5, there have been three major versions in approximately 80 months. So, you could say that major versions arrive approximately every 26 months:
  - **Drupal 5:** January 2007
  - **Drupal 6:** February 2008

- **Drupal 7:** January 2011
- **Drupal 8:** Late 2013 or early 2014

- **Updating:** Unfortunately, updating between major versions is difficult. Each new Drupal version is substantially different from the last. The more complicated the site, the more difficult it is to update. After you choose a version, it will probably be the version that your site uses for several years. A useful blog post on understanding Drupal's philosophy on updates is http://www.buytaert.net/backward-compatibility, written by Dries Buytaert. In that post, he explains that the priority for each major Drupal version is to get the technology right, and that is more important than backward compatibility. Other website software has the opposite priority and values backward compatibility over the latest technology. There isn't a right or wrong answer when discussing which should be the higher priority, but you need to know what Drupal's priorities are.

Minor Versions

Minor versions are released irregularly but often and provide small fixes to existing features:

- **Numbering:** Each major version has minor versions, such as 7.1, 7.2, 7.3, 7.4, and so on. For major versions that are out for a long time, these can add up so that the final version of 5 was 5.23, and the current version of 6 is 6.27. The current version of 7 is 7.18.

- **Reason for new minor versions:** To fix security problems and bugs.

- **Importance:** Is it important to use the latest minor version? Yes, absolutely. Because new minor versions are often released to fix security problems, it is vital to make sure you use the latest version.

- **Release dates:** These versions are released approximately every 1 to 2 months or as needed.

- **Updating:** In Drupal, you need to download the files for the new version and carefully upload them to replace your current files.

What Version Do I Have?

Now that you understand what the numbers mean, you need to see how to apply updates.

Log in to your site as administrator, and go to Reports and then Status Report. You can see what version number you currently have. In Figure 14.1, the site is at version 7.16.

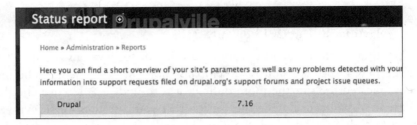

Figure 14.1   The version number of your Drupal site

How Do I Get Notified About Updates?

Drupal gives you plenty of warning notices about updates. If there is an update and you're logged in as administrator, you see a red message across the top of all admin screens, as shown in Figure 14.2.

Figure 14.2   A warning message for Drupal updates

You can have Drupal automatically send you emails whenever there's an update. Go to Reports, Available updates, and click the Settings tab. You see a screen, as shown in Figure 14.3. Enter an email address here, and Drupal can send you daily emails whenever it finds an update.

How Do I Update?

The site shown in Figure 14.1 uses 7.16, which is out-of-date. Here's the process you can use to update the core Drupal files on your site:

1. Take your Drupal site offline briefly so that visitors don't see any error messages as you update. To do this, go to Configuration, Maintenance mode, and check the box marked Put Site into Maintenance Mode. Click Save Configuration.

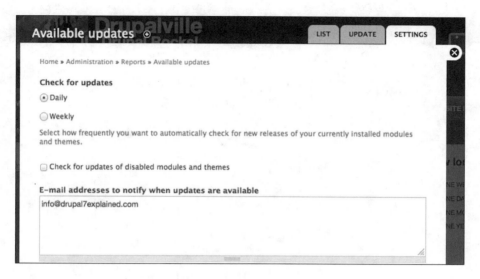

Figure 14.3   Emails about Drupal updates

2. Back up your site, as explained in the section, "Backing Up Your Site Explained," later in this chapter.

3. Go to Reports and Available Updates.

4. Click Download in the red warning area, as shown in Figure 14.4.

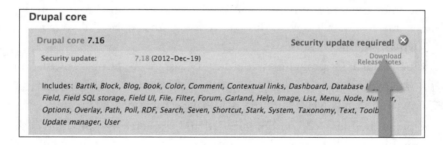

Figure 14.4   Downloading a Drupal core update

5. Save the files to your desktop.

6. Extract the files that you just downloaded. The folder should look like Figure 14.5.

Figure 14.5   A folder containing Drupal core files

7. Delete the /sites/ folder from the folders in the new version shown in Figure 14.5. IMPORTANT! Please do not ignore this step. The /sites/ folder contains everything that is unique to your site: all the uploaded modules, themes, and files. If you don't delete the /sites/ folder in the new version now, you'll upload this empty folder and replace all your modules, themes, and files.

8. Open your FTP program as you did in Chapter 3, "Drupal Installations Explained." Browse to find your existing site files.

9. One more time: Make sure that you have a backup of your site!

10. Upload the files that you downloaded and extracted. Simply upload the new files over the top of the existing ones. This may take anywhere from a few seconds to a few minutes to complete, depending on the speed of your connection.

11. When the upload is complete, go to Reports, Available Updates again. Drupal now shows that the Drupal core is up to date, as shown in Figure 14.6.

12. Go to Configuration, Maintenance mode, uncheck the box marked Put Site into Maintenance Mode, and click Save Configuration.

Figure 14.6   A successful update to the latest Drupal version

Updating Your Modules and Themes Explained

To keep your site safe, you need to update your modules and themes as well as the main Drupal version.

Fortunately, Drupal 7 makes updating modules and themes much easier than updating the core files. Here's how to do it:

1. Back up your site.
2. Go to Reports, Available Updates. Look for any modules or themes that are marked in red, as shown with the Zero Point theme in Figure 14.7.

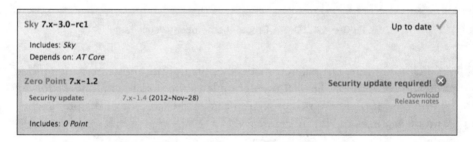

Figure 14.7   The Zero Point theme needs updating.

3. Click the Update tab in the top-right corner.
4. Check the box next to the updates you want to make, as shown in Figure 14.8.
5. Click Download These Updates. You'll see a progress bar as your sites are updated, as shown in Figure 14.9.
6. When the update finishes, you see a message saying Updates Downloaded Successfully, as shown in Figure 14.10.

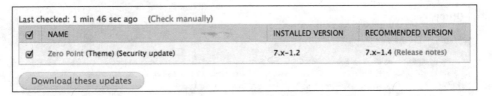

Figure 14.8   Choosing to update the Zero Point theme

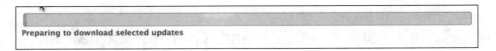

Figure 14.9   Updating a Drupal theme

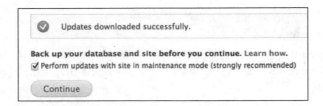

Figure 14.10   A Drupal theme update successful

7. Click Continue. Drupal automatically puts the site in maintenance mode during this process. Drupal then completes the update and checks for any problems. If there are no problems, it takes the site out of maintenance mode again, as shown in Figure 14.11.

8. Click Run Database Updates. This is the final step in the update. You see the screen shown in Figure 14.11.

9. Click Continue.

10. Click Apply Pending Updates if any updates are found, as shown in Figure 14.12.

If all goes well, you won't see any error messages. You just see a screen like Figure 14.13. Click the Front Page or Administration Pages links to return to your site.

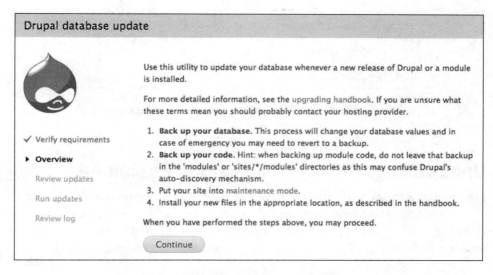

Figure 14.11   Drupal database updates

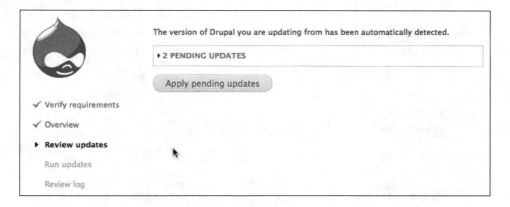

Figure 14.12   Pending database updates

If you see error messages, do your best to follow the instructions given. If the instructions aren't clear, enter the error message into Google or the search box at Drupal.org to see if anyone has encountered similar problems and found a solution.

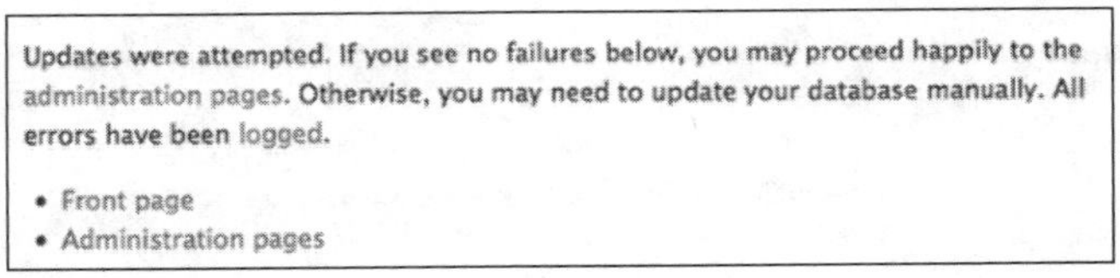

> Updates were attempted. If you see no failures below, you may proceed happily to the administration pages. Otherwise, you may need to update your database manually. All errors have been logged.
>
> - Front page
> - Administration pages

Figure 14.13   Your Drupal site after attempting updates

Uninstalling Modules or Themes Explained

For security reasons, you must uninstall any modules or themes that you're not using. If modules or themes are unused, you're more likely to forget about updating them. Older software that hasn't been regularly updated is more likely to suffer from security holes. Here's how you can remove unused modules:

1. Go to Modules on the Administration menu.
2. Uncheck the box next to the module you want to uninstall, and then click Save Configuration. If you can't uncheck it, it is because another module is relying on it. Look next to the module you want to uninstall and see what is listed in the Required By area. For example, in Figure 14.14, you can't disable the Devel module, because it is required by the Devel generate module. First, you need to disable Devel generate.

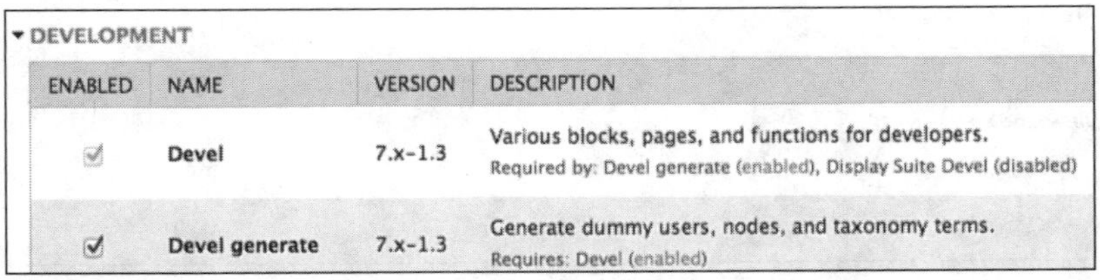

ENABLED	NAME	VERSION	DESCRIPTION
☑	**Devel**	7.x-1.3	Various blocks, pages, and functions for developers. Required by: Devel generate (enabled), Display Suite Devel (disabled)
☑	**Devel generate**	7.x-1.3	Generate dummy users, nodes, and taxonomy terms. Requires: Devel (enabled)

Figure 14.14 The Devel module can't be disabled.

3. Click the Uninstall tab in the top-right corner.
4. You'll see a list of modules that you can uninstall. As with the disabling, they sometimes must be done in a particular order. Check the boxes next to the modules you want to uninstall, as shown in Figure 14.15.
5. Click Uninstall.
6. Drupal warns you that all data from these modules will be lost. Click Uninstall and the process finishes.

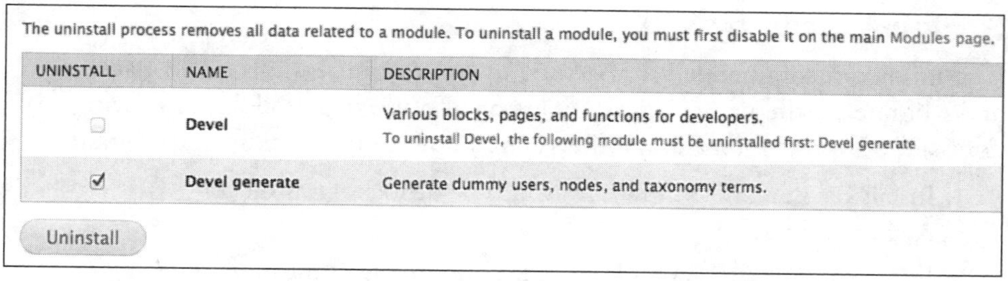

UNINSTALL	NAME	DESCRIPTION
The uninstall process removes all data related to a module. To uninstall a module, you must first disable it on the main Modules page.		
☐	Devel	Various blocks, pages, and functions for developers. To uninstall Devel, the following module must be uninstalled first: Devel generate
☑	Devel generate	Generate dummy users, nodes, and taxonomy terms.

Uninstall

Figure 14.15 Uninstalling a module from your site

The process of uninstalling a theme is different:

1. Go the Appearance tab on the Administration menu, and click Disable next to the theme you want to uninstall.

2. Log in to your site via FTP.

3. Browse to the /sites/all/themes/ or sites/default/themes/ folder to find your theme.

4. Find the folder for the theme you want to uninstall. It will probably have exactly the same name as the theme.

5. Either remove or delete the theme folder, and you will have successfully uninstalled the theme.

Backing Up Your Site Explained

You need to keep your site secure and up to date, but even the best sites can run into problems, and even the best site administrators can make mistakes. To recover from serious problems and errors, you need to have backups. There are two main ways to make backups: Your hosting company can do it, and you can do it yourself. I recommend that you set up both options.

Backups Made by Your Hosting Company

Many of the best hosting companies make backups for their clients. Some of the best hosting companies not only make the backups, but also give you the ability to restore a backup in place of the current site. Some others make the backups but require that you contact them and ask for the backup to be restored. Finally, some hosts won't make any backups available to you because they create backups to recover from server failure and not your mistakes.

You need to know the backup policy of your host, whether it's good, mediocre, or bad.

Backups Made by You

The module recommended for backing up your Drupal site is called Backup and Migrate. As the name suggests, you can also use this module for moving your site from one server to another. Here's how to use Backup and Migrate:

1. Install Backup and Migrate from http://drupal.org/project/ backup_migrate.

2. Install the Backup and Migrate Files module from http://drupal.org/ project/backup_migrate_files.

3. Enable both modules.

4. Go to Configuration and then File System.

5. Enter a private file system path. This is a folder at a higher directory than the public files on your website. If you can access this folder via an http:// URL, it's not a private path. The reason for doing this is that your database might contain sensitive information, and it's a good security precaution to store database backups where they cannot be easily accessed. If you're stuck on finding this path, ask the people in charge of your server or click the link labeled More Information About Securing Private Files.

6. Go to Configuration and then Backup and Migrate.

   You can easily make a backup of your database and files from this screen, as shown in Figure 14.16. You can simply click Backup Now to download a copy of your database.

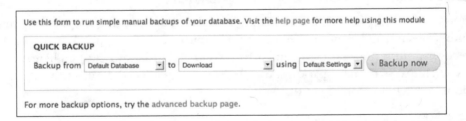

Figure 14.16 The Backup and Migrate module

To download a copy of your files, simply change the Database drop-down to Public Files Directory, and click Backup Now. This can take longer than downloading your database.

You need to make a backup before you update your core files, modules, and themes. You also must make regular, scheduled backups. Here's how to do that:

1. Go to Configuration, Backup, Migrate.
2. Click the Schedules tab.
3. Click Add schedule.
   - **Schedule Name:** Give the schedule a name such as Daily Database Backup.
   - **Backup source:** Default Database.
4. Click Save Schedule.
5. Repeat this to set up a backup for your files. The only difference is that files can take up more space and probably change less often. So, it's not uncommon to back up your database daily and back up your files weekly.

Additional Measures to Protect Your Site

The previous two chapters covered four of the most important security processes for your Drupal site: permissions, regular updates, deleting unused software, and taking regular backups. To further enhance the security of your site, use the Security Review module. This module won't actually secure your site, but it can give you great advice on how to do it.

Here's how to use the Security Review module:

1. Install and enable the module from http://drupal.org/project/security_review.
2. Go to Reports and then Security Review.
3. Click Run Checklist. It gives you some suggestions on problems to fix, as shown in Figure 14.17. Click Details to get information on fixing the problems.

Review results from last run

Here you can review the results from the last run of the checklist. Checks are not always perfectly correct in their procedure and result. You can keep a check from running by clicking the 'Skip' link beside it. You can run the checklist again by expanding the fieldset above.

Untrusted roles do not have administrative or trusted Drupal permissions.	Details	Skip
Error reporting set to log only.	Details	Skip
Dangerous tags were not found in any submitted content (fields).	Details	Skip
Some files and directories in your install are writable by the server.	Details	Skip
Untrusted users are not allowed to input dangerous HTML tags.	Details	Skip
Only safe extensions are allowed for uploaded files and images.	Details	Skip

Figure 14.17 The Security Review checklist

What's Next?

Congratulations! You've reached the end of Drupal 7 Explained.

So, what's next?

- **Practice:** The only way to get better at Drupal is to build Drupal sites. Decide on your first Drupal project and start practicing.

- **Practice now:** You will forget most of what you've read in this book. That's human nature and doesn't make me a bad teacher or you a bad learner. The longer you wait to practice Drupal, the more you'll forget. Why not start right away?

- **Learn more:** I guarantee that there are things you will come across while using Drupal that haven't been included in this book. This book has only a limited number of pages, and we focused on only the most important things about Drupal. We also tried to avoid any code so that the barrier to entry for using Drupal is as low as possible. However, one of the great things about Drupal being so popular is that almost every problem you run into has been encountered by other people. Many of those people have asked for or posted a solution to their problem online. If you ever get stuck, here are the first two places you should go to for help:

  - **http://www.google.com:** If you get an error message or encounter a problem, type it directly into a search engine, and there's a good chance you'll find a solution.

  - **http://drupal.org/forum:** The Drupal forums have more than a million posts at the time of writing, so you can find a lot of solutions. Search for a solution to your question: if you don't find it, write a new post. There's sure to be someone who can help you.

- **Join the Drupal community:** Drupal doesn't rely on money; it relies on people like you. Whether you attend a local Drupal event, post solutions you find on the forum, or even say thank you to someone who's helped you, there are many easy ways to become part of the Drupal community. The more you rely on Drupal for your website or your business, the more it can benefit you to become part of the community.

I hope to see you around in the Drupal community, and I wish you all the best in your use of Drupal!

Index

F